T0385209

THE
LIAR

THE LIAR

How a Double Agent in the CIA Became the Cold War's Last Honest Man

Benjamin Cunningham

PUBLICAFFAIRS

NEW YORK

PublicAffairs
Hachette Book Group
1290 Avenue of the Americas, New York, NY 10104
www.publicaffairsbooks.com
@Public_Affairs

Printed in the United States of America

First Edition: August 2022

Published by PublicAffairs, an imprint of Perseus Books, LLC, a subsidiary of
Hachette Book Group, Inc. The PublicAffairs name and logo is a trademark of the
Hachette Book Group.

The Hachette Speakers Bureau provides a wide range of authors for speaking events.
To find out more, go to www.hachettespeakersbureau.com or call (866) 376-6591.

The publisher is not responsible for websites (or their content) that are not owned by
the publisher.

Library of Congress Control Number: 2022937759

ISBNs: 9781541700796 (hardcover), 9781541700819 (ebook)

LSC-C

Printing 1, 2022

To Bibi, for meeting me halfway

"*A man who lies to himself, and believes his own lies becomes unable to recognize truth, either in himself or in anyone else, and he ends up losing respect for himself and others. When he has no respect for anyone, he can no longer love, and in him, he yields to his impulses, indulges in the lowest form of pleasure, and behaves in the end like an animal in satisfying his vices. And it all comes from lying—to others and to yourself.*"

—Fyodor Dostoyevsky

CONTENTS

Author's Note   ix

Prologue   1

1   Rebel Without a Cause   15

2   Existential Struggle   30

3   Joining Up   42

4   Passing the Test   55

5   Innocents Abroad   67

6   The End of the Beginning   81

7   Double Agent   93

8   Company Man   113

9   Highs and Lows   130

10   Behind the Curtain   144

11   Trigon   158

12   The Beginning of the End   177

13   Out of the Wilderness   194

14   Exchange   209

Epilogue   227

Acknowledgments   241

Bibliography   243

Notes   251

Index   261

Photo insert appears after page 112

AUTHOR'S NOTE

This is a true story. Names, places, and incidents are real. Some of the interpretation is my own.

Quotations from secondary sources are cited in endnotes, and the texts are compiled in the bibliography. Quotations that do not come with a specific citation either came from interviews (also listed in the bibliography) or from archival documents from the Czech Republic's State Security Archives.

Quotations from those archival documents are translated into English, but the original material consisted generally of Czech (occasionally Slovak, and very occasionally German or Russian) language documents. On occasion, juggling multiple languages presented some special challenges.

For example, the dialogue that appears in the prologue originally occurred in a variety of languages. There are, amazingly, actual audio recordings of this encounter. However, much of this—as might be expected of reel-to-reel recording tape stored with little care by the Communist regime—is of low quality. There are transcripts of the discussion translated into Czech. I reviewed both, but the dialogue presented here comes primarily from Czech transcripts translated into English. They were, by necessity, edited for context and clarity but with every intention of keeping the original meaning intact. Other similar small challenges arose throughout the writing process.

AUTHOR'S NOTE

In my view, a good many Cold War stories fall into lazy binary narratives, and twentieth-century history is often projected through caricatures of famous people. This book does its best to avoid both.

PROLOGUE

"Heroes don't exist, only cattle for the slaughter and the butchers in the general staffs."
—Jaroslav Hašek

SEPTEMBER 10, 1976
Čtyřkoly, Czechoslovakia

About twenty miles outside Prague, in a riverside village of little distinction, Karel finds himself in a room with dull walls and a cold, dead fireplace. He doesn't know why he is there.

The unexceptional-looking house sits empty most of the time, but the neighbors tend to stay away anyway. Occasionally they see people milling about the cottage; the black government-issued Tatra 603s parked outside signal they aren't up to anything good. Best to go the long way around when walking the dog or heading out for a beer. Across the river, there's a pub with outdoor tables. Like something out of Greek mythology, a boatman with a pole can take you across.

The cool and breezy September day offers a welcome respite from New York's scalding August. But as Karel smooths the collar on his Brooks Brothers jacket, it strikes him that he hasn't seen his passport since they crossed the border. That cannot be good.

Karel is making small talk when another well-dressed man enters the room. His suit is dark—not exactly stylish, but well cut, tie in a full Windsor knot. Old-fashioned looking, to be sure, but clean, serious. No doubt official. The man's receding hair is slicked back with pomade. Like

1

Karel, he looks to be in his early forties—prodigiously young for a KGB general. His name is Oleg Kalugin. He is a spy, and he's arrived to interrogate another spy.

"Sorry I am late; do you speak Russian?" Kalugin asks as he enters the room.

"I understand it fine, but I don't speak all that well," Karel says. "In America, there's no one to speak Russian with."

Kalugin stops on Karel's side of the table and turns to look him in the face. Karel Koecher stays seated but sizes up Kalugin's thick silhouette framed in the light of an open window. Karel doesn't know it, but Kalugin has defied Moscow Center orders to be here today. As far as KGB chief Yuri Andropov is concerned, Czechoslovak intelligence is conducting this interview on their own.

Standing up straight, chest out, looking confident—cocky, even— Kalugin gives no impression he's worried about the consequences of his insubordination. In fact, it stands to reason that Kalugin has his own reasons for being there, but they are not obvious, and he does not reveal them.

Like Karel, Kalugin is fluent in a gaggle of languages. As he continues in English, his nondescript patrician lilt sounds a bit like Cary Grant—but heavy, pedantic, and stripped of bounce. Kalugin pulls a chair from the table, rotates it to face Karel, takes a seat, and begins a stiff greeting that answers a few questions before he raises a host of new ones.

"I am glad to welcome you in the name of Soviet-Czechoslovakian friendship. I am a guest here on invitation of our Czechoslovak friends, and I have to say, as a representative of a friendly service and collaborator, I am glad to meet you," Kalugin says. "I have heard and read a lot about you. And now I hope my company is going to be useful for clearing up the doubts we share, as well as our common interests. I have some questions related to your personal security. Because the top priority for us is always the success of our people, no matter where they work."

Karel looks over Kalugin's shoulder again, to the open window. It's now drizzling outside. Karel adjusts his stainless-steel glasses. His light-gray suit with flared slacks and his vibrant extra-wide tie look alien amid the humorless monochromes. Kalugin's eyes are captivated by the stripes on Karel's tie, as if they haven't seen color in a decade or so. A bunch of Philistines, Karel thinks as he turns his chair, brushing his fingers through his salt-and-pepper mustache. He makes eye contact with Kalugin but stays quiet.

"I might be repeating some things because I came in late," Kalugin continues. "Well, that's okay; hopefully it's not going to be too unpleasant. How are you? How is your health?"

"Good," a wary Karel says. "Let's see in the evening."

Karel's vision is worse than it used to be, and the Koecher clan has a history of diabetes. As a kid Karel had ear infections that were bad enough to later help exempt him from military service. As a grown man, though, he is something of a fitness nut. In New York, he runs the Central Park Reservoir almost daily and likes to pump iron at the 92nd Street Y.

"The way I understood it, you found it difficult to accept living in the American way," Kalugin goes on. "It is vital to be patient and to build long-term relationships, especially when it comes to working with people from abroad. Earlier, I reviewed the materials and your situation. Correct me if I am wrong, but it was 1973 when you first started working for the CIA. Before that you got the doctorate, that must have been 1970, and then you worked at Radio Free Europe?"

Not quite, Karel explains, briefly recounting his résumé: a fellowship at Indiana University in 1966, then PhD work at Columbia, Radio Free Europe until 1969, American citizenship in 1971, and a smattering of university teaching jobs. "That was until 1972 or 1973. And then I was able to get into the CIA," he says with a touch of impatience.

"Yes, the Pentagon was probably the first serious work, and that was 1973, right?"

"Yes, 1973."

Kalugin asks for more. Was Karel working for the Department of Defense or the CIA or what? He wants details.

Karel explains that he interviewed for work at the Pentagon, but it turned out to be part of the screening process to work for the CIA. The job had only lasted a few weeks. Officially speaking, the US government still claims he works for the Defense Department, but that is just cover.

"Do you remember the number of the office?" Kalugin asks about Karel's visits to the Pentagon.

"It was a small room."

"No, I mean the numbers of the rooms. Do you remember them? Or the floor?"

"Third, I think."

"In what part? What wing of the building was it? Do you remember?"

"I don't remember. I was only there briefly."

After obsessing for a while about the building's layout, Kalugin switches to asking what Karel was doing there: "Huh, okay, so what was your focus?"

"I was translating some materials from the newspaper. Newspaper articles and sometimes also tapes."

"Russian?"

"And Czech," Karel says.

The first recordings were rudimentary, Karel continues. Czechs speaking in a room in East Germany. They had just visited the West to shop in Frankfurt, buying all sorts of stuff. They kept going on about the array of choices. The voices faded in and out, and the clarity was poor. There was an echo; you couldn't get every word, but enough to make it intelligible. Anyway, these were not exactly matters of national security.

"The Russian-language ones, they were phone taps," Karel goes on, "from Latin America. Probably they just wanted to know whether I would be able to translate well."

"Was it a big operation? Were there a lot of people?"

"Yes, there were a lot of people. But I was alone in a small room."

"Who was your neighbor? Do you remember who they were? Were they Americans?"

"I never really spoke with them much, but Americans, yes."

"There weren't any other Soviets or Czechs there. Were you there alone?"

"Yes, alone."

Office numbers, dates, names, addresses. Can Kalugin really be interested in all these minutiae? How can he expect Karel to remember such details from three years ago? Doesn't he appreciate the pressure Karel lives under every day, pretending to be someone he is not?

Kalugin is looking for something—for contradictions, probably. But why? Karel calms himself and answers directly. Keep it simple. Interrogators circle back to the same questions over and over again. More details mean more chances to slip up.

At some point another guy comes in to adjust the tape on a reel-to-reel recording device. Zítek, the StB man sitting in on the interrogation but saying nothing, helps adjust the machine. When Kalugin leaves the room for a minute, Karel makes small talk with Zítek and the guy fiddling with the recorder. Why not? There is nothing to be nervous about. Just the night before, the Czechs had all sat together drinking beer around this same table.

When Kalugin returns, he leans his elbow on the white tablecloth and points the microphone at Karel. The chatting halts, and pointed questions resume:

"Okay, so we finished the chapter with the Pentagon. What is the next step?"

"In the next step, I started working in the CIA unit transcribing the phone interviews. They suggested that if I was interested, they could use someone to do that."

"So that is how you got to the team. And judging by photographs and other materials, there was a team."

Someone had been taking pictures at last year's Christmas party, and Karel took hold of the film. He told the photographer that he knew a guy up in New York who could get the photos developed real cheap. Then he made duplicates and sent the second batch back to Prague, writing the names of his CIA colleagues on the back.

"Yes, and it was a big team," Karel says.

"That means you also signed some document."

"You mean a contract?"

"Yes."

"No, it was the same one I had from earlier. The original contract was for two years, I think."

"That means the same contract you had in the Pentagon?"

"Yes."

Karel hadn't known what to think when Zítek surprised him with the news they were going back to Czechoslovakia. Now here, Karel wishes that he wasn't. It feels foreign, even hostile. That is unexpected.

"Judging by your messages, you knew the geographical locations of where they were tapping the phones," Kalugin continues, legs crossed.

"It was written on the boxes where the tapes were stored."

"And those were phone taps?"

"Yes, phones. And there were some other people working on recordings that came from bugs in rooms themselves."

"So where is the unit based?"

"In Arlington, on North Street Road and Route 50," Karel says.

"A big building?"

"Yes, a big building, twelve to fifteen floors."

Kalugin pushes for still more details. "So a glass one. Did you occupy the whole building?"

"No, just a part of it. Seven floors."

"And the rest of it?"

"The rest belonged to some phone company."

"Then in 1975 your contract finished."

"We added six months. There was an extension."

"I believe in the summer of 1975 the contract was up."

"Yes, the original end of the contract was in February, but I prolonged it six months."

Kalugin's probing is polite but relentless: "So does this mean that they did not wish to extend the contract or that you did not wish to extend it?"

"I wanted to extend it for another six months, but then they didn't want me anymore. In the end, I managed to get the contract in the CIA's Office of Political Research instead."

"So in your opinion, which office offers us greater benefits?"

"If I manage to work for a while in the Office of Political Research, we will benefit more there," Karel says.

Less than two years old, the Office of Political Research (OPR) is a department within the CIA that tasks analysts with writing big-picture interpretations of strategic political trends.

"Do you work with a team of people?"

"No, I don't work in a team."

"So what exactly is your situation? How would you describe it?"

"I write reports from home."

"Where do you get the source material?"

"When there are materials, I get them from Langley."

"How often are you there?"

"Once a month."

"Once a month—that is not very often." Kalugin sounds a little disappointed. "What do you get when you go there?"

"I wrote about the ideological aspects of the Soviet leadership. So I wanted materials about the members of the politburo. They gave me materials about Comrade Suslov, for instance. Telegrams from the American embassy in Moscow, what they heard and where. Where is Comrade Suslov? Is he ill? And so on."

As a promising Communist ideologue, Mikhail Suslov had been Josef Stalin's head of propaganda. For a while he worked as the chief editor for the Soviet newspaper *Pravda*. In 1956—along with an all-star cast of up-and-comers, including the current KGB boss, Yuri Andropov—he helped orchestrate the Soviet crackdown on the Hungarian uprising. Like star bureaucrats anywhere, Suslov hedged his bets at the right time, helping oust Nikita Khrushchev in 1964. For better or worse, when Leonid Brezhnev took Khrushchev's place, Suslov became one of the three or four most powerful men in the USSR.

"They gave you telegrams from the embassy. That is interesting."

"Yes, there were telegrams about Suslov."

"Yeah, even in that way they are interesting."

"But they weren't interesting."

"Yes, the comrades know better."

"I think so."

"And what about the material that you wrote, was that well received? Did the Americans like it?" Kalugin asks.

"Yes."

"In that case they should be giving you more work."

"Well, the question is whether they really need me or not . . ."

"What is your impression? I feel like from what you shared last time, they are somewhat distant, cold."

"They have a lot of their own people that need jobs. They are born in America, and from that point of view, I am a foreigner," Karel says. "They can find someone who has a similar education and was born in America, and that person will get preference. Here we have to create our own situation. As these short-term contracts continue for a longer time, the questions begin to escalate. What is this guy doing? Why isn't he looking for some kind of more secure position? He is getting old."

"What do you suggest?"

"I don't have many suggestions. What I suggest, the best thing, is to try and artificially manufacture some arrangement."

"But how?"

"I can share one idea that could be very interesting. I would suggest to them some kind of extraordinary operation. For example, to meet with Czechs and feed disinformation back to them. Maybe I could move to Germany. I could propose something like that and start making operations abroad, because all CIA operations are abroad."

Kalugin is skeptical: "For example, what kind of activity? Maybe in Radio Free Europe? We can evaluate that, but in my personal opinion, maybe we should focus on something more stable, more simple. Do you have any friends from American society, just people, that you could turn to for help finding a job?"

"I have done that five or six times, and I have not been able to get anywhere."

Kalugin shifts the conversation to Zbigniew Brzezinski, who leads a research institute at Columbia University. Jimmy Carter will be facing Gerald Ford in the coming November election. If he wins, Brzezinski could play a prominent role in a Carter White House. Karel knows him well. As a philosophy PhD student at Columbia, Karel had also taught seminars at Brzezinski's elite, university-embedded think tank focused on Russian affairs.

"He worked for the CIA?" Kalugin asks of Brzezinski.

"No."

"But he cooperated with them, right?"

"No."

"Do you have a personal relationship? Friendly?"

"Personal? I would not say that."

"How does he know you?"

"Well, I have been to his workshops about the problems of Communism. He liked what I wrote. And then I went to his institute."

"You have never had any personal contact with him?"

"Only at the institute."

"As a student?"

"No, not as a student. But as a teacher at the institute. It is a small institute, twelve people."

"If someone asked Brzezinski for a reference about you, would he recommend you?"

"Yes."

"Maybe you could get a little closer to Brzezinski then? You both have Eastern European roots. You started in his institute. The topics you are now writing about would seem to be relevant. Because Brzezinski would not be merely a professor if Carter is elected. Maybe he will not be anyone important, but you never know."

"Maybe an advisor, but not a member of the cabinet."

"No, not in the cabinet, but let's say national security."

"National security advisor," Karel agrees.

"Yes, that is possible. That is big. My, or our, advice would be to get him interested, write him a letter, write that 'I am your student,' that this is the type of problem you are writing about, and that you can exchange some thoughts. He is a creative person, they like this sort of thing."

"It's probably possible to send him some of my current work."

"I think it is realistic. Because if he evaluates your work positively, it could be a big move for you. That can really strengthen your scientific reputation. At the same time, this will be noticed by people in the CIA too, so it can bring something for us."

As the discussion moves on to Karel's doctoral advisor at Columbia, Charles Frankel, Karel can't help but notice a tasteless vase on the mantel and a cheap floral painting on the wall.

"That was my professor," he says. "He was an assistant secretary of state during the time of Johnson."

"Wasn't he involved in culture?" Kalugin asks.

"Yes. Bureau of Educational and Cultural Affairs."

"Good relations?"

"Yes."

"So here we have more hope that he could be in the new government. Of course, it seems like besides this interest in continuing with the CIA, there are other positions that we need to solidify. Think about trying to get a position as a scientist, sociologist, or historian."

Karel doubts this is a realistic option: "That would be great but really difficult, in my opinion."

"But it is possible. That's why you need to further elaborate this initial backstory. You came from Czechoslovakia, you reached a position, you have a post. You finished Columbia. You can write a thesis. I have read it, and I can tell you it is a good read."

"The CIA wants to recommend part of my work to be published." Karel nods at Zítek, who sits across the table from the other two. "It will take a while, possibly a year, but it will come out in an academic journal."

"If I was in your spot, and this is just my advice," Kalugin sermonizes, "you are a man, not a boy, and it would be good if you take some kind of strong stand. Maybe right now you are not so much into academia, but it's an option. You have a wife, a home. It is important to have a strong position. You know, you tell the CIA, 'I am writing for you now, but I am hesitant. I am okay with continuing the work, but I would want it to become more stable. Nothing is totally stable, but as stable as possible.'"

"I already spoke to them, told them that I am looking for a stable, long-term position."

Perhaps it's Kalugin's stale cologne, but Karel is feeling disoriented. It has been eight years since the Soviets invaded Czechoslovakia, and geopolitics aside, he's still unable to accept the stooges they put in charge. And yet, Karel had to admit, life had gotten better once he started working more closely with the Russians. They were more professional than the Czechs. Andropov had sent him $20,000 toward his new apartment in New York City's Upper East Side—a block and a half from the Guggenheim and Central Park.

"Where do you live now, Washington or New York?" Kalugin presses on.

"In New York."

"You did not want to be in Washington? I would think you would want to be there more often."

"No."

"And how often do you go to Washington, to the CIA? Once in two months?"

"Maybe once, sometimes twice."

"And you have no relationship with the New York CIA office?"

"No relationship."

"Our people were on 79th Street," Kalugin volunteers.

"That is not far from the Czechoslovak mission."

"I mean the corner of 3rd Avenue and 79th, but that is already a long time ago." Kalugin sounds almost wistful. "There is the Berlin Bar on 2nd or 3rd Avenue. On the corner there they have good hot dogs. Geography is a big deal. If you lived in Washington, you would be closer to everything that is important. Washington is the center. New York is a totally different center. From the perspective of state politics and intelligence, Washington is the place."

Karel shrugs. Not long ago he had lived in a Washington, DC, commuter suburb. As far as he could tell, Falls Church wasn't the center of much. Karel's wife stayed in New York, so as soon as the option to work remotely popped up, they took Andropov's loot and bought the one-bedroom apartment at 50 East 89th Street. Robert Redford stores his Jaguar in the basement garage. The DC suburbs can hardly compete.

As Karel has told his bosses again and again, the only way to get in with American society types is to convince them you are part of the club. He simply needs them to send more money. It's all about keeping up appearances.

As the conversation peters out, Karel and Kalugin revert to pleasantries. Kalugin starts on about a trip to a nearby castle. "You should go to Konopiště. Have you been there?"

Germany's Kaiser Wilhelm II visited Archduke Franz Ferdinand at Konopiště back in June 1914, the very month the Austro-Hungarian Empire's heir apparent was assassinated in Sarajevo. Franz Ferdinand had never cared much for Vienna and had hoped to lord over his kingdom from the Prague suburbs. But by 1976, kaisers and archdukes are remnants of a different age.

"No, I haven't," Karel says.

"Oh, what a gorgeous place. We were there yesterday. It's a small Switzerland, you could say."

And with that the awkward meeting ends. Karel retires to his room on the other side of the villa. His wife, Hana, is waiting. She asks how it went. Not well, he tells her. In the meantime, Kalugin heads off to consult with Karel's Czechoslovak intelligence colleagues. There, he tells them that he believes Karel Koecher has changed sides—that Karel is now working for the Americans against Czechoslovakia and the Soviet Union.

As the KGB's very own crown prince, whatever Kalugin says goes. So the report on the meeting concludes that Karel's interrogation "proves that he was and is an enemy and an instrument of the American secret services."

As he prepares to return to the States, Karel is ordered to stop working at the CIA. He leaves the villa with a blunt threat ringing in his ears: no trouble, or prepare for consequences—up to and including liquidation.

1

REBEL WITHOUT A CAUSE

"The small nation is one whose very existence may be put in question at any moment; a small nation can disappear and it knows it. A French, a Russian, or an English man is not used to asking questions about the very survival of his nation. His anthems speak only of grandeur and eternity. The Polish anthem, however, starts with the verse: 'Poland has not yet perished.'"
—MILAN KUNDERA

By the time Karel František Koecher was born on September 21, 1934, his Austrian-born father, Jaroslav, and Jewish mother, Irena, were already fringe players in the adolescent First Czechoslovak Republic. Carved from the defeated Habsburg Empire in the wake of the Great War, for the right kind of person, Czechoslovakia was a fine place to be.

Between 1922 and 1929, the Czechoslovak economy grew at an annualized rate of 5.4 percent,[1] and the country ranked tenth in the world in industrial output.[2] The western region of Bohemia had been ready-made for export-driven industrial capitalism from day one. Bohemians forged steel and manufactured cars, trains, and weapons. Even the soon-to-be infamous panzer tank started out as a Czech product. The very fact that these goods epitomized progress warned that a new—ruthlessly efficient and mechanized—conflict was coming. But nationalist myth, not to mention money, has a way of blurring people's vision.

At last untethered from their imperial anchor, Czechoslovaks saw themselves as free to join their rightful place among the world's great nations. Parliament was chosen based on proportional representation in regular multiparty elections. Women had the right to vote.

Though plenty of Czechoslovaks thrived, prosperity and political power were not spread evenly. In a diverse, multinational state cobbled together at the Versailles peace conference, Czechs made up less than half the population while exercising disproportionate political power. The country of 13.5 million housed more Germans than Slovaks, along with healthy helpings of Hungarians, Romany, Ruthenians, Poles, and more than one hundred thousand Jews. And each ethnic group carried its own bag of suppressed animus: Slovaks resented Czechs, the Czechs disliked the Germans, and everybody looked down on the Roma and the Jews.

Irena birthed baby Karel in the Slovak capital of Bratislava. Six years younger than Jaroslav, she hailed from nearby Trnava. Her father had worked in a sugar factory, and her parents were unmarried when she was born. Jaroslav was a devout Catholic and Anglophile who also spoke French. In 1914, he had stumbled from military school graduation into the slaughterhouse of trench warfare.

Young Karel was equally unlucky. Six weeks before his birth, Germany's once-distinct offices of chancellor and president were merged into one, with the occupant now called "führer." What appeared a minor bureaucratic technicality would soon have ramifications for Czechoslovakia, the region, and the world.

"It is an iron law of history that those who will be caught up in the great movements that determine the course of their own times always fail to recognize them in their early stages. So I cannot remember when I first heard the name Adolf Hitler,"[3] wrote Stefan Zweig, a famed Jewish Viennese author who fled Austria for England in 1934, the same year Karel was born.

By 1934, hostility toward Jews—the exact definition of which shifted by the day—was rising throughout the old Austro-Hungarian Empire.

As tensions grew, and Irena faced increased threats, the Koechers decided to move west to cosmopolitan Prague—only to find the environment less welcoming than hoped. By 1938, in the Czech capital, "every feature of liberalism and democracy," a young American diplomat in Prague named George Kennan wrote, had been "hopelessly and irretrievably discredited," and "the atmosphere was already that of war."[4]

On September 30, 1938, Germany, the United Kingdom, France, and Italy signed the Munich Agreement, ceding a good chunk of Czechoslovak territory to Nazi Germany. Hitler had insisted on claiming the parts of Czechoslovakia populated by ethnic Germans. The biggest contiguous chunk was the so-called Sudetenland, a term invented in 1918 to designate a crescent-shaped portion of the country bordering Germany. At the Munich meeting, Czechoslovak president Edvard Beneš was compelled to sacrifice eight hundred thousand citizens and eleven thousand square miles of territory to the Nazis without ever signing on to the final agreement. UK prime minister Neville Chamberlain famously asserted the deal guaranteed "peace for our time."

Chamberlain was right—for all of 334 days. For Czechoslovakia, 1938 would prove the first in a series of instances whereby the West sacrificed a nascent democracy and its peoples in order to dodge principled conflict.

Jaroslav had worked at the Bratislava post office and took up the same work in Prague. By the time the Koechers moved to a two-room apartment in the capital's Vinohrady district, both the craven and clairvoyant were posting swastikas in their windows. In the meantime, Jewish refugees streamed into the city from Germany, Austria, and the newly occupied Sudetenland. At 4:30 a.m. on the Ides of March, 1939, Czechoslovak radio announced German troops would cross their frontier later that day. Kennan took in the creeping Nazi takeover from the US embassy.

"Motorized units pounded and roared over the cobblestone streets; hundreds of vehicles plastered with snow, the faces of their occupants red with what some thought was shame but what I fear was in most cases merely the cold," he wrote. "By evening the occupation was complete and the people were chased off the streets by an eight o'clock curfew."[5]

An impulsive Hitler marked the occasion with an impromptu trip to Prague. On March 16, he visited the coal-mining region of Silesia, then stopped by the university town of Olomouc and the second-biggest Czech city, Brno. By March 17, he was on to the capital of his native Austria.[6] Though the Nazis would hold Prague for more than six years, until May 1945, this was Hitler's only visit.

Kennan assessed the bleak prospects for the Czechoslovaks: "The fate of a small nation already occupied and suppressed by the Germans was not of great interest to the metropolitan dailies of the Western countries. Czechoslovakia had gone down the drain, and that was that."[7]

But things were not so matter-of-fact for the natives on the ground. Children from Karel's generation still replay the life-changing events of the time like a movie in their head. "I remember my mom holding me and looking at the soldiers marching by," said Pavel Illner, a childhood neighbor of the Koechers in Prague. "You soon realize that there is this dark power that could grab you at any time."

What was left of the Czech lands became the Protectorate of Bohemia and Moravia, to be administered by a Nazi *Reichsprotektor*. In Slovakia, a gang of "pseudo-Nazi elements the Germans had assisted to power," as Kennan put it, declared independence and formed a Nazi-allied puppet state. A Catholic priest named Josef Tiso took charge. "Inflation, impoverishment, economic disruption, bitterness, lack of confidence, and the moral disintegration of public administration can reap no good harvest either for the victors or the vanquished," Kennan opined in May 1939.[8]

Within a month, new rules further restricted the role of Jews in public life. Anyone with three or more Jewish grandparents was classified as a Jew. That meant Irena was, but Karel was not, and the Koechers were fortunate that the initial crackdown focused on tracking Austrian and German Jews who had fled. Assimilated Czechs, or Slovaks, were not yet a priority, and the family was further abetted by the fact that

Jaroslav, like the führer himself, was an Austrian veteran of World War I. Even still, a fully packed suitcase would remain at the ready in the family's front closet for years.

On August 23, the Nazis and Soviets signed the Molotov-Ribbentrop Pact. This helped nullify opposition to the Nazi occupation from grass-roots Communists in Prague, but it didn't stop party leader Klement Gottwald and friends from fleeing the country to wait out the war in the Soviet Union. Pact or no pact, the Nazis were not about to treat potential rivals for power kindly. Gottwald and his crew set about planning in the meantime.

The First Czechoslovak Republic had collapsed, and the last of the interwar status quo evaporated with it.

"There is probably no country in Europe where war—and war at the earliest possible date—is so universally desired as in the Protectorate of Bohemia and Moravia," Kennan wrote. Before long the United States had closed its Prague embassy and Kennan was transferred to Berlin. "Whether there is war or not, the Bohemia and Moravia of the future will never quite be the same," he wrote in his final dispatch. "Misfortune has left many marks; and among them is a deep sense of the necessity for unity and discipline in a small people so unhappily situated as themselves."[9]

On September 1, the Nazis invaded Poland. Two days later, Britain and France declared war on Germany. In November 1939, the Nazis closed all Czech universities and kept them shuttered for the duration of the war. Karel started attending a local elementary school the next year, and the milestones toppled fast. In June 1940, Paris fell. A year later the Nazis turned on the Soviets and attacked. In September 1941, Reinhard Heydrich, the architect of the final solution and former deputy to Heinrich Himmler, became *Reichsprotektor* for Bohemia and Moravia. Adolf Eichmann was brought in to oversee Prague's Central Office for Jewish Emigration, and the repression of Jews and Roma accelerated.

"Your restriction is not a necessary sacrifice which you are making for the sake of your country, your army, your struggle," one Czech, who would later join a Communist Party workers' militia, said of the perverse experience of occupation. "You are starving so that the men you hate are well fed."[10] In November 1941, forty miles from Prague, the entire Czech town of Terezín was cleared and converted into a concentration camp. Some 140,000 Jews would cycle through during the war; more than 90,000 were transported onward to death camps like Auschwitz.

Though hardly rich, Karel and his family survived on his father's post office salary. At the time, it was also enough to afford a live-in Polish maid. So long as Irena could keep her Semitic roots hidden, they would not be persecuted.

In December 1941, nine Czechoslovaks trained in Scotland parachuted into the Protectorate of Bohemia and Moravia, where they met up with resistance fighters already on the ground and began planning. On May 27, 1942, as Reichsprotektor Heydrich set off on his morning commute to Prague Castle, would-be assassins waited to strike his armor-plated yet open-topped Mercedes. As it slowed to take a curve, the first shooter's gun jammed, so a second tossed a grenade into the car. It hit the mark, and though Heydrich lived eight more agonizing days, he eventually succumbed to his injuries. Czech children of Karel's age saw Operation Anthropoid as a real-life example of swashbuckling bravery—even if they also learned such heroism came at a price.

"They would announce, in the streets, the names of the people who had been executed for supposedly assisting the assassination," Karel's childhood associate Pavel Illner recalled. "Everybody who lived in an apartment building was in a book, and the Gestapo went house to house."

A week after the attack on Heydrich in Prague, flawed intelligence connected the assassins to the nearby village of Lidice. The Nazis razed the town, shooting 173 men and deporting 196 women to concentration camps. Of the 95 children in Lidice, 7 were sent to live with German families and the remainder were gassed at Chełmno. All told, 1,357 people were killed in the wake of Operation Anthropoid, with another

3,188 arrested. The assassins themselves took cover in the basement of Saints Cyril and Methodius Cathedral in central Prague. The walls still show the bullet marks from the ensuing shootout. The Nazis flooded the crypt in hopes of flushing out or drowning the assassins, some of whom were killed by gunfire, while others committed suicide to avoid being taken alive. All the assassins perished.[11]

Though Prague was spared the air raids that obliterated many other Central and Eastern European cities, preserving the medieval center as a tourist draw to this day, the human cost of the war was nonetheless high. Up to 89 percent of the prewar Jewish population in the Czech lands perished during the war and some 83 percent of Slovak Jews.[12] Even those who defied the odds and survived the concentration camps often returned to find their homes occupied by someone else.

In September 1944, the first units of the Red Army crossed into Eastern Slovakia. On May 5, 1945, with the Red Army on the outskirts of the city, the Prague uprising began. The next day, sixty miles west, US general George Patton's Third Army liberated the city of Plzeň and its famed Pilsner Urquell brewery. After quaffing a celebratory *pivo* or two, Patton and company halted their advance eighteen miles short of Prague before retreating back across the German border. The victorious allies had allocated Czechoslovakia to the Soviet zone of occupation, and for many in Czechoslovakia, the word *Yalta*—the location of the February 1945 conference that outlined the postwar occupation plans—joined *Munich* as shorthand for betrayal.

The first Russians into Prague were led by General Andrei Vlasov. Earlier in the war, his units—a ragtag bunch of right-wingers, ex-czarist aristocracy, and veterans of the White Army that had battled and lost to the Bolsheviks during the Russian Civil War—had sided with the Nazis to fight against the Red Army. Once it became clear the Nazis would lose, the "Vlasovci," as they are known in Czech, switched sides. Hoping to surrender to the Americans rather than the Soviets, the Vlasovci turned their guns back on the Germans and fought their way west. For Vlasov at least, the plan failed. He was captured by the Soviets, transferred to Moscow, and executed. But a good number of soldiers from this rogue unit survived, fled to the United States, and found employment with the CIA—where Russian speakers who hated reds were always in high demand. Karel and the Vlasovci would meet again some three decades hence.

In April 1945, a provisional Czechoslovak government passed a law revoking citizenship for all ethnic Germans and Hungarians. Nine of the twenty-five ministers in that government were members of the Communist Party, but that ratio was about to change. At the time of liberation, the Czechoslovak Communist Party had just fifty thousand members, but eleven months later, there were more than 1.2 million members. By 1948, the party counted 2.5 million acolytes—one of every three adults.

Starting in June 1945, people's courts tried alleged Nazi collaborators—97 percent of the accused were convicted.[13] More than 660,000 ethnic Germans were removed from the country in the first burst of an ethnic cleansing orgy. A further 20,000 were executed. In August 1945, the Beneš Decrees, named after the reinstalled president, codified the earlier law stripping Germans and Hungarians of citizenship. During 1946, 2.8 million more ethnic Germans were forcibly removed from Czechoslovakia.[14] Property in the Sudetenland, now returned to Czechoslovakia, was seized from ethnic Germans and collaborators. Accounting for one-quarter of the national wealth, it was turned over to 1.5 million ethnic Slavs who were brought in from elsewhere in the country.

In the autumn of 1945, eleven-year-old Karel, by now speaking English "more or less fluently," was one of many enduring postwar hardship. A government report from January 1946 found seven hundred thousand children in Czechoslovakia living in poverty; half had tuberculosis. Young Karel suffered from severe middle ear infections. At the time they were treated by poking a hole behind the ear to drain fluid. Karel would bear those scars for the rest of his life.

Even though Czechoslovakia was counted as part of the Soviet sphere, and the Communist Party was in the ascendancy, politics remained democratically contestable for at least three years after the war. In the May 1946 elections, the Communists received the most votes, with a 38 percent share. Gottwald, the Communist leader who had fled in 1938, returned to lead an eight-party coalition government as prime minister. Beneš, a Social Democrat, stayed on as president. In the meantime, the Communists were infiltrating institutions from the ground up.

A university student named Rita Klimová, then an ardent Stalinist who—in a classic Cold War about-face—later embraced free market zealotry to become Czechoslovakia's first post-Communist ambassador to the United States, tried to recruit a young Karel to spy on his classmates. "She told me I could have anything I wanted, party membership when you are fifteen or a diplomatic career, or whatever," Karel said. "I told her to go fuck herself."

Karel was already proving himself a willful, to put it kindly, individualist. "I got into trouble right away with some of the other kids. We were protesting the hanging of Stalin's picture on the wall." In 1946, that was impolitic, and Karel was briefly expelled from school. "I guess the Communists were still not strong enough, so I succeeded with an appeal," Karel recalled.

He joined a scouting group, traveling to England in 1946 and France two years later. "Until my fourteenth year, I was raised by my father. I was a boy just like all other boys—perhaps only more mischievous, for I have a very lively temperament," he would later write of himself in a university admissions essay. "I joined the scouts, and it was good for me, because I came in contact with a group of boys my age and I had to adjust my behavior accordingly."

The people of Prague also wondered how best to behave in this new status quo. With little idea of what else to do, they naturally reverted to prewar cultural norms. Karel recalled that he "went to church regularly, because my father is a fanatical Catholic." That practice was to continue "until I was thirteen to fourteen years old. After that, the church's teachings were too strong even for my adolescent head and I became a heathen, which I remain to this day."

As well as his metaphysical doubts, Karel had another good reason to stop attending Mass. The church, like many other traditional Czechoslovak institutions, was about to be eclipsed by the Communist Party. On February 26, 1948, the headline in the Communist Party's *Rudé pravo* newspaper read, "The People Cleanse the Republic of Saboteurs, Traitors and Unreliable Elements," as the Communists asserted full control.[15] Non-Communist ministers in the coalition government had resigned over a dispute about policing. They had hoped the tactical move would force a policy shift, cabinet reshuffle, or new elections, but instead the remaining Communist ministers simply continued governing without them.

"The parties of order, as they call themselves, died by the legal state they created," Jan Kozák, a member of the Communist Party's central committee, wrote as the soft coup of February 1948 hardened.[16]

Under Soviet guidance Karel's future employer, the Státní bezpečnost (State Security, or the StB), was created—merging intelligence, counterintelligence, and internal security in a single organization. On March 10, Jan Masaryk, Czechoslovakia's foreign minister and son of the country's founder-president, died after a mysterious fall from a ministry window. On May 9, the Communists imposed a new constitution. In the May 30 elections, more than 87 percent of Czech votes and some 85 percent of Slovaks supported Communist-allied candidates. On September 3, 1948, Beneš—the last prewar president, leader of the wartime government in exile, first postwar president, and bridge to the golden age of the First Republic—died.

Confident that friends and fellow travelers now controlled Czechoslovakia, the Soviets asserted themselves elsewhere in the region. In hopes of subsuming British-, American-, and French-occupied West Berlin into what was otherwise Soviet-controlled terrain, on June 24, 1948, the Soviets blockaded the allied zone from the rest of the world. Two days later, the United States launched the Berlin Airlift, flying in thousands of tons of supplies every day. It proved mere overture to the division of Germany into the Western-allied Federal Republic and the Soviet-backed Democratic Republic the next year. All-powerful

Germany had splintered in two and hardened into the front line of a new kind of war.

On June 28, Yugoslavia was expelled from Cominform, the Soviet-led body directing the global Communist movement. Yugoslav leader Josip Broz Tito had liberated his country from the Nazis without Soviet assistance and thus insisted on maintaining independence from Moscow. In response, Stalin cut him off, and henceforth the term *Titoist* became shorthand for any supposed conspirator or terrorist deserving of death in Eastern Europe.

Spotting an opportunity, the United States countered by supplying Tito's Yugoslavia with aid, and early moves by both sides upped the ante to codify the early Cold War. In 1947, the CIA was created, and the next year, the US National Security Council expanded the CIA's modest mandate to include "propaganda, economic warfare; preventative direct action, including sabotage, anti-sabotage, demolition and evacuation measures; subversion against hostile states, including assistance to underground resistance movements, guerrillas and refugee liberation groups, and support of indigenous anti-communist elements in threatened countries of the free world."[17]

The political tumult, a grotesque amalgamation of rigidity and absurdity, was dizzying, especially for a teenage boy. So young Karel Koecher battled away on the home front. In 1949, he started attending the French lycée in Prague, a school full of "girls who were beautiful because their mothers were beautiful," Karel recalled. As he and eight other newcomers joined up, they were considered "social nobodies." Still, Karel picked up the new language fast. Out of his element, Karel's burgeoning disdain for authority surfaced following a round of staffing changes, after which "the teachers' department started reeking of undisguised philistinism," he would write.

"I found it revolting to flatter the professors and then later slander them behind their backs, to nod obediently to everything and never say what I think, not even to my classmate. So I was always in a fight with the school rules. That lasted until my graduation," he continued.

Karel took his rebellious schoolyard persona out into the streets too. In November 1949, he met up with classmate Jiří Kodeš in Prague's Wenceslas Square. There, they connected with a third student, Michal Tanabauer. "We decided to form this illegal group where we would be doing all sorts of things against the current regime," fifteen-year-old Karel later admitted under interrogation from the StB.

A week after their first meeting, Karel received a letter setting a second rendezvous for Wednesday night on Prague's famed Charles Bridge. At six o'clock, Karel joined up with his coconspirators, and the group moved to the shadows of a nearby park to plot. The next week, they met again. A student who identified himself as Josef Urban "stressed that on January 1 it is all going to burst and that we need to prepare ourselves. He further said we are expecting a lot of money," Karel said later. "He also said he has some weapons hidden in his chimney and that he will lend them to us if we need them. After Christmas we were together in Prokopské údolí [a wooded recreational area in Prague], where Urban showed us an old revolver and an old gun. He fired it twice."

According to StB files, Urban implored the rest of the group to scan their neighborhoods for gun shops or potential weapons caches. "Prior to Urban leaving for the New Year holidays, he mentioned that he knows a certain person who has some connections to the American embassy. After his return he told us he managed to get the name of this person and his name is Bach," Karel later told his interrogators.

Early in January, in an attempt to find this mysterious, possibly mythical Bach, Karel, Urban, and others visited the US embassy. They were turned away. "When it comes to the weapons or the guns, he would always talk about seven guns, revolvers, that he was hiding at home," Karel told the StB.

In a trial run of clandestine meetings to come, Josef Urban asked Karel and Michal Tanabauer to go to the Romanian wine bar on Rybná Street to congregate with another rebel group. The meeting was set for 9:00 p.m. "They were supposed to give us some sort of a letter," Karel later told the StB. "We were supposed to wait until three young men came to the bar and then we were supposed to ask them for matches. Then they were supposed to give us the answer that they don't smoke and offer us something to drink. Then they were supposed to give us a letter. We never saw any of those young men; we waited for about an hour."

Instead, Karel and his friends were arrested and hauled in for questioning. The StB files make it clear that the group had been penetrated by informants from the beginning. Karel was eventually released without charges—even Stalinists, it seems, make exceptions for inane teenagers—but he had already acquired a permanent StB file.

"I have joined this group against the state, which was further supposed to initiate some actions against the state and the democratic systems in the Czechoslovak state. I apologize for my behavior," Karel confessed to the StB. "I did not actually take the whole thing seriously in any way. I understood it as a romantic adventure. I have not alerted the security apparatus; I have not told them about the existence of such a group and that was because I did not want to let my friends down."

Karel's social circle was hardly the only one penetrated by Communist agents. "It was all over by 1950," he recalled. "They had spies everywhere. It was absolutely impossible to resist, especially in an armed way."

Cold War paranoia was at an all-time high everywhere. The Korean War kicked off in June, and the view from Eastern Europe was scary. In 1950, the Soviet economy was about 30 percent the size of that of the United States.[18] Americans had 369 operational atomic bombs; the Soviets had 5.[19] The same year, another US National Security Council directive, NSC-68, cleared the way for the American government to use "any measures, overt or covert, violent or nonviolent," in the name of national security.

The gloves were off, and over the next three years, the number of covert CIA staffers increased from 302 to 2,812, with another 3,142 contractors working abroad. Seven CIA stations became forty-seven, and the budget for covert activities ballooned from $4.7 million to $82 million. On November 1, 1952, the United States tested its first hydrogen bomb. Ten months later the Soviets did the same. In 1953, the CIA overthrew the democratically elected leftist Mohammed Mosaddegh in Iran as the "third world" emerged as a Cold War battlefront.

Under Communist leadership, Karel's homeland underwent radical change. "The consequences of the communist social revolution had been felt more dramatically in Czechoslovakia than elsewhere, in large part because it really was a developed, bourgeois society—in contrast with every other country subjected to Soviet rule," historian Tony Judt wrote.[20]

In 1948, 60 percent of Czechoslovakia's trade had been with the non-Communist world, but five years later, that number had fallen to 21 percent.[21] In 1953, currency reform decimated the savings of everyone with anything left. As Soviet security advisors asserted control over the StB, political purges accelerated. During the 1950s, there were an estimated one hundred thousand political prisoners in a country of thirteen million people.[22] Titoists, Trotskyites, and bourgeois nationalists were the targets. As of spring 1951, the Soviets directed Prague to root out so-called Zionists too, including Rudolf Slánský, the Communist Party's second-in-command. As if to guard against anyone presuming Slánský innocent following his November 1951 arrest, he was branded with a sterile, yet prejudicial, nickname in the press—"The Spy Slánský."

A spate of similar arrests followed, and the resulting trials were broadcast on national radio between November 20 and 27, 1952. Eleven of the fourteen accused in the Slánský trial were Jewish. The indictment alone took three hours to read, with the defendants accused of being "Trotskyists-Titoists-Zionists, bourgeois nationalists and enemies of the Czech people," alleged to be working "in the service of American imperialists and under the leadership of Western intelligence services."[23]

All fourteen were convicted. Three received life sentences, and the rest were executed, their ashes scattered on an icy road outside Prague.[24] In a preposterous twist, the Communists tried to spin the Slánský episode as emblematic of their love for the Jewish people. "Normally bankers, industrialists, and former kulaks don't get into our Party,"

President Klement Gottwald said. "But if they were of Jewish origin and Zionist orientation, little attention among us was paid to their class origins. This state of affairs arose from our repulsion of anti-Semitism and our respect for the suffering of the Jews."[25]

Some estimate more than one million Communists were killed in Eastern Bloc purges during the years 1949 to 1953.[26] With comrades like that, who needed enemies? As the violent birth pangs of a new totalitarian age subsided, a certain repressive banality set in. Then, on March 5, 1953, Josef Stalin died. Among his final words, muttered from the depths of a paranoid confusion he had managed to institutionalize, he said, "I'm finished. I don't even trust myself."[27]

2

EXISTENTIAL STRUGGLE

"The only way to deal with an unfree world is to become so absolutely free that your very existence is an act of rebellion."
—ALBERT CAMUS

By November 1953, the cover of *Time* magazine was paying tribute to the winner of the Soviet power struggle—new party chief Nikita Khrushchev—under the headline "Russia: The New Direction." He set to work immediately. Between 1953 and 1956, five million prisoners were released from Soviet gulags.[1] In 1954, the Soviets rebranded Stalin's old secret police, the NKVD, as the KGB. Even more consequential, on February 25, 1956, Khrushchev condemned Stalinist atrocities in a secret speech to Communist Party members.

Stalin "used extreme methods and mass repressions at a time when the revolution was already victorious, when the Soviet state was strengthened, when the exploiting classes were already liquidated, and Socialist relations were rooted solidly in all phases of national economy, when our party was politically consolidated and had strengthened itself both numerically and ideologically," Khrushchev told his stunned party colleagues. "It is clear that here Stalin showed in a whole series of cases his intolerance, his brutality, and his abuse of power. Instead of proving his political correctness and mobilizing the masses, he often chose the path of repression and physical annihilation, not only against actual enemies, but also against individuals who had not committed any crimes against the party and the Soviet government."[2]

No one had dared speak that way while Stalin was still alive, and although the speech went unpublished in the Soviet Union until 1988, news of this decisive break from the past trickled out—even making its way to Czechoslovakia. At a writers' congress in April 1956, poet Jaroslav Seifert, a future Nobel Prize winner, spoke optimistically of the dawn of a new age. "Again and again, we hear it said at this Congress that it is necessary for writers to tell the truth. This means that in recent years they did not write the truth," he said. "All that is now over. The nightmare has been exorcised."[3]

In Czechoslovakia Antonín Zápotocký became president, with Antonín Novotný taking over as party chief. In a nod to the changed mood in Moscow, Novotný ordered a commission to review the Slánský trials, but few were surprised when the commission found the verdicts to have been "just and fair."[4] Unlike Khrushchev, Novotný was directly implicated in many of the earlier era's purges. For Novotný, a former blacksmith, building a worker's paradise was a lot like laying railway track. The job called for hammering raw materials—in this case people—into form while staying the course. A true believer undeterred by the new mood in Moscow, Novotný insisted Czechoslovakia continue to celebrate Stalin. On May 1, 1955, the world's largest Stalin statue—fifty-one feet tall—was unveiled in Prague. As it cast a pall over the city from its hilltop overlook, even the sculptor who made it couldn't bear to watch the unveiling, and he killed himself before it was revealed to the public. This stone-faced statue of the "Man of Steel"[5] would inexplicably lord over Prague until 1962.

Fluent in Czech, English, French, and Russian, and with top marks on his leaving exams, Karel Koecher should have been an ideal candidate for Prague's celebrated Charles University. And yet disciplinary troubles, including that darned record with the secret police, made it difficult for him to get into college. To an admissions board, worried about who might be looking over their shoulders and stuffed with party hacks, Karel Koecher's record of rebellion made him a threat. More dangerous than a violent or angry youth, here was a free spirit who refused to recognize the rules of the game.

In those days and during the decades to come, the Czechoslovak state had no recognizable moral center. Everything was contingent. Nothing was clear. Logic was hard to come by. Many things that were ostensibly illegal—bribery, nepotism, or black-market dealings—were de rigueur among the ruling class. Depending on who you knew, not only was it possible to get away with such acts of subterfuge, but they might even be encouraged.

In the meantime, violations of informal political codes could lead to harsh punishment. A violent assault in a *hospoda*—a local pub—warranted a slap on the wrist, but carrying a copy of the wrong book or mocking a public official in the wrong company could cost someone their job or condemn their kids to a lifetime of manual labor. "Progress dines at times on roasted youth," Czech author Bohumil Hrabal wrote of the era[6]—one in which nothing made sense for long, good could become bad overnight, and librettists were pushed to be welders.

Karel had not faced any specific legal sanctions for his involvement in the half-baked teenaged plot to overthrow the Communist regime, but since the Communist Party's tentacles stretched into every aspect of daily life, he was viewed as suspicious until he could prove otherwise. Karel's first application to Charles University was rejected. And so was his second. Finally, in a third application, after one former teacher vouched for his promise as a student, Karel was accepted to study mathematics and physics in 1953.

In a 1956 essay overflowing with self-doubt, Karel explained his technocratic choice of study. "I did not believe that I had enough talent for literary work—I was assured of that both in school and at home," he wrote. "I lacked a concise and clear view of the world, because all politics and philosophy were revolting to me and I wanted to do something which connected to them as little as possible." As Karel tells it, his parents emphasized to him that they were "old and sick" and that there was no way they could support him if he pursued a line of study closer to his instincts—like becoming a writer: "What horror."

So Karel's artistic inclinations were subsumed by a tide of formulas and theorems. He was surrounded by a repressive society at large and consumed by resentment toward his parents at home. He defined himself as different from pretty much everyone: "I am an extreme individualist," he wrote in 1956. "I try to escape from the society I live in, and I do not succeed. . . . I am also increasingly alienated from my family; we have become strangers."

Karel's animus toward his mother meant he showed little sympathy for her wartime scars. Irena had been lucky to survive; nearly all of her extended family had perished in the Holocaust, which was a lifelong source of trauma. During the six-year Nazi occupation, every knock on the door was cause for alarm. Each noise on the street triggered a twitch. There were rumors and innuendo, and—eventually—the sad truth trickled in from Slovakia. One village or another had been cleared out, more friends and relations eradicated. Somehow—likely a combination of bribes, forged documents, and good fortune—Irena avoided deportation. But the experience crippled her and impacted everybody else. "As far as I know, she didn't leave the apartment for the entire war," Karel's childhood neighbor Pavel Illner recalled.

By the 1950s, Irena was spending her days working in a candy store, but the ambience in the apartment stayed bitter. In Karel's adolescence, the tension in the household had only increased, and Irena made Karel sleep in unheated rooms with the windows open. As far as he could tell, "she hated me."[7]

Relations with his father, Jaroslav, were no better. Jaroslav's world of yesterday no longer existed, but he nonetheless meted out corporal punishment as if he were running an Austro-Hungarian military school. "Somehow he did not get along with his parents, and they usually revisit those problems on their children," Karel explained of his father's rough approach. "As a young guy, eleven years old or so, they started sending him to those horrible institutions. Military schools had to be terrible in Austria-Hungary."

The country Jaroslav had served ceased to exist, and Czechoslovakia's army had no interest in an Austro-German mutt of questionable loyalty. The post office had forced Jaroslav into early retirement in 1949. With nowhere to go and nothing to do, he subsisted on a pension of 4,000 Czechoslovak crowns per month. "He never really recovered," Karel says. "Of course he didn't follow how the world was changing. He just didn't understand it. He had absolutely no idea what I was up to."

As Karel got older, he got up to quite a lot. Physical confrontations with Jaroslav were less common, but the pair clashed on any number of fronts. For Karel, it was easier to just keep his distance: "I was a loner as a kid. So I sought refuge elsewhere." Starting at age fifteen, Karel worked as a tour guide in Prague's city center. His language skills, taste for storytelling, and love of history pushed him to apply for the job: "They decided to get rid of those old timers as tourist guides. So they started licensing tourist guides, and they announced a first round of courses. I thought I would learn something. They thought I was a whiz kid. I was getting the best jobs and was asked to do two-hour lectures at the castle."

The work gave Karel a sense of responsibility and a modicum of respect. It appealed to his creative instincts and put him in touch with interesting people—including many visitors from abroad. "Prague is still beautiful, but now it is commercialized," he recalled. "But that was the Golden City, no tourists at all, and it is unbelievable how the history stands out. It gives you shivers, especially if you are sensitive."

Karel never told his father about the work: "He had no idea with whom I was spending the day."

It was at Jaroslav's urging that Karel felt compelled to study math. "He thought that being a physicist would be a good, secure position," Karel said. Perhaps Jaroslav hoped that rules and numbers would confine his wildly undisciplined son and force him to adapt to the increasingly doctrinaire world around him. Equations are all about balance, after all. But for Karel, the impact was the opposite, and life at Charles University only further alienated him from his peers.

He recalled, "I was quite lonely among the students for whom mathematics and physics is everything. I don't make fun of them. I value their work and know that it is not easy. But for me, natural sciences could never become the purpose of my life. It was a desperate conflict, complicated by the situation at home, which had escalated into enmity."

Three years into his physics degree, Karel could no longer repress his creative instincts, and he worked up the courage to apply for a second course of studies at Prague's prestigious film school—FAMU.[8] A young novelist named Milan Kundera taught screenwriting there, and future alumni include accomplished international directors like Miloš Forman, Agnieszka Holland, Emir Kusturica, and Jiří Menzel.

Karel was willing to continue with his physics degree while studying film on the side, pursuing two separate university degrees at two different universities.[9]

"For a while I had no place to rest from everything, didn't have anybody with whom I would feel happy and content. I wanted to stop reading, writing, watching films, going to the theater, seeing exhibitions," Karel wrote of his feelings in the months leading up to the film school application. "I grasped onto existentialism; it excused my fear about solving these problems, and it also gave me the illusion that I am something else, because I have seen the nothingness of this wretched life."

Existentialism was all the rage. The demise of organized religion and the horrors of the Holocaust could not help but generate questions about the meaning of life—and whether there was any meaning at all. Disorientation, confusion, and angst were the starting points for anybody living in an absurd world devoid of purpose. Individuals were forced to define meaning for themselves. To live authentically in an unmoored existence, each person must first create their own self and then do their best to adhere to it.

"There is but one truly serious philosophical problem, and that is suicide," Albert Camus wrote in 1942 in *The Myth of Sisyphus*, a popular existentialist text. "Judging whether life is or is not worth living amounts to answering the fundamental question of philosophy. All the rest—whether or not the world has three dimensions, whether the mind has nine or twelve categories—comes afterwards."[10]

To Karel, this kind of thinking was attractive. "I had some money, which I made mostly as a guide and interpreter," he wrote in his 1956 essay. "Despite this I despised it all, but I thought that perhaps I shouldn't care."

And so the moral vacuum yawned a little wider, for Karel and many others. The upheaval of recent decades prompted existential crises for men and women of all ages. As Karel applied to film school, his father played his angst out in real time, penning his own letter to the admissions committee. Its tone was hostile, frustrated, and unhinged, and it left little doubt about the environment Karel was forced to endure at home. Jaroslav began by taking offense at not being consulted about his son's plans to study film.

"It is possible to say, that as an adult person, he has the right to do so," Jaroslav wrote. "Parents, who with a great strain enable studying, can however hardly be denied having a say in the matter."

Vitriol spills from every sentence, and it's confounding why any parent—even with these feelings—would find it necessary to put them in writing and share them with the outside world. Jaroslav sought revenge on somebody, for something, and Karel became the target.

"He now treats us rudely and disrespectfully," Jaroslav's letter continued. "It seems that he tries by this to get a larger sum of money from us, especially from his mother, so that he can move away and live on his own. This has caused some unpleasant scenes, although he knows that we cannot afford it, he makes our lives intentionally unbearable."

Karel's father went on to denigrate his son's potential as a filmmaker. It is clear that Jaroslav was not just venting but trying to discourage FAMU from allowing Karel to study. Put another way, he actively tried to sabotage his son's prospects. "[Karel] has an average talent in many things, but stands out in none. He never forms a deep connection to any subject he studies. As soon as he somewhat masters the subject, he loses interest," Jaroslav went on. "He is interested in superficial, cheap success and the admiration of his peers at any cost. Another thing preventing him from standing out is his absolute lack of creative abilities."

By the time Jaroslav wrote his letter, Karel had already passed the FAMU entrance exam and submitted his personal essay, in which he had already advised the admissions team of the troubled father-son relationship: "My father, as I recall, has always had a rather hostile view of the world, which only increased with his old age and decreasing health."

It's unclear what the admissions committee made of Jaroslav's bizarre paternal intervention, but it was painful for Karel. He recalled that it "hurt me badly. I guess he was also frustrated with me. I wasn't following in his footsteps. And it was all the evils of the modern world that I was clinging to." The letter's presence in the StB files indicates that the security services found it worth keeping on hand. Jaroslav's insinuation that Karel was driven to obtain personal success even had a political tone, using code words to insinuate that Karel was partial to Western-style decadence. It became yet another blemish on his record.

Jaroslav was hardly the only member of his generation to experience extreme alienation, and it's difficult to believe he was the only one taking it out on his family. In the United States, this same sort of disorientation was a major topic for Karel's future PhD advisor, the American philosopher Charles Frankel.

"In no other age have men lived with so dizzying a sense of change, or seen their basic material and social environment being made over, and made over again, so steadily," Frankel wrote in a 1956 book called *The Case for Modern Man*. "Technology, plainly, is the fundamental dynamic element in modern society."[11]

By the 1950s, most middle-aged adults had spent a good part of their life struggling through the deprivation of depression and war. This made Soviet-style Communism, with its claim to guarantee stability, employment, and subsistence for all, appear a viable alternative to free market capitalism. It was the latter that had caused the Great Depression, and it was the right-wing Nazis, not the left-wing Bolsheviks, who were the instigators of World War II.

"To keep hope alive one must, in spite of all mistakes, horrors, and crimes, recognize the obvious superiority of the socialist camp," another famed existentialist, Jean Paul Sartre, wrote.[12] In 1958, the French Communist Party won nearly 20 percent of the vote, and the Italian Communists won 22 percent the same year. As long as one was willing to ignore the human casualties and the near total repression of free expression, even Eastern Bloc Communists could produce some numbers to argue that working-class life was getting better.

Between 1950 and 1960, per capita earnings in the Soviet Union grew 5.2 percent (though Moscow claimed a much higher 10.8 percent). In Czechoslovakia, the victims of the purges of the 1950s were likely to be middle-class intellectuals, and so the poor, uneducated, and apolitical were less likely to have experienced repression firsthand. In the meantime, living standards rose. Between 1948 and 1952, the number of people forced to make a living in agriculture dropped 18 percent.[13] Whereas less than 10 percent of Czech and Slovak working-class children were enrolled in nonvocational higher education in 1938, by 1956 that number had risen to 31 percent. Four years after that, it topped 40 percent.[14]

In the developing world, data like this, boosted by the prospect of Soviet aid, had a lot of appeal. The Statue of Liberty beckoned to the world's tired, poor, huddled masses, but so too did Lenin's promise of peace, bread, and land. As the so-called third world toyed with state-centric economics, Cold War ideologues in Washington and elsewhere got ever more nervous.

In 1947, George Kennan had penned an influential article under the pseudonym of X, and it became the early model for American postwar policy. "The main element of any United States policy toward the Soviet

Union must be that of a long-term, patient but firm and vigilant containment of Russian expansive tendencies,"[15] he wrote, going on to argue that the patient application of such policies would not only limit damage to the global system but buy time until the inevitable happened. "The possibility remains (and in the opinion of this writer it is a strong one) that Soviet power, like the capitalist world of its conception, bears within it the seeds of its own decay, and that the sprouting of these seeds is well advanced,"[16] he continued.

But by the mid-1950s, some of Kennan's ideas were mutating into something much more aggressive. In 1954, President Dwight D. Eisenhower was presented with what came to be known as the Doolittle Report, named for the general who wrote it. "We are facing an implacable enemy whose avowed objective is world domination," it argued. "There are no rules in such a game. Hitherto acceptable norms of human conduct do not apply."[17]

Befitting the tenor of the times, the Cold War now amounted to an existential struggle in its own right. In response, the United States redefined itself and the perception of its own role in the world. Morality became fungible so long as it resulted in a net loss to the Soviet Union. The struggle was underway at all times and in all places, no matter how remote.

In 1954, the CIA overthrew democratically elected Jacobo Arbenz Guzmán in Guatemala. The United Fruit Company was farming just 15 percent of the land it owned while generating annual profits that were twice the revenue of the Guatemalan government. They also controlled all the country's railroads and the main port. Arbenz tried to buy the unused land back at the price the United Fruit Company had claimed it was worth in annual tax declarations.[18] Having intentionally undervalued the land to lower its tax bill, the United Fruit Company deemed the offer unacceptable and was able to use connections at the State Department and CIA (CIA director Allen Dulles had formerly served on the company's board of directors)[19] to replace Arbenz with a military junta.

Decades of brutal dictatorship followed, helping codify the term *banana republic* to represent a country with unstable, stratified politics based on extracting private profit from natural resources.

"We had to get rid of a Communist government which had taken over," Eisenhower later said.[20]

That same year, Ho Chi Minh pushed the colonizing French out of the northern part of his country and created North Vietnam. The United States had backed French war efforts, but after signing a peace agreement with Ho on July 12, 1954, in Geneva, the French withdrew from the region altogether. The United States took on the burden of propping up a corrupt but anti-Communist government in the southern part of the country, wading ever deeper into the rice paddies and jungles of Southeast Asia—a fitting metaphor for the practical and ethical quagmire from which American foreign policy thinkers would struggle to emerge for two decades.

When asked to justify the otherwise unjustifiable, US policy makers asserted the need to combat the global spread of Communism—though it was never clear how US troops could successfully confront an ideological concept. It was an argument befitting the Cold War's convoluted but infectious rationale. It explained why "one set of conflicts repeated over and over again," as historian Odd Arne Westad later put it, "and why all other contestants for power—material or ideological—had to relate to" this larger dynamic.[21]

Physical manifestations of ideological confrontations trickled down to the street level, and as a young man of independent aspirations, but lacking the means, Karel Koecher saw his ambition thwarted by Cold War logic at every turn. Along with the normal uncertainties of young adulthood, it was enough to make him question his own sanity.

In concluding his ultimately successful application essay for film school, Karel summed up his life to that point. "I discovered this: that I have no right to complain, that I am twenty years old and that means something, that I have to fight for what I want, that there are other people in this world and I can offer them something, that it is in fact my duty to do so, and that a man has to have his work that he enjoys as a first priority," he wrote. "It took me a long time to work my way to all these perspectives, and I cannot imagine ever abandoning them."

Karel's use of the first-person pronoun nine times in just the last few lines of the essay is notable. He was caught up in a global conflict of ideas, and it looked as if he had already decided to go it alone.

3

JOINING UP

"History is a preceptor of prudence, not of principles."
—Edmund Burke

Sometime during his second or third year at the school of physics, Karel got the call. After seven years guiding tours in the City of Spires, this would be the twenty-one-year-old's biggest assignment yet.

As instructed, Karel waited in Prague's Wenceslas Square. A tall man exited the Ambassador Hotel and introduced himself.[1] American, not British, Karel thought after hearing his accent. Professor George Kline worked in the philosophy department at Columbia University in New York City. As a specialist in Eastern Europe, he made regular research trips to the region. Later, Kline would smuggle manuscripts by Russian poet Josef Brodsky to the United States, helping the future Nobel Prize winner find a global audience.

As Kline and Karel began to chat, the bespectacled professor showed keen interest in Prague's literary heritage too. "He says to me, 'Kafka was from Prague; ever heard of him?'" Karel recalled. "At the time, I swear there would not have been anybody else my age that would have heard of Kafka."

For a host of reasons, Franz Kafka's texts were still rare in his native Prague. As a Jew who wrote in German, his stories recalled a Bohemia that predated Nazi occupation and the Communist takeover. For the new regime, these were times best ignored: the present could never live up to the mythology of that earlier era. Perhaps least convenient to the powers that be, Kafka's themes—alienation, disorientation, absurdity—seemed to anticipate the worst aspects of a totalitarian dystopia. This was a case of life imitating art.

In one of Kafka's best-known works, *The Trial*, a clerk named Josef K. is arrested by two anonymous agents employed by an unidentified power. Josef K. cannot recall committing a crime and is allowed to roam free while awaiting his judicial proceedings. In a way, this uncertain state of being proves worse than incarceration, for Josef K. is left to speculate about what is going on and what might happen. The court never even informs Josef K. of what he stands accused. It is psychologically tortuous.

Josef K.'s anxiety grows when he learns that nobody has ever been acquitted by the mysterious court tasked with adjudicating his case. Like the victims of the Stalinist show trials of the 1950s, Josef K. finds himself caught up in a convoluted, almost hallucinatory, bureaucratic process. Eventually, he is executed—"Like a Dog!" Kafka writes.[2]

As he lay dying of tuberculosis in 1924, Kafka asked his friend Max Brod to burn his unpublished manuscripts. Brod ignored the request, publishing a few in German before fleeing Czechoslovakia for Palestine in 1939. The first Czech translation of *The Trial* did not appear until 1958, and a good many of Kafka's writings only began circulating in Czech as samizdat—literature clandestinely copied and distributed to dodge state censors—publications during the early 1960s.[3] The first major academic conference on Kafka did not occur until 1963, and by then Kafka's discovery by a wider readership signaled the brief flowering of liberal culture in Czechoslovakia that would culminate in 1968's Prague Spring.

But all that was still years away when Karel and Kline met up in 1956, as a series of coincidences toppled like dominoes to alter the course of Karel's life. He happened, by chance, to be dating a woman named Jana Černá at the time. She, in turn, happened to be the daughter of the late journalist and writer Milena Jesenská—who had once been Kafka's lover and his first Czech translator. Jesenská died in a concentration camp in 1944, but Jana was alive and well. She had told Karel about Kafka. Kline had, as Karel put it, "met perhaps the one guy in the whole country" prepared to have an informed English-language conversation about Kafka.

Kline asked if Karel, the tour guide, knew where Kafka was buried. He did. Karel recalled, "So I took him to his grave."

Kline would not forget Karel. The professor returned to Prague in 1957 and 1960, and the two of them met up each time. Karel introduced Kline to people he knew from film school. They drank in bars, and Kline shared books. During the 1957 trip, Kline introduced Karel to Yaroslava Surmach. The daughter of Ukrainian immigrants to the States, she was a painter roving Eastern Europe researching folk culture. Karel became romantically involved with Surmach and tagged along on a trip she took to Warsaw. They were eating in a restaurant when another American— the innovative sociologist C. Wright Mills—sat at a table nearby.

When Mills overheard Koecher and Surmach speaking English, he couldn't resist introducing himself to the attractive artist. As far as Yaroslava was concerned, Karel was no longer the most interesting man in the room. Surmach would later marry Mills. "Through Kline, [Karel] in 1957 met, amid interesting circumstances another US citizen, [Yaroslava] Surmach, later the wife of author Wright Mills, with whom he maintained intimate relations and whom he accompanied on her journey in Poland. He then maintained written contact with her," read a later StB account of the events.

Regular interaction with foreigners, never mind exotic English speakers, was not the norm for young Czechoslovaks. Russian, German, and French were all more common second languages for Czechs, and it would be decades before Prague made it onto the college backpacking circuit. Not only did Karel's English skills and his tour guide job put him in touch with a bevy of cosmopolitan visitors, but his genuine curiosity about the outside world and thirst for risk meant he pushed these relationships further than others might.

Unfamiliar as Karel was with life beyond Czechoslovakia, he was nonetheless imbued with a sense that he might find opportunity amid the uncertainty. As he looked around at his lack of prospects in Prague, at minimum he already saw the outside world as a place worth exploring. Amid frustration in his personal life, with his ambition crashing into barriers at every turn, something was telling him to get out. Though that remained an impossible prospect for the time being, there was at last a flicker of light in an otherwise dark tunnel.

Karel began viewing his own country, and the world, in a way that was different from his compatriots. Contrary to most of his peers, he saw the apparently all-encompassing power of the Czechoslovak Communist Party for what it really was—transient and limited. Whereas most of his physics classmates approached encounters with the state or party with a sense of foreboding, Karel more or less refused to recognize, or at least chose to ignore, their authority. In 1957, Karel was primed for two years of mandatory service in the Czechoslovak army. He had a psychologist friend write a note claiming that he was psychologically disturbed. Along with his history of ear infections, that was enough to dodge the draft.

On the night of September 29, 1958, a police officer (from the domestic security agency the VB) spotted twenty-four-year-old Koecher kissing twenty-year-old Maria Nováková good night on her front doorstep. The two had been out on a date, and as Karel moved to depart, the officer approached. "He was met with insulting words from Karel Koecher," a district court document from the time reads. "He told him he should be ashamed, that he is a voyeur, that he is just looking on as he is meeting with a woman."

According to the officer's testimony, he had tried to reason with Karel, but "Koecher continued with the insults." Karel was detained and taken to the police station, and though he "admitted he said those things," he denied "that they were insulting in any way." Eventually, Karel "was sentenced conditionally to three months to one year [in jail] for insulting a public official."

Though the worst of Czechoslovakia's Stalinist purges were over, incidents like this lent the later 1950s a more Kafkaesque feel. In 1957, Czechoslovakia's president, Antonín Zápotocký, a former stone mason, died. Communist Party chairman Antonín Novotný, the ex-blacksmith, took on the role. As president and party chief, Novotný now controlled most levers of power. He wasn't executing people by the dozens, but he nonetheless eschewed Khrushchev's softened approach to domestic repression.[4]

"Even among the unglamorous company of communist leaders," an article in the *New York Times Magazine* read, Novotný "manages to carry the concept of squareness well through the cube and on into a quadrilateral fourth dimension."[5]

In 1960, a new constitution officially changed the name of the country to the Czechoslovak Socialist Republic (ČSSR), making Czechoslovakia the second country (after the Soviet Union) to claim it had achieved pure socialism. The name change no doubt meant to signal achievement but had the unintentional consequence of time-stamping the exact moment the regime gave up all pretense of progress and exposed itself as committed to a rigid defense of the socialist status quo.

Even as Novotný did his best to keep Czechoslovakia frozen in place, the Cold War was heating up like rocket fuel. On October 4, 1957, the Soviet Union launched the Sputnik satellite, and the starting gun on the superpower space race had been fired. In November 1958, Khrushchev demanded the West retreat from West Berlin, prompting a war scare just two hundred miles from Prague. On December 31, 1958, Cuban dictator Fulgencio Batista fled his country, and a week later, a triumphant Fidel Castro rode into Havana with a ragtag band of cigar-chomping guerillas. By the end of 1959, US president Dwight D. Eisenhower mused that if a nuclear war started—an increasingly realistic prospect—"you might as well go out and shoot everyone you see and then shoot yourself."[6] Not the most optimistic of images.

Karel finished his physics degree in 1958 and continued with film school while taking on work as a television journalist. Even there he couldn't toe the line: "It made me sick, all that lying and trying to make things appear beautiful. Eventually, I refused some assignment and got blacklisted." In September 1959, he started teaching at a vocational school near Prague's picturesque Náměstí Míru. He also taught math part time at Czech Technical University and thought it prudent to apply for membership in the Communist Party. "I did admire, and still do, Khrushchev's refutation of Stalin," Karel said. "It was a heroic act to step out and say that Stalin was an insane maniac; what is more, [Khrushchev] opened the gates of the Gulag."

Many a citizen of Czechoslovakia looked to score party membership by the early 1960s. Some indeed still believed in socialism's prospects for creating a just society, while others hoped to gain power and exploit it. For the vast majority of people, though, party membership was little more than a pass into what equated to elite society, not unlike a diploma from the right boarding school or a titular inheritance in other countries.

In a remote Czechoslovak village, party membership might determine who got the job teaching seven-year-olds their multiplication tables. Or a parent's party status might prove decisive as teens competed for limited spots at a university. For adults, membership might lead to a well-paid, untaxing job or guarantee they could afford a small weekend cottage in the countryside.

This was clear as day to anyone paying attention, and Karel surrendered to the notion after a teaching colleague at the vocational school convinced him it would be easier to join the party than not. At last, Karel just might belong to something. Karel did not so much believe in the cause as he was willing to ally himself with the party in order to carve out some autonomy for himself. Applying for party membership was easy, but getting it was easier said than done. As Karel's application was under consideration and the party deliberated his already spotty record, more ghosts from the past emerged.

A former classmate from the French lycée in Prague, one Vladivoj Tomek, had recently mentioned Karel's name in an StB interrogation. Back in 1952, when he was sixteen, Tomek and three accomplices had ambushed four Czechoslovak soldiers on a tram and tried to steal their guns. One of the soldiers was shot and killed. Tomek went on the run and somehow managed to avoid arrest for years. In the meantime, he needed a way to make a living, so he took up a trade: counterfeiting money. In December 1959, Tomek was finally arrested for printing fake Czechoslovak crowns. By January 1960, the StB had managed to connect him with the 1952 shooting, and in the midst of a security service grilling, Tomek mentioned that he had met Karel Koecher just before the encounter with the soldiers on the tram.

Tomek holds two dubious historical distinctions. His confession was the first ever recorded on tape in Czechoslovakia. And after a court ruled that his "retention in human society would further endanger the people's democratic social order and people's lives," Tomek is often said to have been the country's last political execution. He was hanged on November 17, 1960.

"He was fat, not very smart, sick, with bad body odor," Karel recalled. "Nobody wanted to associate with him. As I said, the French lycée was an elite school, mostly girls from prominent families. Eventually, nobody would even sit next to him. I, asshole that I am, sat with him. I felt sorry for him.

"He missed quite a few classes, particularly mathematics," Karel continued. "So Tomek asked me if I could lend him my notes and maybe I could help teach him. So he came to my place." Tomek shot the soldier on his way home from the tutoring session. Though Karel had nothing to do with it, combined with his own youthful dalliance with armed rebellion, carefully noted in the StB records, Karel looked a lot like a repeat offender.

The StB opened another file on Karel. They called this one "Učitel"—the Czech word for teacher. More harassment and frustration followed, and Karel started to feel that it would never end. He did not belong, and perhaps he never would. He had tried going his own way, and he had tried following the rules and joining the party—neither had worked. Karel's dream of leaving the country started becoming more concrete. He was one of a growing number of young people from the Eastern Bloc looking for a way out.

By 1961, some 2.7 million East Germans had already fled their country through the open border to the West. The refugees were disproportionately educated and ambitious, the very people necessary to sustain an economy. To prevent the loss of more valuable human capital, East Germany sealed the border. On the night of August 12, they threw up a makeshift barrier running through the center of Berlin. The fence was meant to be temporary, but as it was fortified with concrete, razor wire, Dobermans, and guard towers, it became a fact of life for the next twenty-eight years. Everybody was locked in or out.

Though Karel did not have to vault over a wall to get out of his country, the impediments were still significant. He did not have a passport. Even if he managed to get outside the Eastern Bloc, there were limits on the amount of hard currency Karel could travel with—and he didn't possess much hard currency to begin with. After crossing the border into booming Austria or West Germany, he would have to live like a pauper.

Still, Karel did what he could. He applied to join a group of teachers going on an exchange program to Mali. Though he secured a spot, his besmirched record meant the authorities denied him a passport. In September 1961, he started teaching math at the technical university full time, and in October he won a UNESCO competition that would have seen French-speaking Karel teach for a year as a goodwill ambassador in Cameroon. In November, he signed a contract with UNESCO, and for a few days, he even allowed himself to get excited about the prospects of travel.

"He wasn't allowed a journey to Cameroon in the year 1961 as a teacher," a later StB file noted. "Although he had a legally concluded deal with UNESCO, as stated the reason for this was that considering his past, although he was a candidate for [Communist Party membership], he can't be seen as mature enough for this job."

Karel had applied for party membership and had gone through official channels as he tried to land a substantive job. For a reflexive antiauthoritarian like himself, this felt like a great personal concession to the powers that be. While Karel had always clashed with his parents and teachers, he at last had to acknowledge that the Communist Party was in charge. He could not beat them, so Karel concluded he had little choice but to join them. As the party rejected him anyway, he knew for a certainty that he was alone in this world.

The Czechoslovak government "tried to make me sign something that would say I was sick or something," Karel recalled of his failed bid to join UNESCO. "I told them to go fuck themselves." It would not be the last time.

Stuck stewing at home, Karel watched with interest as the world teetered on the brink of nuclear conflict. On his way out of office, US president Dwight D. Eisenhower delivered a farewell address on January 17, 1961. "Until the latest of our world conflicts, the United States had no armaments industry," he noted, before going on to say that the country had been "compelled to create a permanent armaments industry of vast proportions." This, he insisted, was unique in the American experience and thus something worth keeping an eye on. Eisenhower worried about a creeping "military-industrial complex" in which the economic influence of weapon companies was helping fuel American aggression in the world.

"We annually spend on military security alone more than the net income of all United States corporations," Eisenhower continued. "We must not fail to comprehend its grave implications. Our toil, resources, and livelihood are all involved. So is the very structure of our society."[7]

Even Eisenhower, a former career soldier who had dedicated his life to training for, planning, and executing war, considered emerging Cold War norms—a massive standing army, troops permanently deployed to bases abroad, and an economy predicated on the production of destructive weapons—as a dangerous deviation from the American way of life.

But nobody was listening. A few months later, in April 1961, the CIA used B-26 bombers to attack Cuban airfields. Two days later, fourteen hundred CIA-trained paramilitaries stormed the island's beaches, with the main invasion force landing at the Bay of Pigs. As the Cuban army made quick work of the invading force, US president John F. Kennedy was branded a foreign-policy neophyte, and US-Cuban antagonism was cemented for decades to come.

More Cold War clashes followed. On February 10, 1962, captured American pilot Gary Powers was exchanged for KGB spy Rudolf Abel on the Glienicke Bridge in Berlin. Twenty-one months earlier, Powers had been shot down over Soviet territory while taking reconnaissance photos in his U-2 spy plane. Karel didn't know it yet, but twenty-four years later—nearly to the day—he too would be exchanged on the legendary "Bridge of Spies."

Kennedy had campaigned for the American presidency in 1960 touting a supposed "missile gap"—the idea that the United States was falling behind the Soviet Union in its nuclear capabilities. In truth, by 1962 the United States had somewhere between eight and seventeen times more operational nukes than the Soviets.[8] The American advantage in intercontinental ballistic missiles (ICBM), projectiles that could be fired from each country's home territory and reach their enemy's respective territory, was even more pronounced: the Soviets possessed just twenty capable of striking the American continent.[9]

In Castro's Cuba, Khrushchev sensed an opportunity. Kennedy had already shown himself paranoid about the prospect of a Communist state just ninety miles from the US border, and in early 1962, Khrushchev wondered aloud, "Why not throw a hedgehog in Uncle Sam's pants?"[10]

By September 1962, the Soviet Union was constructing launch sites for medium- and intermediate-range ballistic missiles on the island. This forward deployment would compensate for the Americans' superior missile numbers and increased range. Some Soviet missiles destined for Cuba were capable of striking as far as twenty-eight hundred miles away. If they had been based on Soviet territory, they would have minimal strategic value in a hot war with the United States. But stationed in Cuba, most of the contiguous forty-eight states were within striking distance.

In October, the one-month standoff that came to be known as the Cuban Missile Crisis began. That same month, Prague finally removed its fifty-one-foot-tall statue of Stalin. Appropriate to Communism's lack of direction and mounting apathy in the world's second fully socialist state, the pedestal on which Stalin had once stood remained empty until 1991—when it was replaced by a metronome.

In Prague, Karel's personal battle with authority intensified as yet another StB report noted: "In the year 1962 he committed a criminal activity of a moral character, when he violated the moral code in the company of underage girls, and was convicted for eight months [jail time], probation for three years, after an appeal he was put on probation for 2 years."

The charges—initially statutory rape—were trumped up, Karel insisted, and the police files are convoluted enough to signal that something strange was going on. It seems clear Karel was partying with a group of young girls. Everybody was consuming alcohol, and one of the girls was underaged. Fifty-plus years later, it's impossible to know what happened, but two other women in the room later recanted their initial stories and told police that Karel had done nothing wrong.

Karel believed the StB was looking to frame him as a way of justifying his permanent exclusion from the Communist Party: "If you rape someone, they put you in jail." But Karel did not go to jail, and the episode reinforced in him the idea that the authorities would harass him no matter what he did.

Amid his other work, Karel had always managed to write. In fact, his desire to be a writer bubbled to the surface time and again throughout his life. In the early 1960s, he wrote book reviews and essays; later he wrote detective fiction as a hobby. By 1962, he was also toying with radio plays. Karel's father had pushed him to study hard sciences, but Karel's sojourn into film school made him think he just might make it as an artist. As he looked around at the competition, he realized he had at least as good a chance as some of his classmates.

Those hopes were ever so briefly validated when state-run radio hired him on as a full-time writer in the spring of 1962. "It was in the department in charge of satirical and humorous material," Karel said. "I had already written some stuff. I was doing pretty well, but by then state security was already after me."

After the reports that he was "keeping company with underaged girls" reached a local Communist Party committee, they raised hell, and Karel's superiors at the radio station had no choice but to fire him. "His conviction meant a discharge from the [list of Communist Party] candidates," as well as "much more trouble," the StB concluded.

Around that time Karel "realized that something terrible was going on, that it's like a Hitchcock movie. They tried again to make me out as some kind of criminal. So I couldn't get a job, and at that time, it was a felony not to be employed."

After a period of struggle, Karel managed to get work as a night watchman: "There was an old farm, and they used it for storing construction equipment. It was a job that priests would do. So I got it through one of the back channels at the seminary. It was an easy job; you could read the Bible."

Karel might have been content that he had avoided prison. But laying low just wasn't his style. At once assertive and pragmatic, he set out to rehabilitate his reputation: "I had a friend from the film school, he was studying production. A good guy. They offered him a job with the StB, snooping. Like snooping on actors and filmmakers. The first thing he did when he got there was look at my file. That is how we found out."

Karel's friend was named Jan Liška. In 1968, he would defect to Sweden, but in 1962 Liška came across Karel Koecher's swelling dossier. Each and every misdemeanor had been itemized.

So Karel and Jan cooked up a plan. What if they could get Karel a job at the StB? This could help tidy up Karel's otherwise sullied records.

It was impossible to erase the past, but working as an StB agent might allow him to dilute the worst of it in a torrent of bureaucratic verbiage. Handled in the right way, Karel just might avoid a lifetime of harassment and menial labor. The only alternative—surrendering to mediocrity—was just not an option.

Liška worked in counterintelligence, the branch of the StB that focused on opposing intelligence threats from abroad. As the name indicates, this is the opposite of standard intelligence work, which seeks to collect new information from hostile and friendly states alike. But the lines can be poorly defined. Liška, for example, was meant to keep an eye on artists and intellectuals inside Czechoslovakia to make sure foreign intelligence agencies were not using them to execute an agenda.

Early on, Karel also had his eye on counterintelligence work. Thwarting foreign adversaries sounded a lot better than informing on fellow citizens. So Liška started dropping Karel's name around the office while talking up his cunning and language skills. Then he began inviting Karel to a cafeteria where StB officials liked to lunch. In Czechoslovakia the midday meal was (and is) the day's main source of sustenance. *Piva*—beers, not beer—were routinely consumed. Well fed and just a little bit lubricated, even otherwise humorless StB officers were open to making new friends. So Karel would stop in to the cafeteria: "I thought, hell, if they got interested in me, they wouldn't just keep me here; they might send me abroad."

The plan worked: "Eventually they just knocked on the door."

It sounded like opportunity.

4

PASSING THE TEST

"Men make their own history. They do not make it just as they please.
They do not make it under circumstances chosen by themselves, but under
circumstances directly found, given and transmitted from the past."
—KARL MARX

Karel met twice with the StB in November 1962, but the first detailed record in the files comes from a third meeting at Prague's Demínka pub in early December with Lieutenant Miloslav Gvozdek, code-named Grulich (the German word for gruesome). Gvozdek would become Karel Koecher's first supervisor as a spy, but before the StB could trust their new recruit, they needed to put him to the test.

Gvozdek's summary of the meeting listed several contacts that Karel already had in the United States, including George L. Kline and Yaroslava Surmach. Though the summary does not explicitly spell it out, it's obvious that the authorities already thought of Karel as a candidate for a risky mission abroad to confront the country the Soviets preferred to call the "Main Enemy"—that is, the United States. Just a week after Gvozdek filed his report, on January 31, 1963, Karel signed a document formally launching his career in the Czechoslovak intelligence. He was code-named Pedro.

The StB wanted Karel to spy on Germans. If he happened to encounter a dramaturge dancing with imperialists or choreographers canoodling with capitalists, it was his duty to report them too. But Germans—West Germans—were his real targets.

It had been just a few years since Germany had invaded and occupied Czechoslovakia. Even before the smoke had cleared, starting in 1949, West Germany began implementing the so-called Vergangenheitspolitik, or "policy for the past," that offered amnesties to former Nazi officials and reintegrated them into public administration. "At that time West Germany was extremely hostile," Karel remembered. "Not like stealing technology or whatever, but refusing to extradite war criminals, refusing to pay restitution to people who were in concentration camps. So that was the job. I learned a hell of a lot."

Briefing, training, and instruction followed, and on the morning of April 5, the StB put Karel through his paces. They phoned Karel at home, where his mother, Irena, answered. She told the caller that Karel was not home and took a message from a man who spoke German with a Viennese accent. The man had something to give Karel. He wanted a meeting. Tell your son to call me, he told Irena.

Around midday Karel managed to connect with the mysterious caller, and they convened in Wenceslas Square fifteen minutes later. As agreed, the mystery man carried a copy of the West German magazine *Stern* to identify himself. He was, as Karel noted in a report, "around 35, tall about 170 cm, fat - weight 100 kg or more." He had "a round face, hair scarce at the back of the head, almost bald, hair quite prominent on the sides of the head, dark brown or black. Eyebrows light brown, not very thick, eyes dark brown, glasses, the black hoop of which covers only the top part of the glasses, golden above the nose; a small nose, strong lips, double chin, a massive back of the neck."

Clean shaven, with odd earlobes that clung close to his skull, his "skin stretched tight to the face," the man had a wart "above the right corner of his lips, a 3 cm long scar stretches itself from the left eye upwards." His hands were "small" with "fat fingers, nails kept shipshape, a slim gold wedding ring on his right hand." He smoked cigars and had "a swinging way of walking."

The pair ambled to a nearby restaurant, where the man told Karel he had a letter for him. New to the job, Karel grew nervous. What sort of letter? What could it be about? Was this some kind of trap? The restaurant was crowded, and Karel was wary of making an exchange in the midst of unknown people. What if someone were watching?

Karel suggested they might go somewhere else to talk. Back on the street, the man handed over the letter. Karel pocketed it as they made their way to the Demínka pub, home to great pilsner and bad coffee and where, at that midafternoon hour, they were likely to find themselves more or less alone. Karel took a table in the back corner and ordered coffee for two.

In Karel's estimation the man was "jovial, obviously enjoys good food and drinks, not very interested in women. Not very intelligent, to put it more accurately street smart, probably a capable merchant." And Karel got the "impression, that for benefits in business he would be willing to offer minor help for any side; he would be afraid of bigger tasks and wouldn't be capable enough to execute them."

Karel opened the letter. It was written in English. In it the man stated that he was a businessman from Munich interested in buying and selling raw materials, metals, especially steel. It appeared that a West German capitalist with a Viennese accent was interested in doing black-market business in Czechoslovakia.

The StB's new recruit pocketed the letter. He made small talk as the stranger shared colorful stories about his recent nights on the town in Bratislava. Karel couldn't get over the impression that there was something off about him, something more than those unusual earlobes. As the man continued on about his after-hours exploits in the Slovak capital, Czech idioms pockmarked his speech. He had pretended not to know Czech, and yet these colloquialisms appeared at odd times. Something was amiss, Karel decided, and indeed it was. The stranger was an StB plant—in other words, a test. Karel had passed, and the StB paid him one hundred crowns for his work. "Pedro is serious and can be fully trusted," Gvozdek concluded.

Even as he began work as an StB agent, Karel continued with other humdrum jobs—as a night watchman and then at the planetarium. Labor in the agricultural sector, all in the service of the people's revolution, of course, was a résumé builder for anyone hoping to impress the Communist authorities. So Karel's work at the farm warehouse helped rehabilitate his official standing. It was an utterly unremarkable task except that in September 1963, at a party in the warehouse, twenty-nine-year-old Karel met a nineteen-year-old beauty with short, dark hair and twinkling eyes. When Hana Pardamcová's teeth peeked out through her thin lips in an open-mouthed smile, Karel was all in. It was love at first sight.

Karel was drawn to Hana's beauty, not her breeding. But if anyone had been raised to be a Communist spy abroad, it was her. Born on January 8, 1944, in the South Bohemian town of Tábor, Hana came from hearty Communist stock: her father, Josef, had joined the ascendant Communist Party in 1945—a time when the party was not recruiting on the basis of ambition or intelligence but looking to enroll anyone aggrieved at those possessing either. "A real Communist asshole," was how Karel found him. "Horrible."

Hana's mother also joined up, and Josef's enthusiasm for the proletarian revolution helped him climb the ranks. Soon enough he was heading a local party branch, and a decade or so later, he scored a key spot in the national party infrastructure. Such loyalty guaranteed a plum day job managing a switchboard for the national warehousing company.

The Pardamcoví eventually settled in Prague, where Hana grew up with twin siblings—a boy and a girl, Pavel and Petra. Hanka—as friends and family called her—was no scholar and a touch shy, but she made up for it with savvy and discipline. Conspicuously pretty, Hana studied French in high school and passed the state exam for Russian language. Her family background put her on the fast track for Communist Party membership.

Hana's "upbringing (from the family, educational and social point of view) was in the spirit of absolute devotion to the socialist movement in the ČSSR," an StB background file declared. In 1962, at eighteen years old, Hana joined the party in her own right. After high school graduation, Hana got a job translating Russian technical manuals at an aviation repair shop. Later, she worked as a secretary at a publishing house. When Hana met Karel in 1963, his confidence and intellect were unlike anything she had encountered before. The boys she met in her parents' social circle were a lot less interesting. A demure young woman with limited ambition, she couldn't help but feel flattered by the older, more sophisticated attention she received from cosmopolitan Karel. "From the very beginning of her acquaintance," the StB judged, "she was directly dependent on [Karel], her relationship with him was in many ways completely uncritical."

Karel adored Hana, and she was up for adventure. "I was forbidden to tell her that I was working for the StB, but I told her anyway," he admitted. "We were getting married, so I could not exactly hide it."

The Koechers got hitched the same month John F. Kennedy and South Vietnam's president Ngo Dinh Diem were assassinated. Lyndon Johnson took over as US president, and he proceeded to fan the flames of conflict in Vietnam. Though Hana didn't know it quite yet, it would not be long before she and Karel witnessed the political fallout firsthand.

At StB headquarters, the formalities for deploying Karel across the Atlantic were already under discussion. The StB files indicate Hana was marked to join Karel for "active development" early on. The supervisors had good reason to believe her capable of such a mission. Along with the family's "perfect background," Hana also had a strategically useful cousin.[1] Named Josef like her father but with his surname Germanized to Pardametz, he lived in Austria, and the StB saw him as a possible backdoor exit to the West. The Koechers could go visit Hana's "Uncle Josef" in Austria, and a rough draft of a plan emerged.

"In an interview, I confirmed the findings that she is completely dependent on her husband, who is her first and last authority," Gvozdek wrote of Hana by way of confirming she would be a reliable companion. "There is no danger of defection."

Karel's work for the StB was, by its nature, secretive. Even local bureaucrats, police, and other low-level StB informants were unaware that Karel was now working alongside them. As a result, parts of the state apparatus continued making his life difficult. For fear of blowing Karel's cover, the StB balked at alleviating these day-to-day nuisances. If they did, when Karel made his move abroad, it might have been obvious that he was being deployed as an agent.

Though hardly planned and plenty unpleasant, this continued harassment provided helpful backstory for Karel's future ventures. It would, after all, make sense that somebody so unreasonably persecuted by the Communist apparatus would develop resentments. A quadrilingual philosopher-physicist forced to do manual labor at ridiculous working hours would, on the surface, have ample reason to seek his fortune elsewhere.

But for the time being, bad jobs still meant bad pay. Karel's job at the planetarium in Prague's Stromovka park was a step up from the agricultural detail, but he came to believe lecturing ungrateful schoolchildren was a waste of time—for very little money. Gazing up at the stars on the planetarium ceiling, he wondered if this was really all the universe had in store for him. It was far from the last time he would consider his skills underappreciated.

In their new married life, the only things Karel and Hana could claim to own outright were "a radio, typewriter, small collection of books, and some modest shirts,"[2] according to the StB. The newlyweds lived with Karel's parents to start. Given Karel's struggles with his parents as an adolescent, it's not hard to fathom the intensity of the enmity the grew during the early days of married life, with Karel, now approaching thirty, reduced to sleeping in his childhood bedroom with his alluring wife.

"Koecher is a very ambitious and principled man," his old film school friend Jan Liška wrote in support of Karel's burgeoning StB career. "The greatest desire of his life is to make full use of his extraordinary abilities, because he longs for recognition from the people he cares about and respects."

But in the meantime, Karel was seething. It felt as if the pointless pretense would never end. Bad jobs, bad pay, a bad home life. The authorities were always on his ass. He had joined the StB to do real work, something of substance. And then, one day, he got a break. "Honza"— Jan Liška's nickname—"heard about it, and we had discussed it," Karel said. "I knew they were going to offer me something."

Two StB officials came to Karel's parents' apartment. They wanted him to go to the United States. Karel was stunned.

"What should I do there?" he asked.

"You are going to penetrate the CIA," the case officer replied, as if it were as simple as buying a movie ticket.

"How?"

"That's up to you."

Incredibly, the StB plan didn't go much further. They offered no guidance or advice because nobody giving the orders had the faintest idea how somebody might function in the United States in the mid-1960s. But for the odd diplomat, few in Czechoslovakia, never mind anybody leading the StB, had spent significant time in the West. In the great American tradition, Karel—part guinea pig, part sacrificial lamb—would be a pioneer.

As Karel sat there in his parents' apartment, he thought the proposal felt like "sort of a dare. . . . To this day I don't know whether it was naïveté or not." But the idea of the Statue of Liberty or Empire State Building must have seemed pretty enticing from Mom and Dad's living room. It took Karel all of three seconds to agree to go. He was up for the challenge: "I wanted to see if I could do it. And if I can do it, I would put myself in an extremely influential position."

Twenty-year-old Hana took the news well: "We were in love, and there would be adventure, and I assured her that it would be fine," Karel said. As Hana remembered, "He promised me it would never be boring, and he was right." The StB's soulless summary fails to capture the young couple's excitement, as their report declared that Hana "without objections understood the correctness of her husband's activity."

And so the real adventures of Karel Koecher, code name Pedro, began. The StB looked on approvingly as Karel reached out to his American contacts: "Between agent 'Pedro' and 'Kline' a very good relationship has developed. It was therefore decided to use this relationship for counterintelligence goals—agent 'Pedro' wrote a letter to Kline, in which he stated his intention to emigrate to the USA and asked if Kline could help him build a new existence there."

However, Kline was already traveling in Eastern Europe. So instead the two of them connected face-to-face in December. As the StB put it, Kline "endorsed 'Pedro's' decision to emigrate and promised him help in building a new life." Even better, George Kline had some connections with the Ford Foundation and thought Karel could earn some early money working on Czech-to-English translations. "Before leaving the ČSSR he asked 'Pedro' to send him a list of plays and published works he has written, noting that it would ease his start in the USA and give him a basis for being a US student/scholarship holder."

The seed had been planted, and while it was true that Kline seemed eager to help a friend, he—like everybody in this tale—also looked to have ulterior motives. The StB suspected that Kline might be working for American military intelligence.[3] File after file reveals Soviet intelligence had long marked Kline as working for the Pentagon's Defense Intelligence Agency (DIA). "Based on the reports of 'Pedro' we made a further investigation of Kline, and it was said by Soviet Friends, that he is a US military spy, who during his time in the Soviet Union took part in recruiting a Soviet citizen and prepared more citizens as targets for US intelligence," the StB noted.

Karel and Kline shared intellectual interests and a genuine rapport, but Karel also had his own suspicions about Kline's possible ties to American intelligence: "You put it together: Kline came for the first time, and he had a list of names. Those were the very, very top intellectual elite that formed the political opposition. He couldn't possibly have come up with that by himself. That was professional work."

Karel's earlier indiscretions faded from relevance if not memory. The StB dismissed them as the acts of someone who was "young and silly with a strong temperament." Instead, the intelligence service was excited at the daring prospect of taking on the CIA, even if they found it nearly impossible to imagine how Karel might succeed in his mission.

"We are talking about a highly educated and unusually skilled person. He knows physics, mathematics, culture, journalism, films and languages. His demeanor is rather pleasant. He is really smart and bright. He shows a lot of interests," one file read. "One of his significant characteristics is that he can get angry about the little things, but he forgets about it quite quickly. After that he is able to communicate about that matter further. He is responsible and precise in fulfilling tasks. He has really good general knowledge, he knows what's going on in the world, in current affairs, especially what's going on in the United States."

Phase one of the budding plan was complete: "Kline during his visit in the year 1964 spoke with 'Pedro' about his contact with Surmach and promised to talk to her about help for 'Pedro,'" the StB affirmed.

The next step was to plot the Koechers' departure. They would exit Czechoslovakia via Austria, with Hana's uncle Josef instrumentalized as an unwitting intermediary. Once in Austria, Karel would go to the US embassy to claim that he and Hana were fleeing and wished for asylum. They were not political; they simply sought opportunity—that was the line. Karel was not vociferously anti-Communist, but his professional persecution and thwarted ambition left him no choice but to seek a better life elsewhere. The beauty of the backstory is that it was more or less true.

In October 1964, the same month Nikita Khrushchev was replaced by Leonid Brezhnev in Moscow, Hana and Karel took a trip to see Uncle Josef in Austria. De jure, it was an eleven-day visit to the Pardametz family. De facto, the trip laid the groundwork for the Koechers' great escape one year later.

A forty-three-year-old proprietor of a midsize construction company, Pardametz was little more than a pawn. He hosted the Koechers in his home in the village of Saint Valentin, about one hundred miles west of Vienna—where the Danube's southern tributary, the Enns, conflates with the main river. They talked about their plans to defect, but Pardametz had no idea the Koechers were spies. Uncle Josef accepted their cover story, believed them legitimate refugees, and said he was willing to help. "That is the worst thing about all this, the deception," Karel reflected later. "I feel bad to this day. It depends on the kind of person you are, but if you are basically a decent person, you are terribly ashamed."

Months of preparations followed. Both Hana and Karel spent their days walking the streets of Prague, learning to recognize when—or if— they were being followed. They practiced losing a tail and making handoffs and dead drops. Field operatives had to be prepared to make exchanges even as they were being tracked. One basic evasive tactic was to circle city blocks repeatedly until they had a good idea of who (and how many) might be following. Then the Koechers were taught to make multiple sharp turns around street corners in quick succession—not to fully shake off their trackers but to create a little more distance between them with each turn. On the final turn, when they had opened up enough of a gap and were able to disappear from sight for a few key seconds, they would make an exchange. Karel's training also saw him learn to beat lie detector tests by manipulating his heart rate. This would come in handy.

As defection day approached, an StB document, dated July 15, 1965, summarized Karel's mission:

> He will try to settle in the eastern part of the US. Agent "Pedro" will try to get, through his friends in the US, near the environment of artistic, journalistic and scientific circles. We are interested in him establishing social contact with people who have relations to others from US state offices and persons who are employed in scientific

institutions, where materials for state offices are being processed, etc. In the case where he studies at a US university, agent "Pedro" would establish contacts with students, assistants and professors, carry out a selection and connect mainly with persons who are likely to join state services.

On September 11, 1965, Hana and Karel boarded a 7:00 a.m. train from Prague. To appear as legitimate refugees, they traveled with almost no cash. Karel carried a bar of soap with a pad of coded ciphers embedded inside. The StB held on to a matching pad.[4] Known as a one-time pad, this miniature notebook contained numbered pages with varied codes on each page. Readers used modular addition to combine the letters on the pad with the letters in the message received, and only those possessing the matching pad could decrypt the messages.

Hana's father, whose impeccable Communist credentials suited him for the role of official contact point for the Koechers, was the only civilian informed of the Koechers' mission. Code-named Valentín—a sly reference to the Austrian village where Uncle Josef lived—the Koechers could signal their current status to headquarters in postcards and letters that they would mail to Valentín's sixth-floor apartment in Prague's Vinohrady district.

Karel was meant to communicate things like a change of home address or a new job. In letters where he needed to communicate in code, Hana's name would appear as the return addressee. If Karel felt he was being followed, he was to send a letter that included one word in English. The code varied if he had been called in for investigation and everything was okay (two English words) or if there was still reason for concern (three English words). If Karel believed operational prospects were improving, he was to use four English words. If American intelligence had approached Karel or attempted to recruit him to spy on Czechoslovakia, he was meant to include the number twenty-one. If he needed to use an English word but intended no coded meaning, he was to put the Czech translation of the word in parentheses. Should Karel want to call his own meeting, he had to send a postcard that had been signed by both him and Hana, whereupon a meeting would take place fifteen days from the date on the postage stamp, at 7:00 p.m. New York time, at the Mayflower Coffee Shop at 777 5th Avenue, on the corner of 59th Street.

By late morning on September 11, the Koechers had already passed the border and were greeted by Uncle Josef. Within minutes, Karel was considering abandoning the plan altogether. Perhaps he could just simplify things and really claim asylum, he thought. After a few days, Karel began to visit embassies in Vienna to probe the possibilities. But the fear that the StB might simply reveal that he was a spy, and the concern that his and Hana's families would be punished, kept him on track. In the end, Karel stuck to the script.

He went to the American embassy, which Kline had alerted in advance. As the Koechers set off, the StB couldn't help but wonder if they had made the right decision. "'Pedro's' political reliability is not at the level this case would need," one file read. "Although the checks of his collaboration with the Interior Ministry and other circumstances indicate honesty and competence, we do need to take this into consideration."

As Karel Koecher departed for the States with visions—or delusions— of changing the course of the Cold War, an StB psychological evaluation concluded he was "over-confident, hypersensitive, hostile toward people, money driven, showing a strong inclination to instability, emotionally volatile, possessing an anti-social almost psychopathic personality, touchy, intolerant of authoritarianism." Maybe not the ideal man to take on the task of posing as a dissident, penetrating the CIA, and then operating as a double agent. Or perhaps it was just what this treacherous mission demanded.

5

INNOCENTS ABROAD

"First you invent yourself, then you get to believe your invention. That is not a process that is compatible with self-knowledge."
—JOHN LE CARRÉ[1]

Though plenty risk their lives for cause, country, and—more than occasionally—conceit, for the most part intelligence work amounts to amalgamating, sorting, and analyzing details flowing in from disparate sources. It's one thing to place an espionage asset, another to know what to look for, and still a third to make sense of what they find.

Though Czechoslovakia's security services had proven themselves adept at repressing domestic political dissent by the mid-1960s, their activities abroad looked amateurish by comparison. The aging apparatchiks leading the country had forged their worldview during the Depression and World War II. Much like their Western counterparts, they had effectively zero knowledge of life on the other side of what Winston Churchill first termed as the Iron Curtain. Such willful ignorance of the world would have been humorous had so many human lives not lain in the balance.

Within days of touching down on American soil in 1965, Karel was already one of the StB's most knowledgable people about the United States. But even he was flying by the seat of his inexpensive, sensible, mass-produced pants. "You never quite know what your next step will be, so you decide along the way—it's not a straight line," he recalled of those early days. "It's like playing cards."

Karel did not have much of a hand to play, and his inexperience meant he had no idea what he was in for. The StB supervisors had offered scant guidance—how could they? Karel's mission was to penetrate the upper echelons of American government by any means necessary. If Karel succeeded in his mission, great; if he failed, he was no great loss. His past history as a roguish agitator offered ready-made deniability should the Americans ever get suspicious. The bosses in Prague would simply tell the Americans Karel did not work for them, take the lessons they learned, reshuffle the deck, and give some other poor slob a seat at the table. There wasn't much to lose. And with Karel out of the country, there would be one less delinquent to worry about at home.

The StB files suggest hope that Karel might become the prototype for many future spies, and they outlined five operational questions Karel's mission was meant to answer:

1. Does a Czechoslovak citizen with an education, who is known for his progressive views but also his reservations toward the current regime in the ČSSR, represent a suitable object for deployment in the USA, and can he get into the object of interest in the USA?
2. How should the backstory of deployment (emigration from ČSSR) be built? Is it expedient to have advanced contact with US citizens who can be useful or helpful in the process of settling in the USA?
3. What should the preparation for a candidate for deployment be in terms of general preparation, intended occupation, and operative and psychological aspects?
4. What should be his qualities, personal and professional, from the perspective of competition in the American environment?

5. How should contacts or connections with him be prepared or carried out?

Even legitimate diplomats—tasked with learning about the countries in which they serve so policy makers can understand what goes on—only passively engage in local life. Guaranteed salaries, short-term deployments, perks that cushion life abroad, and social circles populated by other diplomats limit integration by design. It's a cushy way to travel, and most professional intelligence operatives work under diplomatic cover, with day jobs in embassies and the immunity from prosecution that this affords.

Karel and Hana had no such luxuries. They were traveling to the States as so-called illegals—spies operating without any kind of diplomatic or other protection. Like other immigrants or refugees, they had to interview for jobs and pay security deposits on apartments, and they could never be entirely sure where their next meal was coming from. Every move was freighted with risk. Spies with diplomatic cover were deported if caught; illegals risked prison or death.

When Karel and Hana were in Austria, all but penniless, Karel wrote to Kline, who knew of his link to Yaroslava Surmach—that woman Karel had once escorted to Warsaw. She was now forty years old and widowed. Her sociologist husband, C. Wright Mills, had died suddenly of a heart attack in 1962. His prescient 1956 book, *The Power Elite*, argued that an amorphous multigenerational class of corporate, political, and military types was concentrating power in the United States. Karel's mission, on one level, was to test Mills's thesis.

By the time Karel and Hana set out for the States, Yaroslava had become a successful professional painter. As they waited in Vienna, she wired them $200 (more than $1,700 in 2021 dollars). Although she was in London at the time, her house just outside New York City was empty, and Yaroslava connected the Koechers with her brother, who lived downtown.

On December 5, 1965, the Koechers arrived on a charter flight organized by the American Fund for Czechoslovak Refugees. They dialed Yaroslava's brother, Myron Jr., and made their way to Manhattan's eclectic East Village, where Myron ran the Surma Book & Music Company—a cultural hub in what some still call the Ukrainian Village neighborhood.

Just two doors down from the legendary McSorley's Old Ale House and a few steps from the Cooper Union for the Advancement of Science and Art, the shop occupied the ground floor of a five-story building. The Koechers spent a few nights in an apartment above the store at 11 East 7th Street. They looked out their window onto the pulsating epicenter of the nascent American counterculture.

Myron eventually dug up the extra set of keys to Surmach-Mills's home in West Nyack. Life in the suburbs demanded wheels, so Yaroslava had also granted Karel access to her Volkswagen Beetle.

By the mid-1960s, the American economy was rife with opportunity, and apparently everyone—even newly arrived immigrants—had access to a house and car. In 1965, the unemployment rate was 4 percent, and the economy grew at 6.5 percent. Though the US Army's presence in Vietnam jumped from 23,300 to 184,300 troops over the course of the year, the grim news remained a mere trickle, and the mood was upbeat. At year's end, the number one song was "Wooly Bully" by Sam the Sham and the Pharaohs, and *Mary Poppins* topped the cinema box office.

These were simpler, optimistic times, and the light mood was a sharp contrast to the land Karel and Hana had left behind. In America, ambition was more than encouraged; it was rewarded—and Karel felt empowered. He had left Czechoslovakia hoping to shape world events, and now he started to really believe he could: "My idea was to help the cause at home, and I believed that the Russians were also moving in a positive way."

In early 1966, George Kline paid the Koechers a visit in Nyack. Kline told Karel about a fellowship that was available at Indiana University. Kline knew people there, and he offered to write Karel a letter of recommendation. "The beginning of his action in the US was favorable from the aspect of the deployment's end goal," the StB wrote of the mission's early days. They issued Karel a new code name too. "Pedro" was now "Tulián": "Tulián used some of his long-term acquaintances with US citizens from the ČSSR, especially his acquaintance G. L. Kline, a professor at Columbia University (according to the knowledge of our Soviet friends he is also a US military spy) who became his guarantor during his application for an immigration permit, introduced him at Columbia University and helped him acquire a scholarship."

Not all of Karel's preparations proved especially useful. The StB's set of codes embedded in the bar of soap served no obvious purpose, and they felt like a potential liability should the wrong germaphobe spend too long washing their hands. So Karel found a spot in the forest near Surmach-Mills's home and buried it.[2]

In Nyack, the Koechers stood out like a goulash stain on a white tennis shirt, but that came with unexpected benefits. The community of recent Czech émigrés to the States was somewhat limited. One day, as Karel and Hana spoke Czech outside a grocery store, another Czech transplant overheard. They got to talking, and he helped Hana land a job at Harry Winston's landmark jewelry shop on 5th Avenue.[3] Winston was already famous for his diamonds. Maybe America was not so hard to crack after all.

Hana started in the sorting room, working hours every day examining raw diamonds for color, clarity, and flaws through a loupe—that thick magnifying monocle preferred by jewelers. Each day the diamonds were removed from the safe and laid out on the table, and the examining room's jet-black floor made it easy to find stones that happened to fall to the ground. It was laborious, repetitive work—but Hana had the eye for it, and the training proved valuable.

The men who dominated the diamond trade took a shine to Hana. She was young, beautiful, and exotic. As long as she could also differentiate between a VVS1 and VVS2 diamond, a well-timed wink and a smile might net thousands of dollars in a given diamond trade.

In the meantime, Karel used his connection to Kline to start work at the New York office of Radio Free Europe (RFE), a CIA-run broadcaster tasked with providing pro-American news and analysis to the Communist Bloc.[4] The KGB worried that broadcasters like RFE and the UK's BBC caused "immense" harm to their cause. Worst of all, "the broadcasts were popular with the intelligentsia and young people" in Eastern Europe and the Soviet Union.[5] RFE's staff of dissidents, intellectuals, second-generation émigrés, and outright spies made it an ideal port of call for the StB's new man on the ground.

Hana was paid $100 per month, and Karel made about $250, which was enough to move into an apartment on 55th Street near 8th Avenue. Rent was $160 per month, and the modest building still has a liquor store, nail salon, and dry cleaners on the ground floor today. The Koechers bought a used Chevy on an installment plan, paying $50 a month. In mid-1960s New York, refugee citizens of nowhere had no problem getting credit lines, drivers' licenses, even a Midtown lease. At thirty-one, Karel felt, perhaps for the first time in his life, a sense of youthful optimism. With adventure in the air and formal expectations from his handlers in Prague still low, Karel's primary task was to ingratiate himself with some Americans.

Karel would maintain an on-again, off-again relationship with RFE for years. The StB urged him to inform on his coworkers, but he never really got around to delivering. Something always seemed to get in the way. Even though Radio Free Europe was "an operation run by the CIA," Karel recognized that it supported a kind of "dissent and opposition" that he more or less agreed with. "I did not want to work against that. I could not possibly snitch on the people who were associated with it."

Considering he worked as a spy for an official state agency, Karel's claim to sympathize with Czechoslovakia's political opposition must be taken with a hefty dose of salt. At the same time, in 1966 some of the staunchest dissension in Czechoslovakia came from within the Communist Party itself. As elsewhere in the world, there was a growing gap between the views of young people and their aging political leaders. In

Czechoslovakia, the early thaw of what came to be known as the Prague Spring was already underway.

Though socialist realism remained the only officially sanctioned form of art in Czechoslovakia, the party intervened less, and other styles emerged. In 1964, the American folk singer Pete Seeger toured the country.[6] Playwright Václav Havel was calling for a more radical break from the Communist regime.

The film *Closely Watched Trains* was released in Czechoslovak theaters in 1966. Based on a 1965 novella by the underrated author Bohumil Hrabal, it told the story of a Czech railway apprentice who worked at a small train station during the Nazi occupation. Though set in an earlier time, it offered a sly critique of ideological dogma and bureaucracy. These same themes had more than passing relevance with contemporary audiences and were already dominant motifs in the satirical Austro-Hungarian–era literature of Jaroslav Hašek and others. Released internationally the next year, the film, directed by Jiří Menzel, went on to win Best International Feature Film at the 1968 Academy Awards.

Though the atmosphere could hardly be considered progressive, it was at least a little less retrograde. After Khrushchev revived Soviet ties with Yugoslavia, it felt less ominous to deviate from Moscow's official line throughout Central and Eastern Europe. In Poland, in January 1964, the conservative future pope Karol Wotyla was appointed archbishop of Krakow, with the full approval of the country's Communist Party.[7]

Whether Karel actually sympathized with reformist currents or not, his commitment to his colleagues at RFE stayed solid for the most part. As Karel began meeting with his StB handlers more often, he rarely offered insights on his coworkers, and StB reports from the time complain about his refusal to inform: "The processing of the knowledge that he gave about the headquarters of Radio Free Europe in New York and some Czechoslovak immigrants wasn't of high quality."

On June 22, 1966, Karel stood near Columbus Circle with the front section of the *New York Times* in his hand. The headlines read "Hanoi

Said to Bar Latest U.S. Offer for Peace Parley" and "Philadelphia, Miss., Whites and Negroes Trade Shots." After a few minutes, a man approached and introduced himself as Mirek. The pair decamped to the Mayflower Coffee Shop.

"As you ramble on thru Life, Brother, Whatever be your Goal, Keep your Eye upon the Doughnut And not upon the Hole!" the Mayflower's menu crowed. Karel and Mirek somehow passed on the tempting sixty-cent quarter-pound cheeseburger on a toasted bun with coleslaw and relish, opting instead for two ten-cent cups of coffee. Then they took separate taxis to the East River embankment near United Nations headquarters at 45th Street.

Mirek, full name Miroslav Polreich and code-named Patera, knew the area well. As an officer at the StB's New York residency, he posed as a UN diplomat and carried full diplomatic immunity. After speaking for a while outdoors, they went to eat sausages at a German restaurant on 46th Street, where Karel informed Patera of his prospective fellowship in Indiana and expounded on the general plan to use the meritocracy of American academia to integrate himself with elites. Patera reported their conversation, noting that "getting a degree at one of the best and most prestigious universities was part of the plan as it is an attractive place to start with agency work," as part of his summary recorded in the files.

During their talks, Karel also mentioned a certain professor at Columbia University, Zbigniew Brzezinski. His name would come up again. As they parted, Polreich gave Karel $300. When they met again the next month, Polreich gave Karel $600 more and set another meeting for August.

Up until his September move to Indiana University, Karel continued working at RFE. In August, a security official named Millingen summoned Karel to his office. Karel was asked directly whether he had been visited by an employee of the Czechoslovak permanent mission or a Czechoslovak UN Secretariat official. Karel denied he had but began to worry that someone had followed him to his meetings with Polreich. Millingen advised Karel that new arrivals, especially those who start working at RFE, were frequently approached by the intelligence agencies of their native countries. Millingen also reminded Karel that if he was approached, it was his duty to report the contact immediately.

As Karel and Hana prepared to pack their Chevy and head to Bloomington, Indiana, in September 1966, StB officials were equal parts optimistic and confused. "From the highest status it is clear that T[ulián].'s deployment in the USA happened successfully and that the legend supporting his emigration is credible," they wrote. "The negative signal is his still unclear interview with Millingen, which could have consequences during Tulián's further action in the US and the connection of Tulián's attempt to obtain work in the object of our interest."

As 1966 rolled on, geopolitics belied the Mary Poppins optimism that began the year. The American troop presence in Vietnam doubled on the previous year, with 385,300 soldiers now deployed. In March, France withdrew from NATO's integrated military command, and NATO moved its headquarters from Paris to Brussels. Hitting closer to home for the Koechers, the Austrian police visited Hana's uncle Josef.

"During this check it came to light that the Austrian police could not explain to themselves the reasons and circumstance of the relatively quick and, for them, the relatively easy leaving of T. and H. to the USA," the StB wrote. "Suspicion arose that they could be connected to espionage. After an explanation from Hanka's uncle that he supplied them with help as a relative, and that they executed their leaving on their own through the American Embassy in Vienna and that they are in the USA to study," the Austrian police told Uncle Josef that he should alert them whenever the Koechers returned from their study trip.

But the Koechers had no plans to go to Austria any time soon. Instead, they were going west to Indiana. Hana traded her job in diamonds for one as a librarian's assistant, and that pretty much epitomized the year the couple spent in Indiana. It was earnest—in his second semester Karel took his GRE—but dull: "I really was a sleeper agent."

Bloomington couldn't compete with Manhattan, so by the spring of 1967, Karel had reached out to Kline to ask for his help in finding a way back to New York and into Columbia University. Karel hoped to complete a PhD in philosophy, so Kline connected him with a Columbia professor named Loren Graham. Graham specialized in the history of science, with a particular focus on Soviet science, and would go on to have a lengthy academic career at Harvard and MIT.

Graham remembered talking quantum physics with Karel: "He was a very intelligent man. His interest was not pretense. He was really interested in science. He knew what he was talking about." Karel was admitted to Columbia, where he worked a good deal with Graham out of the history department but had philosopher Charles Frankel as his main dissertation advisor. After some years in government, Frankel had resigned from the Johnson administration over his opposition to the Vietnam War.

In Frankel's 1956 magnum opus, *The Case for Modern Man*, he deliberated on the central issues facing the generation of Westerners reaching maturity after World War II, a cohort that Karel hoped to become part of.

"Ten years after a victorious war, and in the midst of unusual prosperity, an extraordinary number of men, here and abroad, are asking whether our civilization has not been on the wrong path for a long time," Frankel wrote. "They are searching for a faith or a cause, they suspect that we have placed too much trust in the benevolence of the human will and the objectivity of the human mind."[8]

By the end of two prosaic semesters in Indiana, Karel learned that he would receive a research stipend for the next school year at Columbia, along with the opportunity to work at Columbia's Russian Institute, run by Zbigniew Brzezinski: "I had to pass an exam; they took just ten people." Back in New York, he also resumed work with RFE—contributing as a freelancer.

On June 15, 1967, Karel stood waiting to meet Polreich, his StB supervisor who posed as a UN diplomat. He carried a copy of the *New York Times* as a signal that it was safe for the meeting to go forward.

President Johnson was moving to further escalate the Vietnam War, and the headline read, "Senate Approves Draft Bill, 72–23; President Curbed." At the same time, another nearby column screamed, "Security Council Bars Soviet Move to Censure Israel." The Koechers were about to travel to Europe, and this meeting laid the groundwork for a more relaxed get-together planned for Paris in three weeks.

There was some talk of Karel trying to get a job at RFE's main headquarters in Munich. It was arranged for Karel to meet with the RFE's head of Czechoslovak broadcasting during the time that he was in Europe. Polreich told Karel that StB headquarters thought he should consider taking the job. Karel was reluctant. He wanted to study at Columbia, and he insisted that this was a more promising route to gather intelligence. Karel also began to complain about a lack of money—this would become a regular lament—and Polreich gave him $600.

A few weeks later, with Polreich less worried about blowing his cover as a UN diplomat, Karel and Polreich had a series of meetings in Paris. Polreich produced a more systematic report on Karel's strengths and weaknesses as an agent. "[Karel] said that he knew that he was not a systematic worker, that as a thinker he would not stand out," he wrote. "Most of the time his knowledge is only scratching the surface, and that's why he wants to build things on connections rather than skills."

Agents Tulián and Patera agreed on future signaling protocols in the United States. Should the StB want to set up a meeting with Karel, they would call his apartment and say, "I'd like to talk with Marilyn,"[9] at which point Karel would respond that they had the wrong number. Both parties would then hang up but know they were meant to meet at 7:00 p.m. the same night. As they parted, Polreich gave Karel $1,000 to bankroll his travel.

The next day Polreich met with Hana for the first time, and he was not impressed. He thought her "more a girl than a woman," and he surmised that "she is not doing so well" learning English. For security reasons, he noted they probably should not have met. "Our first meeting should also be our last meeting," Polreich concluded.

As a man intent on blazing his own trail, Karel declined the job in Munich. From Paris the Koechers went to visit Hana's uncle Josef Pardametz in Vienna, where he told them how the Austrian police had come looking for them after their departure. Josef told them he was supposed to report their return.

Cold War machinations continued all around, producing reverberations that would—eventually—impact the Koechers. In 1967, Yuri Andropov became head of the KGB and Karol Wotyla, archbishop of Krakow, a cardinal. In 1967, the US Army deployed 100,000 more soldiers to Southeast Asia, bringing the total to 485,600. By the fall of 1967, Czechoslovakia was also attracting attention. In a lengthy story in the *New York Times Magazine*, critic Richard Eder wrote of "Some Interesting Happenings in Prague."[10]

"Nowhere else in Eastern Europe has a political polemic been conducted in recent years with the clarity and force shown by the writers and intellectuals of Czechoslovakia," he wrote.

Between 1960 and 1965, Soviet per capita GDP grew 6.5 percent.[11] But in Czechoslovakia, which had the highest standard of living in the entire Eastern Bloc, the creaking state-planned economy was slowing. In 1963, both GDP and real wages declined.[12] In 1965, the Communists adopted a plan that would allow some decentralized market mechanisms to function in the cracks between massive state manufacturing enterprises. And yet the Czechoslovak Communists' leader, Novotný, and his inner circle of hard-liners delayed implementing the reforms.

Discontent among young people grew. Previously little more than an appendage of the Communist Party's central committee, the official writers' union in Czechoslovakia saw a new generation pushing for increased independence, and the debate foreshadowed larger events to come. The *New York Times Magazine*'s Eder conducted a lengthy interview with the playwright Václav Havel, then thirty-one years old.

"When I was going to school in the 1950s it was dangerous to read Joyce or Kafka. We would get books secretly from older friends and pass them around among ourselves. If you were caught you could be thrown out of school or find yourself in worse trouble. But nowadays the young people can read anything they want," Havel explained to Eder. "They read everything, they do everything, and none of it matters much. And it keeps them well under control, even if the old guard is outraged when it sees them strolling around. The best allies of the system are those who submit to it without respecting it. It is the believers who are dangerous.

"The Communists think the truth belongs only to them," he continued. "When they knew everything, everybody else was wrong. Now that they don't know, they think everyone doesn't know. They think their mistakes are better than other people's mistakes. We are much more cynical here than in the West. Look what happened when the Shah of Iran visited West Berlin. The young people came out, protested, fought the police. When the Shah came here no one stirred. They don't care."[13]

After the ebullient start to his days in the States, Karel was contending with his own brand of ennui. He had secured a position as a research assistant for Loren Graham at Columbia, where he would be paid $3,000 a year (the equivalent of $24,000 in 2021). Though the money was nothing to ignore, it remained a paltry sum for a man trying to climb the social ladder. Academics may well have been social elites, but not elite enough. Karel again complained to his StB superiors about money troubles, noting that his youthful contemporaries in academia were generally subsidized by wealthy families.

Years later Karel would recall these early years in America fondly—"The happiest years in my life were when I was in graduate school at Columbia. Fantastic."—but it didn't necessarily feel that way at the time. Much as it did to Kafka's Josef K., extended periods of uncertainty produce their own brand of strain. Storm clouds were gathering over Czechoslovakia and in Karel and Hana's relationship. In the midst of political and financial precarity, Karel sent a letter home to his parents.

"I am considering giving up studying, because managing to work and study at such a hard school is truly exhausting," he wrote in November 1967, continuing:

> Not that I wouldn't expect this before, but I was relying on Hanka having a bit more understanding for the given situation than she appears to have. If I am to manage this how I should, I just can't come home in the evening tired, and find out that there is no dinner or to have to clean and wash the dishes in the morning before I can have my breakfast. I am also fed up with the eternal complaints about her not having enough dresses. I think that if I am earning $850 dollars per month, then that is sufficient. I got carried away a bit, but my nerves are really being tried and it's my most serious problem right now.

The moment felt problematic enough for Karel to exhibit an uncharacteristic insecurity: "If I don't have topnotch results this semester, my year in Bloomington won't be acknowledged, which is something I can't afford. And given the situation, I am doubting the topnotch results."

Around the same time, Hana wrote to her sister, Petra, who had recently married. The StB summarized her correspondence: "She writes life advice and simultaneously contemplates her own life. She writes that everybody must live their own destiny, know how to swim and save a space in their heart for themselves—only for herself. As for the swimming, she herself sometimes has a feeling that she will drown."

6

THE END OF THE BEGINNING

"If we want things to stay as they are, things will have to change."
—Giuseppe de Lampedusa

A few years into their deployment, the Koechers could appreciate New York's vibrance. But there was no escaping the loneliness of big city life in an alien culture. For a grad student and retail clerk—even one working in a shop that happened to sell diamonds—American consumerism remained a spectator sport. The shiny stereos, color televisions, and full-sized chrome-bumper cars outclassed anything on offer in Czechoslovakia. Back home, no one could imagine gems as big as the ones Hana now handled every day.

The Koechers wanted in on the game, but they hadn't figured a way as yet. "In America, you would sell your mother for money," a frustrated Karel told the StB.

Despite a smooth entry to the world of academia, he had started to wonder whether his unique genius might, perhaps, go as underappreciated in the Big Apple as it had been at home. If you can make it there, you can make it anywhere. But what to make of a man who makes it neither here nor there?

Along with operational information, Hana's coded postcards to her father expressed the emotions of these early years. She had been excited for the adventure abroad, but the leap was a big one. In the Koechers' minds, the caricatures of America had been equal parts Main Enemy and the land of dreams. So far, though, the reality had proved more pedestrian. There were prospects, yes, but one's ability to capitalize on those prospects felt directly proportional to how much money was already in the bank.

Financial strain led to marital tension. Like many a newly married woman in 1968, Hana assumed she might soon have a baby. But as the partner of a secret agent on a mission, she had accepted that motherhood must wait. Though work kept her occupied, a general sense of purposelessness weighed on her. Hana had no idea how long the wait for a baby might be: "I left with the idea that I was not going to come home for five years," she later lamented in an StB interview. In the end the Koechers would stay more than two decades in the States.

Hana's early struggles with English translated into added estrangement but—on occasion—also proved a blessing in disguise. Unlike the often irascible Karel, her easy nature drew people in, and her lack of language skills rounded out an aura of innocence. She was beautiful, and her slightly crooked smile captivated all comers. Soon, she developed a taste for fashion. Next, the shy brunette from Tabor became a blonde from the Big Apple as she grew out and lightened her hair. Having returned to her work at Harry Winston jewelry, she also started moonlighting with Solomon Trau—a rabbi, Talmudic scholar, and diamond importer who helped supply Winston. Eventually, Trau lured Hana away, offering her a job with more pay and more responsibility.

Karel continued with graduate school in the meantime, and though the Koechers were by no means rich, they were becoming a bit less penurious. Consorting with diamond dealers and professors at an elite university meant they had climbed the social ladder, even if their own wealth hardly matched others in their milieu. Karel and Hana lived more comfortably, but there was room for more comfort still.

Even as Czech intelligence was still filing away positive reports about Hana and Karl—"She is a good and reliable partner to her husband, she subordinates herself to his contacts, helps him and appears as an attractive hostess," one read—by late 1967, the bosses in Prague had begun to worry whether the couple could deliver the goods. Two years after the Koechers had left home, they still seemed to lack interesting contacts in the US. The StB suggested a host of possible characteristics that might be stunting Hana's own progress, including her "inadequate self-confidence, a slight arrogance, egocentricity, ambition, sometimes contemptuous tendencies, introversion, masochistic tendencies," and so on.

Rather than offering an accurate snapshot of Hana at the time, reports like this say a good deal more about the Czechoslovak intelligence service's own disorientation. It seems, for example, illogical to allege that someone is both lacking confidence and prone to arrogance. Reading between the incongruent lines in this and other reports, it's easy to imagine Hana necessarily showing contemptuous tendencies toward handsy StB men—who then go on to file negative reports.

Even in their more insightful moments, the StB leadership struggled to understand their agents abroad, publishing aimless lists of adjectives that offered nothing close to analysis. As the StB parsed every postcard home for clues into the Koechers' mindset, it became clear that they didn't know much about their own agents. So far as the postcard messages reflect anything general, they point to what should have been an obvious truth: some days were better than others for a newish couple still adjusting to life in the world's most exciting city.

Young as she was, Hana was perceptive enough to realize that Karel felt a particular kind of frustration. "Karel is a nice husband. He is not cruel, he is not just some husband who is chasing his own career," she told the StB. "But it is all so complicated. He has double the pressure. On the one hand, you can say, I confess that some of it comes from me. And on the other hand he wants to do something, be more successful for us, for everyone."

Never one to bite his tongue, Karel often allowed his irritation—he could not shake the stubborn belief that someday someone would have to recognize his prodigiousness—to boil over in verbal outbursts. But all told, the turmoil in the Koecher household—dirty dishes, cold dinners—paled in comparison to the volatile changes underway at home in Czechoslovakia.[1]

Even a provocateur playwright like Václav Havel had started to sense that politics were trending in a more liberal direction. Though Novotný was still president and as committed as ever to unreformed Communism's old ways, Havel, who would spend much of the 1970s and 1980s in jail, under house arrest, and continually harassed by Communist authorities, was able to travel freely to New York in July 1966 to attend a writers' conference as part of the PEN International club. Young Czechs in 1966 confronted practical limitations on their freedoms—low salaries and limits on how much cash they could carry abroad—but travel abroad was still possible if you could find a way around them.

While the Czechoslovak economy had moved beyond the deprivations of the postwar era, just getting by was no longer good enough for the country's young people. Czechoslovakia's industrial base made it the envy of the Eastern Bloc, but the combination of stagnating growth and a baby boomer generation coming of age made for an uneasy mix. Like their counterparts in the West, young people radicalized.

As a man lacking political skill, Novotný reacted the only way he knew how: reflexively doubling down on repression. In January 1967, a new law further muzzled the press. By June, the Czechoslovak Union of Writers, a government-sanctioned body, was in revolt. At another conference, attended by Milan Kundera and Havel (Kundera was a party member, Havel was not), a third writer named Ludvík Vaculík gave an inflammatory speech condemning the Communist Party's preeminent role in Czechoslovak society. "Not one human question has been solved in the course of the last twenty years," he said, blaming the Communists for the country's "postwar failure."[2]

By the time Soviet leader Leonid Brezhnev visited Prague on December 8, 1967, it was clear that Novotný was losing control. A reformist movement within his own party, though hardly as liberal as the writers, was already scheming to take power, and Novotný hoped a clear endorsement from Brezhnev might help bolster his credibility. But none was forthcoming.

Hardly the creative type himself, Brezhnev was, however, a skilled enough politician to have colluded in pushing Khrushchev out in 1964. When the dust settled, he had emerged the strongest of the politburo conspirators—and thus ascended to the role of party chairman. To Brezhnev, it was clear Novotný was out of step with the times. The two had never been cordial to begin with, and Brezhnev used his trip to meet with several other politicians, including Alexander Dubček—a Slovak raised in the Soviet Union who helmed the reform wing of the party.

Dubček and his allies had maneuvered around Novotný for months. When Brezhnev declined to back Novotný outright, they made their move. Less than a month after Brezhnev's visit, on January 5, 1968, forty-six-year-old Dubček replaced sixty-four-year-old Novotný as the head of the party—and world-changing events accelerated from there.

In March 1968, the Dubček-led Czechoslovak Communists began dismantling censorship. Novotný had already been ousted as the party head when, on March 8, newspapers printed articles demanding he step down as president too. Two weeks later, he was finished, and two days after that, Dubček attended a meeting with leaders from Bulgaria, Hungary, East Germany, Poland, and the Soviet Union in the East German city of Dresden. These supposed comradely leaders spent the bulk of the time berating Dubček while waving a series of clips from the moderately liberated Czechoslovak press. Dubček, who had been party chief for just ten weeks, was walking a dangerous path, they insisted.[3]

As early as that same month, KGB chief Yuri Andropov—among others—was already calling for an invasion.[4] Andropov had been the Soviet ambassador in Budapest in 1956 and had helped orchestrate the crackdown on the Hungarian uprising. By the time it was all over, twenty-five hundred Hungarians and seven hundred Red Army soldiers were dead. Another two hundred thousand Hungarians fled the country. The West had done nothing in response, and Andropov was willing to bet they would keep their hands in their pockets yet again.

Despite the dressing down in Dresden, Dubček returned to Prague undeterred. On April 5, Czechoslovak Communist leaders agreed to an action plan that Dubček called "socialism with a human face." Among the most radical measures was a planned ten-year transition to a political system that would allow competition from other parties. Other changes sought to depoliticize the security forces, placing the StB under government, rather than party, control. Within six days, Brezhnev sent a furious letter denouncing the latter decision and wondering why he had not been consulted.

By May 1, the date marking International Labor Day and the Soviet Union's national holiday, the Prague Spring had marched past the point of no return. Instead of traditional placards declaring "The kulak is the most stubborn enemy of socialism" or the slightly more modern "Communism has opened the route to the stars," banners carried by the day's parade goers tilted sarcastic. "With the Soviet Union forever—but not a day longer!" read one. "Long live the USSR—but at its own expense!" quipped another.[5]

For those of Karel's generation and younger, for whom World War II was at most a childhood memory and whose formative years came amid the dour 1950s and early 1960s, this so-called Prague Spring created a palpable enthusiasm. "You started to feel like the handcuffs were coming off," Karel's childhood acquaintance Pavel Illner recalled. Illner had attended medical school, eventually taking a job in the gritty industrial city of Ústí nad Labem. By then in his early thirties, Illner recalled, "hope was getting stronger every day. It made you happy to be involved."

Though Karel claimed to sympathize with reformist currents in Czechoslovakia, he nonetheless condemned many of the intellectuals associated with the movement as childlike. In the spring of 1968, Karel met Václav Havel at a party in New York at the home of George Voskovec, an actor who had fled Czechoslovakia in 1939 and went on to star in films like 1957's *12 Angry Men*. Havel was in town for the opening of his play *The Memorandum*.

The plot of the play involves a small group of workers seizing control of a business. Once in charge, they introduce an entirely new language for the company. It is completely nonsensical as a form of communication, but nobody will admit as much publicly. Later, the same managers tasked with implementing the language receive a directive from above to eliminate that language and punish the people who created it in the first place. To cover up the contradictions, a third language (also gibberish) is introduced instead.

"These languages," Havel told the *New York Times*, "stand for all the political and ideological systems made to serve man, but which end by mastering him. It is theater of the absurd, but I'm not sure that is quite the right name."[6]

A May 6, 1968, review in the *Times* found that the themes translated well to the American context. "We must not forget that 'The Memorandum' has a message for us as well as Eastern Europe, because the concept that the human being is more valuable than any bureaucratic organization controlling him is not irrelevant to our own paternalistic corporation-structured society," Clive Barnes wrote.[7] Karel could no doubt sympathize with the plight of the individual caught in the gears of a massive machine, but he nonetheless disdained Havel's stubborn idealism—"a naive and self-centered man who lacked political experience" is what Karel called Havel—and would continue to do so for the rest of his life.

Following the premiere of his play, Havel returned to Europe, where the pace of events gained steam. In June, Dubček fired the pro-Soviet StB chief. On July 15, leaders of the same five countries Dubček had met with in March sent a letter, drafted at a meeting in Warsaw, that warned Czechoslovakia was meandering "off the path of socialism" and therefore risking the "interests of the entire socialist system." This led to a meeting between Dubček and Brezhnev at the end of the month in the eastern Slovak city of Čierna nad Tisou. It did not go well.

On August 13, Dubček and Brezhnev spoke again by telephone. The Soviet leader was still agitated that Czechoslovak newspapers were "doggedly continuing to occupy themselves with the publication of defamatory ravings about the Soviet Union and the other fraternal countries.

"If you are not able to resolve this matter now, then it seems to me that your presidium in general has lost all its power," Brezhnev menaced.[8]

Dubček did his best to mollify Brezhnev, but the Soviet leader ended the call with an unmistakable threat. Continued liberalization in Czechoslovakia might "compel us to reevaluate the whole situation and resort to new independent measures," he said.[9] Four days later the Soviet politburo made the decision to invade. "The invasion will take place even if it leads to a third world war," Soviet defense minister Andrei Grechko told a group of military leaders.

And so it began with a pair of unscheduled Soviet flights landing at Prague's Ruzyně Airport the evening of August 20. Plainclothes officials offloaded, and the aircraft immediately took off again. At around 10:45 p.m., a Soviet general informed Czechoslovakia's defense minister that invasion was imminent and that the troops were coming to offer "fraternal assistance" as part of efforts to prevent "counterrevolution." At around 11:00 p.m., the first ground troops crossed the border. At midnight, large transport planes began landing at Prague's airport, and dozens of soldiers took control of the airfield. For the next half hour, the Soviets landed a plane per minute, dispatching scores of soldiers with every flight. Civilians who just happened to be at the airport were held hostage until 5:30 a.m. and then forced to walk nine or so miles back to central Prague.

As a half-million Warsaw Pact troops (Soviets, Poles, East Germans, Hungarians, and Bulgarians, with Romania's Nicolae Ceausescu refusing to take part) made their way into Czechoslovakia, at 1:00 a.m. on August 21, the Czechoslovak government made a radio announcement. It said the invasion "took place without the knowledge of the government" but urged people to "remain calm" and not to "resist the advancing armies, because the defense of the state borders is now impossible." The country's leaders were said to consider "this action to be contrary not only to the fundamental principles of relations between socialist states but also a denial of the basic norms of international law."[10] Radio transmissions were cut throughout much of Czechoslovakia, so most people only heard a few words. But for one reason or another, the Prague transmitter continued unabated, so night owls in the capital—and anybody awakened by sorties circling overhead—had an inkling of what was underway.

About an hour later, at 8:00 p.m. Washington time, Anatoly Dobrynin, the Soviet ambassador to the United States, was sitting face-to-face with President Lyndon Johnson. He read a dispassionate official message to the president announcing the invasion. Johnson "did not react at all" and was "utterly oblivious of the impact," according to Dobrynin.[11]

Five weeks earlier the United States and the Soviet Union had signed a nuclear nonproliferation treaty, and the White House had been discussing a summit meeting. Johnson was eager to visit the Soviet Union before he left office in January of the next year, and he turned the conversation toward future travel plans. Then, Johnson and Dobrynin drank whiskey together.[12] For Czechs and Slovaks, the president's casual response put 1968 in the same basket of betrayals as Munich and Yalta.

"I was not informed in advance about our plans, but for me it was clear that the invasion would certainly destroy the summit with the United States and spoil our relations with the West in general," Dobrynin wrote later.[13]

The next morning in Prague, Dubček and five other top officials were in the midst of a crisis meeting when his office doors "flew open and about eight soldiers and low ranking officers with machine guns rushed in, surrounded us from behind around a large table and aimed their weapons at the back of our heads."[14] The entire leadership team was arrested and later that night forced onto a plane and taken to Soviet Ukraine, where they were kept isolated from one another.

Karel had been spending the summer working at Radio Free Europe's main headquarters in Munich, a world away but just two hundred or so miles southwest of Prague. Karel first got wind of the invasion on the radio on August 21. He and Hana were traveling in Portugal, where RFE had transmitters. Upon hearing the news, they immediately returned to West Germany.

KGB documents show that Polreich, Koecher's main StB contact in New York who operated under UN diplomatic cover, tried to convince the Czechoslovak foreign minister, Jiří Hájek, to bring the country's case to the UN Security Council, but no such petition was ever made, and Polreich, along with scores of other officials, was purged for being too supportive of the Dubček government. Karel may never have believed that dreamy elitists like Havel could run his homeland, but he had even less patience for the dogmatic yes-men who would now run Czechoslovakia and its intelligence operations: "After the Russian invasion they wrote assessments saying what kind of son of a bitch I am, that I never gave any tips or informed on people."

Along with most of Czechoslovakia, Karel also had trouble accepting that a supposedly friendly nation would invade his homeland. Soviet leaders had expected their tanks would be greeted by grateful citizens. Prior to the invasion, the Soviets had flooded the country with intelligence operatives, but Moscow proved incapable of comprehending the messages that were sent back. "Unlike the leaders of the Soviet Union and the Soviet public, who had no first-hand experience of the world outside the Soviet Bloc, the illegals"—Soviet agents operating undercover in Europe—"knew the West and the reality of life in Czechoslovakia too well to have deluded themselves into believing that they were engaged in a moral crusade to defend Socialist values against Western imperialism," wrote espionage historian Christopher Andrew.[15]

Brezhnev's willingness to invade Czechoslovakia prompted talk of a Brezhnev Doctrine, in which a threat to Communist rule in any Eastern European state was considered a threat to the rest. Time and again this could, and would, be justification for military intervention. "When forces that are hostile to socialism try to turn the development of some socialist country toward capitalism, it becomes not only a problem of the country concerned, but a common problem and concern of all socialist countries," Brezhnev declared during a November 1968 speech in Poland.[16]

Though the doctrine was never fully formalized, "the determination never to permit a socialist country to slip back into the orbit of the West was in essence a true reflection of the sentiments of those who ran the Soviet Union," Dobrynin wrote. "It proved to Moscow that Western governments were not prepared to commit themselves militarily on the territory of the Warsaw Treaty powers."[17]

The world was shocked by this sudden outburst of Soviet brutality, and the reverberations were profound. Even committed Communists were forced to question what they stood for. "One's concept of socialism moves to last place," Zdeněk Mlynář, secretary for the Czechoslovak Communist Party's central committee, said of the invasion. "But at the same time you know that it has a direct connection of some sort with the automatic weapon pointing at your back."[18] It was enough to push some high-level Soviet officials to turn against their country. "It was that dreadful event, that awful day, which determined the course of my own life," said Oleg Gordievsky, a KGB colonel who would go on to feed Soviet secrets to British intelligence from 1974 to 1985.[19]

Reasonable Western leftists could no longer pretend the Soviet model represented any sort of a principled alternative to liberal democracy or that achieving political justice was a simple matter of sanding the rough edges off the Soviet system. Czech author Milan Kundera wrote that the events meant "Czechs and Slovaks placed themselves at the center of world history for the first time since the Middle Ages and addressed the world with their challenge."[20] Kundera, who would himself immigrate to France in 1975, wrote a novel, *The Unbearable Lightness of Being*, about Czechs who fled to Switzerland. It was fiction based on a true story. Some one hundred thousand people, most of them young, left Czechoslovakia within months of the invasion, including

Hana Koecher's twin siblings, Petra and Pavel, who also fled to Switzerland.

Karel's childhood neighbor Pavel Illner also realized that his world would have to change: "Thirty years later I am holding my children, watching the Russians march in, just like my parents were holding me with the Nazis. It occurred to me that this was not the right place to be. Suddenly you are back in a cage." Illner left Czechoslovakia two months later for a research fellowship in Texas. By the end of the year, his family had joined him. Illner has lived in the United States ever since.

Karel was already out of Czechoslovakia, and after the summer break, he and Hana returned to New York. He continued working for RFE and she in the diamond industry. If Karel felt alienated before, in the years immediately following 1968, he was forced to confront profound questions about who he was working for and what their goals were. Everything he had previously taken for granted, not to mention the belief that he might be a major player in a grand project to remake the world, had been crushed under the treads of two thousand Warsaw Pact tanks: "I thought we were on our way in Prague to something that would eventually approach a democratic welfare state. My problems really began after the Russian invasion."

7

DOUBLE AGENT

"From a certain point onward there is no longer any turning back. That is the point that must be reached."
—Franz Kafka

Czechoslovakia was not the only country losing its ethical and political bearings in 1968. In Vietnam, the year began with the Tet Offensive. Amid what was thought to be a natural suspension of fighting for the Vietnamese New Year, a coordinated set of attacks by the North Vietnamese targeted dozens of South Vietnamese cities. In Southeast Asia, at least, total war did not take weekends off.

The attackers went so far as to breach the walls of the US embassy, raining mortar shells down on this outpost of American power for more than six hours. The US Marines beating back the attackers made for popular but shocking television viewing, as reports from ABC, CBS, and NBC permanently altered the public's view of the war and America's place in the world. A Gallup poll immediately before the attack found that 28 percent of Americans opposed the war, while 56 percent were in favor. Just one month later, it was an even 40–40 split.[1]

At last, the public started paying attention, and television executives noticed. Body counts appeared nightly on the news, and it became impossible to ignore that several hundred Americans were dying each and every week. Like shoveling wood chips into a forest fire, the US responded by increasing the American ground troop presence, which peaked at 536,000 soldiers later that year.

Browbeaten by the war, President Lyndon Johnson declined to run for reelection. NSC-68, which allowed the US government to use "any measures, overt or covert, violent or nonviolent," in the name of national security, had created a division between how the US government behaved at home and abroad. But that was all changing. "With the Vietnam War, the line between what was allowed overseas and what was permitted at home disappeared altogether," historian John Lewis Gaddis wrote. "The Johnson administration found it impossible to plan or prosecute the war without repeatedly concealing its intentions from the American people, and yet the decisions it made profoundly affected the American people."[2]

By the time the world lost its illusions about the benevolence of Soviet-style Communism in August 1968, the myth that the war in Vietnam could be won was already seven months dead. In April 1968, Martin Luther King Jr. was assassinated. In May, France erupted into revolt, as student occupations and a general strike brought life in Paris and other major cities to a standstill. At one point, a full quarter of the French workforce took to the picket line. As order disintegrated, President Charles de Gaulle fled the country for orderly West Germany. In June, US presidential candidate Robert Kennedy was killed in Los Angeles.

Karel experienced the radical tumult of late 1960s America firsthand. Violent protests at Columbia cut the spring semester short and saw final exams canceled. "Our young people," said Grayson Kirk, the university's president, "in disturbing numbers appear to reject all forms of authority, from whatever source derived, and they have taken refuge in a turbulent inchoate nihilism whose sole objectives are destructive. I know of no time in our history when the gap between the generations has been wider or potentially more dangerous."[3]

Students occupied Columbia's administration building and took the dean hostage. African Americans from the surrounding neighborhoods joined the protests—opposed to university plans to construct a new gym on Harlem parkland. Demands grew, including a call for the university to end any and all programs that indirectly contributed to the war in Vietnam. Four other buildings were occupied until one thousand New York City police officers were called in to physically remove the occupiers.[4] It would not be the last time state security forces would violently intercede in political protests.

Between June 1966 and the Soviet invasion of Czechoslovakia, Koecher met with the StB eleven times. Nine of those meetings were with the pseudo-UN diplomat Polreich (code name Patera). In one of Polreich's final reports on Karel, he mused about Karel's malleable values: "His political profile is mainly characterized by its easy adaptability to the current situation. In summary, his profile has a very cyclical focus, which is not exactly a good stabilizing feature for a person who is and will be without contact for a long time.

"The main operative goal pursued by deploying T. in the USA isn't yet solved," Polreich continued, "and will be handled in the spring months of 1968 when he will be finishing his studies at Columbia University."

But Polreich would not be long for his job as Karel's handler, nor employment with the StB more generally. After the 1968 invasion, he and many other colleagues were judged as untrustworthy and forced into early retirement. Polreich had reason to find himself in the crosshairs. Unlike most of his cohorts, he was often willing to put his convictions in writing. His attempt to convince the Czechoslovak foreign minister, Jiří Hájek, to bring the country's postinvasion case to the UN Security Council proved damning.

Hájek had refused to do so, and it's doubtful their petition could have made much difference. As a permanent member of the Security Council, the Soviet Union, the country leading that invasion, held veto power over any resolution. Plenty around the world were outraged, but the collective American attention span had moved on in a matter of days—as the Democrats looked to nominate a presidential candidate at their convention in Chicago.

When thousands of protesters descended on the city, Mayor Richard Daley called in twelve thousand police, six thousand members of the National Guard, six thousand US Army soldiers, and one thousand undercover officers from the FBI, CIA, army, and navy.[5] No matter that CIA statutes banned operations on American soil.

On the night of August 28, protesters clashed with cops and federal agents in what came to be colloquially called "The Battle of Michigan Avenue." Scores were injured, and there were more than six hundred arrests. Amid the carnage, CBS newsman Eric Sevareid said that Chicago "runs the city of Prague a close second right now as the world's least attractive tourist destination."[6]

The next month, in September 1968, polls showed that 25 percent of American voters supported segregationist presidential candidate George Wallace—including substantial support in the industrial North.[7] Such numbers were not lost on Richard Nixon, the supposed mainstream Republican candidate and eventual winner of that November's election. His winning coalition of white southerners and aggrieved blue-collar northerners would remain the formula for every winning Republican presidential candidate thereafter. Nixon changed his voter registration from New York to Florida to paint himself a southerner.[8] Nothing was what it seemed.

This kind of rapid change was hard for the Communist Bloc to understand. It seemed to defy all logical projections of where American society might be heading. The South, decisively defeated in a civil war just a century before, now seemed to dictate the direction of the country. In Moscow, it was as if the Mensheviks had seized the Kremlin from the Bolsheviks.

At the same time, all signs pointed to the North—including Karel's adopted hometown of New York City—as being in decline. Starting in the 1960s, manufacturing jobs sprinted for the suburbs, nonunionized southern states, and overseas. In the Big Apple, for every manufacturing job that was replaced by a service-sector job, the city lost $1,000 in annual income taxes. In 1968, the US Federal Reserve raised interest rates to 5.5 percent, the highest rate since 1929. Prices rose at 4 percent per year, and 60 percent of Americans told Gallup that rising cost of living was the number one problem they faced.[9]

In a cheap, cynical inversion of John F. Kennedy's oft-quoted call for public service, Nixon tipped the first domino in what became a half-century-long campaign to promote individual, rather than collective, identity. "In our own lives, let each of us ask—not just what will government do for me, but what can I do for myself?"[10]

America had coarsened, and with Polreich out, so had the new crop of handlers that Karel would be forced to work with in the wake of the 1968 Warsaw Pact invasion. Optimism was in short supply on both sides of the Atlantic; it was enough to make a skeptic of even the most hopeful soul, and Karel was never that. He was particularly unimpressed when his new superiors pressed him again to inform on his colleagues at Radio Free Europe. Karel had ignored these requests before and paid it little more than lip service now, even as the new stiffs in charge at the StB couldn't seem to think about anything else. The record shows Karel doing little more than going through the motions. "He delivered, but the quality of his report is below average," the StB grumbled. "It is submitted without any sign of depth into the subjects of interest for the agency."

American and Soviet relations reached a sort of low-level equilibrium, and Karel allowed himself to wonder if the West's drift toward a welfare state and the East's recognition that basic subsistence demanded some small-scale market activity might indicate that the two systems were converging.

"From a western European and Superpower perspective the idea of stabilizing the Cold War through a gradual lessening of tension between blocs made sense in the late 1960s," historian Odd Arne Westad wrote of this period.[11] In July 1968, the United States, the Soviet Union, and more than fifty other countries signed the Treaty on the Non-Proliferation of Nuclear Weapons.

One additional incentive to avoid war was that it meant everyone everywhere could get a little bit richer. Between 1965 and 1970, the Soviet per capita GDP grew 4.9 percent.[12] At the same time, Americans had accepted that some government intervention in the economy might benefit a wide swathe of the population and generate opportunities for the poor. Programs, many of which were implemented as part of Lyndon Johnson's so-called Great Society platform, reduced the poverty rate from 20 percent in the late 1950s to 12 percent in the early 1970s.[13] Enrollment in American universities tripled between 1955 and 1970 and in the Soviet Union by a factor of 2.5.[14] On July 20, 1969, the Apollo 11 crew landed on the moon.

"Industrial society seemed to pose similar challenges to East and West, the thinking went. Some of the solutions, through technology and social engineering, were also likely to be similar, and therefore the states that carried them out would look more like each other, even if the political context was different," Westad surmised.[15]

The comparisons dipped to less laudable areas too. When it came to surveilling its own citizens, the US government started taking clear steps toward the Soviet model. The new American president's "actions went well beyond the idea that there could be separate standards of behavior at home and abroad: instead he made the homeland itself a Cold War battleground," historian John Lewis Gaddis observed.[16]

In his first term alone, Nixon ordered the secret bombing of another country, attempted to overthrow a democratically elected government, bugged American citizens without court authorization, ordered the burgling of Democratic headquarters, and then engaged in a conspiracy to cover it up.

Still, by any reasonable measure, the environment in Karel's native Czechoslovakia was demonstrably worse. The purge that followed the Prague Spring was more subtle than the bloodlettings of the Stalinist era, but the period that came to be known as *normalizace*—normalization—incapacitated victims with banal body blows rather than an ostentatious knockout punch.

In April 1969, Gustáv Husák replaced Dubček. Husák, amazingly, would lead the party until 1987 and hang on to the title of president all the way through 1989's Velvet Revolution. Once in charge, Husák immediately restored censorship. He set about cleansing the ranks of the Communist Party, and soon enough one-third of party members had lost their jobs—replaced by lackeys and loyalists. "Everyone in counterintelligence was fired, to the man," Karel recalled.

Troublesome intellectuals were no longer shot. They were, however, relocated to obscure country locations, far from the city centers. "The menial work is done by the writers and the teachers and the construction engineers and the construction is run by the drunks and the crooks," Philip Roth wrote after his own visit to Prague.[17] By 1974, Václav Havel found himself hauling barley at a brewery near the Polish border. Writer Ivan Klíma worked as a street sweeper. All told, more than three hundred thousand people were expelled from the Communist Party, and the exodus of young people continued.

In 1969, the radio show that Karel worked on at RFE was canceled. For the better part of four years, the StB had continually pushed him to inform on his RFE coworkers. Karel had resisted. He made little effort to find something else to do at RFE and essentially quit. Karel had not yet completed his PhD, and for the time being, this left the Koechers almost entirely reliant on Hana's salary. Such dependence ate away at Karel, who still saw himself as a man of destiny.

Karel looked for and found a new teaching job at Wagner College. It paid about $12,000 per year, but he was not content. For a man who thought himself a vessel for influencing important events, the job was unsatisfying for any number of reasons. At the small college on Staten Island, he did not find his station in life. "Wagner, he told me, was not good enough," Columbia colleague Loren Graham recalled.

Karel and Hana struggled. Around this time, Czech journalist Vladimír Ševela described an affair that Karel had with another Czech woman, Jana Jandová. The pair had met before Karel had moved to the States. Like Karel, she had studied film. Travel was still possible from Czechoslovakia, and Jana had come to the United States for a film festival. The two met up, and the affair was passionate enough for Jandová to ask that Karel leave Hana. Unsure what to do, Karel told Jandová he was a spy and asked her to go back to Czechoslovakia. Upon her return to Prague, the StB paid Jandová a visit and the relationship ended.[18]

By 1970, Karel found himself reporting to a new StB superior, Václav Kralík—whose day job was first secretary at Czechoslovakia's UN mission. They revamped the protocols for arranging meetings with one another. Postcards and the daily newspaper would still play a role, but so too would more modern telecommunications. The Mayflower Coffee Shop remained a key rendezvous point. Should a superior officer hope to meet with Karel, they would call him by phone, and their conversation would follow a particular script:

StB OFFICER: I have greetings from Irena.
TULIÁN: Is she still in Trnava?
StB OFFICER: No, she is currently working for the radio in Prague.

This discussion could occur in either Czech or English. On the day of the meeting, a second protocol would kick in. As before, Karel should carry a copy of the *New York Times* in his left hand so that the main headline was readable. Another section of the paper was meant to be tucked in the left pocket of his jacket.

On March 30, 1970, Karel received a phone call.

"I'd like to talk to Marylin," the voice said.

"*Jde o omyl*"—wrong number—Karel said, hanging up.

It was understood that a face-to-face meeting had been set at the Mayflower for 7:00 p.m. that same day. If either Karel or his supervisor failed to show up, the rendezvous would be pushed back two days. Amid prevailing uncertainties between headquarters and their frontline secret agent, perhaps it was meant as a test of Karel's reliability. He did not show on March 30 or April 1.

In fact, as Karel finalized his PhD, he had had few direct meetings with his superiors for the better part of two years. A good portion of his dissertation, entitled "Ideology, Philosophy and Science," discussed the nature of truth. Fittingly, for a spy operating as a double agent, Karel argued that truth is relative to context. Put another way, there can be multiple truths at the same time.[19]

"A claim to know 'P' can be justified only if 'P' is true," Karel wrote. "Consequently, if 'P' cannot be considered true, then the claim to know cannot be justified." It is not possible to know something that is false, he argued. The very fact that it is false makes it unknowable.

It was a handy way to think for a man reevaluating—yet again—who he was and what he stood for. The Cold War superpowers were also turning their attentions inward rather than directly menacing one another. "Brezhnev symbolized the spirit of the age within the Cold War," Westad wrote. "In a time when social and economic realities changed very rapidly, the Soviet leader stood out for his unwillingness to conform to the new conditions and his stubborn defense of his country's position in the Cold War system."[20]

Nixon's America, still knee-deep in the rice paddies of Vietnam, was also looking to retrench. The postwar boom years had fizzled out. Karel struggled to find work, and the economic downturn in New York City over this period presaged trends in the rest of the country. In 1962, 77 of the 250 largest American companies were headquartered in New York. By 1970, there were just 19, with most of the companies opting for head-quarters just beyond city limits in lower-tax suburbs.[21] In 1970, the American GDP contracted 0.4 percent.

This malaise, as it would later be called, undermined aspects of American life far beyond the economy. In a survey that spanned 1970 and early 1971, one-third of the college-aged population in the United States felt marriage was obsolete and that having children was not important. There were no such things as heroes anymore, and half held no living American in high regard. Close to 50 percent agreed America was a "sick society."[22]

In a speech on April 30, 1970, Nixon railed against the doubters: "We live in an age of anarchy. We see mindless attacks on all the great institutions which have been created by free civilizations in the last 500 years. Even here in the United States, great universities are being systematically destroyed."[23] Four days later the Ohio National Guard shot four students on the campus of Kent State University. In August 1971, the defense contractor Lockheed received a bailout from the US government, including $250 million in loan guarantees. A few years later, another Republican administration would refuse similar credit to New York City itself.

Despite their struggles, the Koechers managed to get by—even doing so with a typical sense of style. Hana got a bonus from work selling diamonds, and the Koechers spent a good chunk of the summer of 1970 in Europe. The StB hoped to meet Karel in Vienna. By this point of the Cold War, the Austrian capital had developed into a veritable spy haven. Austria avoided prolonged occupation after World War II by declaring neutrality, and borders with Czechoslovakia, Hungary, and Yugoslavia meant Western intelligence agencies could easily access the Communist world. Austrian banks were used to make transactions across the Iron Curtain. Spies from both sides could come and go as they pleased.

The Koechers flew to Paris on June 16 and out on August 28, stopping to visit Hana's relatives in Austria and Switzerland before visiting Munich, Hamburg, Copenhagen, Helsingborg in Sweden, Pisa, Corsica, and Florence. Amid all this travel, and probably not by mistake, Karel ignored his orders and skipped the Vienna rendezvous. Back in the States, he failed to show up for a September meeting with Kralík's New York colleague Richard Zítek too. Karel was still resisting work with the postinvasion intelligence services. It wasn't until October 10 that Karel finally agreed to meet the representatives of the StB.

At 7:00 p.m. he made contact with Kralík at the corner of 42nd and Broadway. It was a Saturday night in Times Square. Kralík told Karel he had already made a reservation at the Continental restaurant at the corner of 58th and 6th. They agreed to reconvene there to speak further. So both set off, taking separate routes. Another StB agent tracked Karel to see if he was being followed and, likely, to make sure Karel would show for a conversation that he had been dodging for months. When Kralík arrived, Karel was already waiting at a table. The encounter that followed lasted nearly three hours.

Kralík filed an appropriately lengthy report: "The first part, probably an hour, was good and calm." Karel had some useful news to impart. He had secured a new job, one that would bring him into the orbit of a potentially influential figure. He was working at Zbigniew Brzezinski's Russian Institute, a think tank operating out of Columbia University. Karel had been attending seminars there for at least two years while completing his PhD. His new role was to analyze ideological "currents" in the Soviet Union.

"At his disposal he had a variety of publications that are easily accessible, materials that they get from the RAND Corporation, some from the Russian Institute and also reports that are processed by the analytics department from [Radio Free Europe]," Kralík noted.

But soon enough the conversation slid out of control, and Karel became increasingly hostile to a startled Kralík: "The second part was, basically, from his side, you could say it was essentially wild, absolutely hostile toward me, explosive. At certain points it was even approaching a scene that was completely unacceptable, especially on ground as hot as the United States."

Though Karel did have a legitimate argument that his strategic positioning, and potential, could be an asset to the StB, such ranting was the worst possible way to get his point across. Czechoslovak intelligence had never successfully planted an illegal among the American elite, but Karel's hostility toward Kralík meant his appeal fell on deaf ears. Financial struggles were among Karel's biggest frustrations, and his effort to get more money from Kralík also failed.

The StB still wanted detailed reports about Czechoslovak émigrés working at Radio Free Europe. Karel had viewed this as menial work for years, and he was even less inclined to cooperate with the StB handlers who had showed up after the 1968 invasion.

By the time Kralík got around to admonishing Karel for not coming to the Vienna meeting in the summer, Karel was ready to explode. He upbraided his handler for choosing a rendezvous in a city that his family could not visit; he complained that his personal expenses for visiting Vienna were not being met. Karel concluded with a screed about the incompetence of the new Czechoslovak administration for good measure.

Karel told Kralík he didn't trust the Czechoslovak government, Czechs specifically—"At the end of the day I am Slovak, and I only trust them"—or the Communist Party. Karel hurled a book across the dinner table in his fury and frustration and declared, "I would rather work with the Soviets directly because they deal with people with more respect." Having finally vented his doubts, Karel kept going: he told Kralík that he suspected somebody, perhaps Kralík himself, must be stealing money that was otherwise meant to help Karel and Hana make their way in America.

Kralík's agent was out of control. When he offered to "put Vienna on the side" and suggested they "move more calmly and deal with all the other stuff," Karel pounced yet again: "Fix it quickly. You fucked up that Vienna thing, and you are going to take all the responsibility for it with your bosses. I am going to raise hell."

After enduring a relentless barrage of accusations, frustrations, and outright abuse, and with the realization there was nothing more he could accomplish that night, Kralík called the meeting to a close. Indeed, Kralík was so exhausted and terrified by Karel's emotional outburst that he feared Karel might attack him on his journey home from the meeting. A cowed Kralík spent an extra two hours taking evasive measures just in case Karel Koecher was willing to take their dispute up another level.

But Kralík couldn't abandon Karel altogether. And like many a good bureaucrat in an unpredictable system, he wasn't sure whether it would serve his interests to try to ruin Karel. His report was a masterpiece of gobbledygook meant to prolong his own institutional survival. Though willing to show himself personally offended by Karel's manic intransigence, Kralík writes like somebody wary of ending up on the wrong side of some leadership change in the department, agency, country, or world order. As with most StB analyses, Kralík's report was reluctant to assert any real opinion. Just when it seemed clear he was leading up to some sort of recommendation, he left himself a back door. He hems, haws, and halts his way forward, telling superiors they (just might) consider (possibly) ordering the Koechers back to Czechoslovakia, but his recommendations are ignored.

Along with achieving acclaim, as a totem of spinelessness, some five decades after he wrote it, Kralík's report acquired a kind of internal StB fame in real time. Future StB reports would frequently refer back to Koecher's "aggressive behavior at the meeting from 10/10/1970." It had become one for the books.

The two men agreed to meet again at the main 42nd Street branch of the New York Public Library a couple months hence. The meeting was set for December 12. Kralík, attempting to reassert authority over his willful and rebellious subordinate, ordered Karel to bring four things to the meeting:

1. Materials from Columbia University. Materials from RAND Corporation and RFE.
2. A written report on the department where he worked, mostly people, their characteristics, and the problems they are working on.
3. A written report about the situation in RFE.
4. A written report about specific immigrants.

This rubbed Karel the wrong way. After five years of living on the margins in America, he was already feeling down and out. Karel had not changed the world in a way that fulfilled his sense of what he could accomplish. His homeland was a mess, and the people he worked for were less than impressive. Who were they to give him orders? Perhaps unsurprisingly, just a few weeks later, in November 1970, Koecher went to an FBI office in New York and told them he had been contacted by Czechoslovak intelligence—by Kralík.

Karel justified contacting the FBI on the spurious grounds that he was unsure who Kralík was: "This new chief of station, I certainly did not know him before." Karel was not foolish enough to tell the FBI everything: "I was sounding out the FBI, because I did not want to tell them the whole story—after all I had violated the law, badly."

The FBI ignored him at first.

"At that time the FBI was used to chasing gangsters, not spies. They were not interested in anything Czech at all, which was disappointing because you think of the invasion as a big deal, and it was no big deal to them." But Karel had initiated a connection, and the FBI came back to him a month or two later asking "about some Czech who wanted asylum." Karel knew the man and told the FBI he was a spy, "no question about it."

At the December New York Public Library meeting, Karel was meant to simply hand over the documents Kralík had requested. There was to be no talking. Kralík would judge Karel's future reliability on whether he fulfilled his assignment or not.

Kralík arrived early and wandered the cavernous marble hallways on the library's second floor. He waited. And waited. Karel "came to the meeting point 10 minutes late when our officer was already about to leave," a report on the meeting read. "He came lightly dressed and even though it was raining all day, he was not wet. It seems like he came to the library by car."

The meeting was brief; Karel had brought nothing. Kralík left, and though his communications with headquarters make it clear he was angry, he—once again, and like so many of his StB colleagues—was reluctant to put any specific recommendations for handling the situation in writing.

Karel's loyalties seemed all over the map. He was actively considering a legitimate defection to the United States. He and Hana had applied for American citizenship, and their cases were pending. A defection might help them: "I was expecting that the FBI would say, 'Hey, listen, are you telling us the whole story? Maybe there is more to it, and if there is more to it, we will guarantee immunity or whatever.' I was trying to squeeze this kind of offer from them. I would have loved to gladly change sides. Because of the invasion, I was furious and hated the scum that took over."

The antagonism was mutual. Ahead of a scheduled meeting on January 21, 1971, the StB considered the possibility of cutting off the Koechers forever. "He has no moral right to treat the officers as he is," a summary document written in Slovak, not the usual Czech, opined. At the same time, the StB expressed a willingness to let Karel's and Hana's mothers visit the States and to pay him more money so long as he produced more.

The document also acknowledged Karel's success at advancing through higher education and gaining direct access to Brzezinski before cushioning that praise: "It is only a vehicle to further cooperation, in no case is it the final target. . . . The ball is in his court."

After spending the Christmas holiday in Martinique with Hana, and in a softer mood, Karel met Kralík in a New York bar. As something of a peace offering, Kralík gave him $300. Karel skipped the February and March meetings and in letters home used the code words "take care" to signify he was being investigated—likely a reference to the FBI contact he had initiated a few months earlier. Karel again resumed contact with Kralík on April 1 at the Brass Rail restaurant on 43rd Street and explained that he and Hana had both undergone interviews as part of their American citizenship process. Karel brought no intelligence information of note to the meeting, but Kralík gave him fifty dollars anyway.

In June, when Koecher met Kralík at Patricia Murphy's restaurant in Midtown, he reported that he wasn't yet a US citizen and as a result would not be coming to Czechoslovakia until he was. No doubt the StB could have found a way to get their man back to Prague, but Karel showed no interest in complying. StB files in the coming months continued to indicate that they found Karel to be a reluctant collaborator. Yet again his bosses demanded that he inform on people from Radio Free Europe and Czech émigrés who had fled the country after the 1968 Warsaw Pact invasion. "He never created those connections," read a report dated September 9, 1971.

"We devoted a lot of time and energy toward his political education and actually Tulián's behavior does not reach the level needed for belonging to the Communist Party or his cooperations with the Interior Ministry," Karel's supervisors determined. The same report added, "Some signals in his reports suggest that Tulián is quite close to Zionist politics in Israel. In the same way, he is involved in Zionist circles in the United States." The sentence was underlined in pen for emphasis.

On September 21, 1971, Karel finally became a citizen of the United States. Hana's more overt ties to the Communist Party in her youth meant her application remained open—she would obtain citizenship the following year. In October, Karel met Kralík for coffee and told him that he and Hana would soon visit Prague for the first time in six years, but, perhaps nervous about what awaited him there, he reneged on the promise, and the Koechers stayed in the States.

Karel did not know what to expect if he returned to Czechoslovakia. He was not acting as a productive agent, and he had treated his superiors with outright hostility. Karel was hesitant to cooperate with the StB and even considered turning himself in to the FBI. At the same time, as a new American citizen, he saw few paths to professional success.

Around this time, the StB issued some tentative answers to the questions they had first posed when sending the Koechers abroad. The answers reflected how difficult they had found Karel and how far from being a perfect agent he had become:

1. *Does a Czechoslovak citizen with an education, who is known for his progressive views but also his reservations toward the current regime in the ČSSR, represent a suitable object for deployment in the USA, and can he get into the object of interest in the USA?* The so far limited experiences with Tulián show that a Czechoslovak citizen can be quite successfully deployed in the USA. In the context of deploying Tulián, whether he can actually settle in long term is a bigger question than we are willing to admit. The other part of the question we cannot yet answer.

2. *How should the backstory of deployment (emigration from ČSSR) be built? Is it expedient to have advanced contact with US citizens who can be useful or helpful in the process of settling in the USA?* It is shown that it is correct to build the immigration backstory already in the ČSSR through contact with well-chosen US citizens in the ČSSR. The experience in the case of Tulián speaks in favor of building this backstory. It has been shown that his contact with an influential US citizen was very important in his stay, immediately after deployment. He introduced him to the Columbia University environment and recommended him. [Note: Alongside the typewritten text, someone has written in pen: "Generalized based on one case?"]

3. *What should the preparation for a candidate for deployment be in terms of general preparation, intended occupation, and operative and psychological aspects?* Candidates should prepare for at least one year under the decisive instruction of the 1st Division [a newly created department in 1969 specializing in illegals], which can ensure the required level of schooling and training for counterintelligence work in the US environment. T.'s preparation was clearly insufficient and early on produced negative results.

4. *What should be his qualities, personal and professional, from the perspective of competition in the American environment?* When choosing a candidate, personal qualities were important. Their qualities should be judged solely by the workers of the 1st Division who have worked in the USA. Into such a difficult operational environment for agents, we should not be sent people who are politically similar to Tulián or personally unstable. From the professional perspective the only candidates must be highly qualified and capable.

5. *How should contacts or connections with him be prepared or carried out?* Connection will always be a problem if it will be maintained by residences operating under official cover, that goes for both personal and nonpersonal. The need arises in the USA to build first an illegal apparatus for connection.

The StB did not trust Karel, and he did not trust them.

But just as both sides considered a divorce, destiny took a hand. Even more so than now, and almost certainly to its detriment, the CIA has routinely drawn candidates from Ivy League institutions. They wanted people from what Karel's old acquaintance C. Wright Mills called the "power elite," and the pattern was so obvious that the higher-ups in Czechoslovak intelligence, people who knew almost nothing else about how the United States functioned, had flagged this as a possible avenue for infiltrating the upper echelons of American government.

Frustrated with his own job prospects, Karel paid a visit to the job-placement office at his alma mater, Columbia. He told them he would be open to working a government job; they suggested he apply to join the CIA in April 1972. Karel says Brzezinski wrote him a letter of reference. So did George Kline. On the strength of the recommendations, Karel was invited to a meeting at a federal building in Manhattan, where he was interviewed by a man named "John Fitzgerald."

All this happened without Czechoslovak intelligence having the slightest idea about Karel's new career path. In June 1972, the StB was still preparing for the worst. "We will need to prepare the mission of discrediting Tulián in his current job because of his betrayal," one report read. "Warn him that we will complicate his life in the United States as much as possible." As Karel was on the verge of joining the West's preeminent spy service, the StB was on the verge of decommissioning him.

Karel filled out questionnaires so the CIA could do a background check. Assuming the FBI must have kept records, he openly described being approached by Kralík and revealed that he had reported this to the New York office of the FBI. Later he was called in to sit for a language exam, which largely consisted of translating Russian to English. In October 1972, he went to Washington to face a lie detector test.

Polygraphs monitor changes in heart rate, respiration, and skin conductivity while a professional asks a structured set of questions. Rapid changes in these psychophysiological indicators are said to indicate the subject of the test is telling a lie.

While there are several types of tests, the most common is called a control question test. Control questions target a person's past and tend toward the general, such as, "Have you ever betrayed anyone who trusted you?" The personal nature of the control questions naturally produces stress, so someone who is telling the truth on the questions the polygraph is hoping to test generally exhibits more stress on the control questions than on the test questions themselves.

This introduces a fundamental flaw: somebody already troubled by their own past would probably exhibit stress about their past. As the American Psychological Society puts it, "An honest person may be nervous when answering truthfully and a dishonest person may be non-anxious." There is also an added complication, as Karel had written in his own PhD thesis: there may well be more than one conception of truth.[24]

Before departing Czechoslovakia, Karel had been trained to beat polygraph tests by summoning certain emotional responses to key questions. On control questions—"Have you ever betrayed anyone who trusted you?"—the examinee intentionally thinks stressful thoughts.

Meanwhile, on difficult questions—"Are you a Communist spy?"—the examinee prepares to think peaceful thoughts. At minimum, this should at least keep the psychophysiological indicators on the test closer together.

In the end, Karel's key to passing the test was telling the truth. The CIA was aware that he had turned up at the FBI office in November 1970 and that he had reported being contacted by a Czechoslovak intelligence agent.

"Have you ever been in touch with a foreign intelligence agency?" the questioner asked Karel.

"Yes," he responded, without undue stress.

Karel was cleared for work with the CIA.

Karel in 1962,
age twenty-eight.
Credit: Karel Koecher.

Karel in Washington, DC, just a few months after arriving in the States. Credit: Karel
Koecher.

Karel and Hana at Staten Island's Wagner College in 1972. Credit: Karel Koecher.

Karel at the airport on the Caribbean island of St. Croix in 1975. Credit: Karel Koecher.

Oleg Kalugin speaking with Karel and Hana in September 1976. Credit: State Security Archives of the Czech Republic.

An StB photo and diagram identifying the Koechers' Upper East Side apartment. Credit: State Security Archives of the Czech Republic.

Hana outside the door of her office in Manhattan's Diamond District. Credit: State Security Archives of the Czech Republic.

StB photos of the inside of the Koechers' 50 East 89th Street apartment. Credit: State Security Archives of the Czech Republic.

Karel approaches
the border with East Germany on the Glienicke Bridge in 1986. Credit: State
Security Archives of the Czech Republic.

Hana smiles after she and Karel were successfully traded for Soviet dissident
Natan Sharansky. Credit: State Security Archives of the Czech Republic.

Karel and Hana celebrate with StB colleagues after returning to the Eastern Bloc. Credit: State Security Archives of the Czech Republic.

8

COMPANY MAN

"For a man who wants to make a profession of good in all regards must come to ruin among so many who are not good. Hence it is necessary for a prince, if he wants to maintain himself, to learn to be able not to be good, and to use this and not use it according to necessity."
—Niccolo Machiavelli

In the months before the calendar turned to 1973, Karel's contact with his StB handlers had been so infrequent that even as he was on the verge of achieving a fantastical objective—full-time employment inside the CIA—Karel's supervisors in Prague were plotting against him. Karel's notoriously "aggressive behavior at the meeting from 10/10/1970" had sure rubbed the higher-ups the wrong way, but it was collective ignorance and institutional paranoia that most obscured the intelligence boon that awaited.

Rather than strategize about how to make the most of this well-placed, albeit volatile, asset, StB reports mused about ways in which Karel could be brought to heel or "taken down," as one document put it. In fact, pretty much all the StB reports from this era are critical of Karel. And yet, perhaps because they did not know what else to do, Czechoslovak intelligence stuck with Karel. Prague had invested more than eight years of effort in agent Tulián, so why give up now? Maybe they just needed to try a little harder.

To stay in Karel's good graces and hopeful they might squeeze out just a bit more effort, the StB finally permitted Karel's and Hana's mothers to travel to the United States in January 1973; Hana's brother, Pavel, who lived in Switzerland, came as well. On the surface, this appeared a conciliatory gesture, as it remedied one of Karel's biggest long-standing resentments. Though it certainly came off as friendly to Karel and Hana, the StB was not in the greeting card business. Decisions often came as part of some cynical trade-off—and this case was no different.

The StB saw an opportunity to exploit Hana's mother's trip to the States. Since Hana's father, Josef, had been left in Prague alone, the family apartment sat empty each day as he went off to work. So in what might best be considered Cold War logic, the StB felt they had little choice but to break in and install listening devices. Anything else would be irresponsible, and it would give them one more way to keep tabs on Karel and Hana. The StB would continue to listen in on and transcribe phone calls to and from the Pardamec house for years to come.

The dearth of contact with Karel prompted StB concerns that he was operating outside the bounds of their control—and he was. But above all, the StB was oblivious. It didn't know that Karel's imminent move to DC would require Hana to give up a promising new job working for a Slovak émigré named Joseph Savion, once again in the heart of Manhattan's Diamond District. The office at 55 West 47th Street was perched on the seventh floor above a sign that read, "World's Largest Jewelry Exchange."

More astonishing still, the StB seemed not entirely sure what Karel was moving to DC to do. As late as January 15, an StB report noted that Karel had obtained "a job in Washington D.C. that is of a half-diplomatic character. . . . The address and the character of his employment is still unknown to central."

As Mr. Koecher went to Washington in February 1973 to begin work at the CIA, the StB sought to plug gaps in its own narrative while seeking comfort in mundane anti-Semitism. Befitting an organization that seemed hell-bent on the idea that some Jewish cabal was pulling the world's strings, the StB decided Karel's semitic roots might help explain his enigmatic behavior. In an interesting take that seemed to ignore the most famous espionage case in the history of the United States—that of Julian and Ethel Rosenberg—the StB surmised that Jewishness acted as some sort of invisibility cloak in the US: "Tulián is a Jew. We are not sure about [Hana]. . . . We have to assume that Tulián and Hanka have such close connection to Zionist circles that it gives them a sense of security while they stay in the US. Considering our knowledge on international Zionism, especially its power in the USA, Tulián does not have to anxiously fear the [CIA] as long as they do not have concrete evidence against him."

Karel signed a two-year contract with the CIA. After passing the polygraph test, he was given a "top secret" security clearance and a cover job. If anybody asked, Karel was to say he worked for the Department of Defense as a translator. The CIA even took him to the Pentagon to show him around his supposed workplace "so I would know what to say."

But Karel's real job was with the CIA's AE Screen department, a top secret branch of what would later be called the Soviet East European (SE) Division. He was tasked with listening to and translating recordings from listening devices placed in assorted Soviet embassies, trade missions, and private homes of diplomats. The work was part of a larger assembly line that looked for, investigated, and then recruited Soviet officials who were willing to cooperate with the CIA.

The department had a playbook. Step one was to have active CIA agents on the ground look for potential recruits among diplomats or KGB or GRU (Soviet military intelligence) officials. "In order to somehow pick somebody for this kind of thing, you have to follow him. You have to listen. Everybody does it," Karel said.

Then, using the wiretaps, Karel and his office colleagues looked for weaknesses that might be exploited to compel the target officials to cooperate. In a best-case scenario, targets would be genuinely motivated to fight against the Soviet system, but if someone had a drinking problem, needed money, or was having an affair, all the better. The CIA could use such pressure points to their advantage.

Karel was perfectly positioned to play the role of double agent, and he took information he accessed during his work for the CIA and fed it back to Communist intelligence agencies. The CIA wanted to recruit Soviets, but Karel could tip them off in advance: "I more or less sabotaged their efforts by telling the Soviets who the targets were and so forth."

Karel's boss at AE Screen, Milos Vukasin, was an American of Croatian descent. The two got along well, and over the next few years, Vukasin proved to be an effective advocate for Karel within the agency. Even after Karel left work at the CIA, the two kept in touch socially. Vukasin was patient with the new recruit, who was not at all patient himself. After only three weeks on the job, Karel was already clamoring for a promotion: "My present position is by no means one which would require a PhD. I am interested in intelligence work, and I want to stay with the agency and do some good work. But I also think it would only be fair to let me do it in a position intellectually far more demanding than the one I have now," he wrote to Vukasin.[1]

Nor was Karel thrilled by some of his colleagues. His department was populated by ex-Vlasovci, members of the rogue Russian army unit that had sided with the Nazis during World War II. Virulent anti-Communists with native Russian-speaking capacity were a valuable commodity, and the CIA had wasted little time drafting them into their ranks. Karel, with his loyalty to the Communist Bloc seemingly renewed, advised the StB that going public with this information might be a way to embarrass the CIA.

"They sympathize with Hitler. And some of them were the absolute worst and did some unspeakable things," Karel told a superior. "And now they are revealing these old war criminals who live in America publicly. You could really surface some nasty things about them. I couldn't even talk to them, I wasn't up to it, so that I wouldn't actually say anything inappropriate. . . . My nerves weren't up to the task. I just think that they are trash."

"Trash?" an StB officer asked.

"Yes, trash. They are actually super gangster types."

Once Karel was on the inside at the CIA, it was nearly a year before the StB made direct contact again. The files show they debated internally over the best way to connect with Karel before eventually deciding it was safest to reach out through Hana.

In August 1973, Karel's code name was changed from Tulián to Petr, and in October, he got yet another code name—Rino—which he would keep for the remainder of his time in the United States. By then, the StB had begun to appreciate the value of their agent, and they were not the only ones. The KGB had noticed Karel too. "Rino" had managed to do what no Soviet agent ever had: he had traveled to the United States as a sleeper agent with no diplomatic cover, penetrated the American government, and found a secure spot within the CIA itself. The Russians were impressed and were not going to let Czechoslovak intelligence have Karel to themselves.

After years at sea, Karel felt as if he had purpose. It was clear that at last he was being taken seriously; Hana, however, could not say the same. The two of them lived in a gated Falls Church, Virginia, complex popular with Beltway bureaucrats and a few other spies. But in a matter of months, when Hana was unable to find a job, Karel and Hana decided that she would move back to New York and start working with Savion again.

Savion was happy to have her back, and Hana took part of her salary off the books—in cash. The girl with a twinkle in her eyes also had an eye for the gleam of a high-grade princess-cut diamond. In November 1973, Savion sent Hana on a buying trip to India, Israel, and Switzerland. Hana was able to afford her own apartment. The Koechers would have a "weekend marriage."

The upturn in Hana's fortunes was in contrast to many Americans, who were worse off than they had been in decades. In late 1973, the economy entered recession. Unemployment rose as inflation ate away at people's savings. Between 1960 and 1975, the number of Americans on welfare doubled to fourteen million. Taking account of other public assistance programs—like food stamps, Medicaid, and public housing—more than twenty-four million Americans were drawing some kind of benefit by the end of the Nixon presidency.[2] Amid an OPEC embargo that came in response to the American support for Israel in that year's Yom Kippur War, oil and gas were in short supply.

In New York City, a poll found that one in three New Yorkers had "no confidence" the police would respond if they called for assistance.[3] The city was an estimated $8.5 billion in debt.[4] Between the late 1960s and the mid-1970s, New York City lost five hundred thousand jobs.[5] The Big Apple was rotting from the inside out. In a sign of things to come elsewhere in the country, the American dream of meritocracy, upward social mobility, and permeable class divisions was dying on the branch. In 1974, there were 1,554 homicides in New York. By the end of the year, the unemployment rate was 7 percent.[6]

Although, by the mid-1970s, President Richard Nixon was pursuing accommodation with the Soviets—building on the Strategic Arms Limitations Talks (SALT) I treaty that he and Brezhnev had signed in May 1972, an agreement that sought to curb the growth in both countries' respective nuclear arsenals—for the first time in a long while, the advocates for the American free market model had reason to fear the challenge posed by the Soviet Union. By 1973, the Soviet economy was making gains on the United States. Though still much poorer, Soviet GDP equated to 36 percent of American output, a gain of six percentage points on a quarter century earlier.

But Nixon was not long for office. Starting with the Watergate break-in of June 1972, a slow drumbeat of scandal began chipping away at his presidency. He finally resigned on August 9, 1974. His condemnation of the welfare state—in his second inaugural, Nixon had thundered, "Let us remember that America was not built by government but by people; not by welfare, but by work"[7]—would become a model talking point for Republicans in the years ahead, but they would increasingly eschew attempts at finding peaceful accommodation with the Soviets.

When the Koechers planned to visit Hana's brother in Switzerland in August 1973, Karel was still not in regular contact with the StB, and he didn't inform them of the trip directly. But the StB had been listening in and monitoring the letters the Koechers were sending home. As Karel arrived at Zurich Airport, he was surprised to see a familiar face—Kralík—waiting for him.

They agreed to meet the next day, August 20, for lunch at the Zurich Kongresshaus. At the restaurant, Karel explained to Kralík—and the StB—for the first time how far he had managed to penetrate American intelligence. For whatever reason, Karel lied to Kralík and told him that he had started working as a civilian employee at the Pentagon the year before, prior to switching over to the CIA. Kralík and Karel met again on August 22. All of a sudden, the StB's suspicions about Karel started to evaporate, and plans to sabotage the Koechers' life in the United States dissipated like a puff of mist.

Karel had more information for Kralík. The CIA was monitoring the KGB station chief at the Soviet embassy in Beirut, including in his apartment, where he was known to conduct business. The agency was also actively monitoring Czechoslovakia's military mission in West Berlin. Perhaps most consequentially, they had taps up and running on four different phone lines at the Soviet embassy in Bogotá, Colombia. Karel said the CIA was preparing to recruit a Soviet diplomat there, but he did not know exactly who. He was able to describe quite precisely the CIA agent in charge of the operation on the ground: "About 26–30 years old, more than 180 cm tall, a former CIA pilot in Vietnam, single."[8]

Karel realized that his new position was a powerful bargaining chip with his Czech employers, who had, he felt, always paid him on the cheap. So having just revealed his triumph in joining the CIA, Karel immediately threatened to resign from the position because he wasn't being adequately compensated—by either intelligence organization. He told Kralík how unsatisfying the work was and that he was looking to pursue academia or perhaps a job with Hana working in diamonds. He was planning to fulfill his CIA contract but not necessarily renew it because the job just wasn't all that interesting. Karel lamented that he and Hana had been forced to live apart and that even with two salaries, they did not have enough money to live comfortably. To round things out, Karel reminded Kralík that he was not young anymore and that Hana wanted to have a baby. Karel told Kralík he was looking for more secure employment and had applied for academic jobs at the New School for Social Research and Sarah Lawrence—where his old friend George Kline was teaching.

The threat to swap the CIA for what had been until 1968 a women's college was a masterful provocation: Kralík realized he would again have to stroke his agent's ego. He did his best, emphasizing that Karel was poised to accomplish great things and that his bosses would expect no less. Kralík also met Hana and reported that "it was discovered during the meetings in Switzerland, [Karel's plan to leave his CIA job] is motivated mostly by the pressure from his wife. She has fully succumbed to chasing money and status."

For what seemed like the first time, as a result of her apparent influence on Karel, the StB started to take a real interest in Hana. Hana would become a cypher for the StB's anxiety over their major asset: when they were anxious that Karel was drifting out of their control, they tended to consider her a malign influence; when Karel did well, she was a blessing. The hapless zigzagging continued: "After evaluating Hanka's attitudes and considering their personal qualities as they appear after the meeting, we suggest excluding Hanka from executing contact meetings after the set October meeting and to maintain contact directly with Rino by hand-over meetings in New York while creating prerequisites for instructional meetings 1x a year outside of US territory," the StB wrote in September 1974 before concluding that they had to now consult with "friends," meaning the Soviets, on future steps.

The "friends" evidently disagreed, because on October 5, 1974, Richard Zítek made contact with Hana in front of the Wienerwald restaurant on 7th Avenue in New York, framed by the dining spot's bright neon-green sign. With a line of people waiting to go into the movie theater next door, Zítek and Hana agreed to meet again three days later. When they did, Hana handed over six small documents hidden in a pack of gum that described the CIA methods for analyzing Soviet wiretaps and included specific information about the CIA's efforts to target Soviet activities in Afghanistan. The Americans were able to monitor the entire Soviet embassy and all the diplomats' apartments, the documents revealed. The StB shared this information with the KGB, which then was able to verify enough of the details in Karel's reporting to determine he was telling the truth.[9] Moscow was becoming more impressed with Rino.

On November 6, Hana met Zítek again. The logistics of setting up the meeting were carried out "with the help of Soviet friends." Again Hana produced documents in a pack of gum, this time a list of CIA phone numbers and a description of how the CIA prevented its own phones from being tapped. The StB became concerned that the documents were so sensitive that Hana could not afford to be caught carrying them, and henceforth they would "focus on oral reproduction of information"—she would tell them what she and Karel knew.

The Koechers also got some positive feedback on their latest work. Zítek handed Hana a magazine with $5,000 tucked inside. The large sum—beyond the scale of anything the StB had ever given them before—indicated that their newest "friends" were prepared to show their gratitude.

Karel's usual way of getting documents out of the CIA was to pretend he needed to copy newspaper articles while bringing a top secret document with him to the copier and then scanning the document instead. Hana duly brought the paperwork to the intelligence contact. Another disclosure included a list of Soviet embassies abroad that had their phones tapped by the CIA, including Accra, Ankara, Athens, Bamako, Beirut, Bogotá, Brasília, Casablanca, Islamabad, Istanbul, Kabul, Karachi, Kinshasa, La Paz, Monrovia, Njamena, Panama, Quito, Rabat, and Tunis.[10]

Sometimes, valuable intelligence turned up unexpectedly. In late 1974, the Koechers stumbled into a windfall of insider information at a CIA office Christmas party. The holiday cheer was free flowing, and many of Karel's coworkers had let their guard down—they were all professionals with a security clearance after all. Somebody decided to capture the festive occasion on camera, and, spotting an opportunity, Karel volunteered to get the film developed. He made duplicate prints, and two months later, Hana was able to pass the extra set of photos to Zítek. On the back of each photo, Karel had written the names of the people in the picture.

In January 1975, Karel learned that his CIA contract would be extended another six months—through July. In the meantime, another New York–based StB operative had begun to take an interest in the Koechers. Jan Fila posed as a UN diplomat. In one way or another, he would remain entangled with Karel and Hana for more than a decade.

Fila had grown up a model Communist. His father worked as a machinist and later as a boss at a starch factory in the railway town of Havlíčkův Brod. His mother was a clerk. Both had joined the party just after the end of World War II. Jan started working for the Czechoslovakian interior ministry in 1963. In 1964, he married Marie Šturmová, a teacher. Fila's code name—Šturma—was derived from Marie's maiden name. Jan joined the party himself in 1966, and between 1967 and 1972, he studied law at Charles University while also working full time. As the StB purged the ranks of anyone thought to have sympathized with the liberalizing currents of the Prague Spring, there was plenty of room for ambitious young officers. They offered this analysis: "During the crucial years 1968–1969 he stood by the official Marxist-Leninist position"—the kind of perspective the postinvasion leadership was looking for.

But Fila was skilled too. He spoke English and Russian, and he was smart. "[Fila] showed very good skills in abstract thinking," an StB report read. "He is mentally stable, extraverted. Very sociable, confident, with a healthy tendency for adventurousness, interest in self-education, cheerful, calm and in control of his behavior." But as StB report writers were wont to do, the author also left himself an out in case Fila made a future mistake, expressing unspecific worries about "inconsistency and carelessness."

In 1973, Fila finished a year in counterintelligence school in Moscow. Upon his return, he started working on cases related to the United States, and in 1975 he deployed to New York, where he would remain for the next seven years. Within a month of arriving, he was the contact for Hana in their handoff meetings.

By this time, Latin America was a focal point for Soviet and American intelligence. The lands south of the border held a special place for American Cold War paranoiacs: "Successive U.S. Administrations saw Latin American radicalism and Soviet-style Communism as natural allies of each other," historian Odd Arne Westad wrote.[11]

As well as Eisenhower's adventures in Guatemala, Kennedy's incursion in Cuba, and Johnson's support of a coup in Brazil in 1964 that ushered in a decades-long military dictatorship, in 1967, the CIA helped capture and kill the revolutionary Che Guevara in Bolivia. In 1970, leftist Salvador Allende won elections in Chile despite ample meddling by the CIA, and by 1973, Nixon had ordered CIA chief Richard Helms to do whatever he could in Chile to "make the economy scream."[12] After a September 11, 1973, coup that brought Augusto Pinochet to power, Nixon supported his new regime—which arrested forty thousand Chileans and killed three thousand more in a matter of months. Military coups followed in Uruguay (1973) and Argentina (1976), and by the end of the 1970s, right-wing military regimes helmed fifteen of twenty-one Latin American countries.[13]

American entanglement in Colombia had its own twisted legacy. In 1903, President Theodore Roosevelt had encouraged the secession of Panama, then a Colombian state, after the Colombian government had opposed his plans to build a canal. In 1928, the threat of a US invasion prompted the Colombian military to kill two thousand striking banana-plantation workers.

Fearing Fidel Castro might inspire nascent Colombian guerrilla movements, the Kennedy administration flooded Colombia with aid starting in 1961 and sent military consultants to design counterinsurgency strategies. Rather than eliminate these disparate bunches of would-be jungle revolutionaries, the intervention pushed them to organize into Revolutionary Armed Forces of Colombia (FARC) and the National Liberation Army (ELN)—with whom the US and Colombian governments would battle for the next half century.[14]

So it was no surprise that the CIA was determined to recruit a Soviet asset from the Bogotá embassy or that the Soviets were especially keen to learn how this process might be carried out. By the mid-1970s, Colombian cocaine that was processed at $1,500 per kilo in jungle laboratories already sold for $50,000 per kilo in the United States—and demand was rising.[15] This made Colombia the testing ground for a US shift away from counterinsurgency toward a counter-narcotics strategy—Nixon's "war on drugs"—in Latin America.

Hindsight shows that much of American policy in Latin America during the Cold War was driven by delusion. Though the KGB maintained a presence via Soviet embassies in the region, other than Cuba, Moscow had little active interest in Latin America. "The main thing," KGB chief Yuri Andropov said, "is to keep our finger on the pulse of events, and obtain multi-faceted and objective information about the situation there."[16]

In a report, Karel told his Soviet handlers that he had no idea who the CIA asset in Bogotá was and stated that he was unlikely to find out. That kind of information was above his pay grade. But he was able to reveal that he knew the attempt to recruit this Soviet asset had likely happened by the summer of 1974.[17] As Soviet diplomats were duty bound to report contacts with the CIA, especially attempts at recruitment, logic held that if nobody at the Bogotá embassy had yet reported being approached by the CIA, the person who had been approached had probably agreed to work for the United States. There would, after all, be no other reason to keep the contact a secret. Though Karel's information was inconclusive, it was said to have "expanded the knowledge" of the

KGB station in Bogotá. The Soviets knew they had a traitor in their midst—perhaps more than one.

In March 1975, Karel and Hana went back to Czechoslovakia, transiting again through the espionage hive of Vienna. It was the first time they had returned to Czechoslovakia since departing nearly ten years earlier. Two days of meetings in Znojmo, a border town just eighty kilometers north of Vienna, followed, and the information Karel provided made its way directly to Moscow.

Much of what Karel shared was focused on CIA operations in Latin America. According to StB files that summarized the meetings, the CIA was targeting a correspondent for the Soviet press office TASS in Brazil—but Karel concluded that the correspondent was resisting their overtures. In Bogotá, the telephones of the political section, the business department, and the apartment of diplomat Viktor V. Fedjanin were being monitored, Karel told the StB. In addition, the CIA showed strong interest in a certain secretary at the embassy named Alexandr Ogorodnik.

If somebody at the Bogotá embassy was cooperating with the CIA, Karel reasoned that it had to be Fedjanin or Ogorodnik. Karel was intrigued by Ogorodnik as a character and wondered whether he might work for the KGB alongside his diplomatic work. Ogorodnik had his own car and always carried plenty of cash, but Karel considered Fedjanin to be the most likely to flip and work as a CIA informant.[18]

Karel had taken the cautionary step of using a fake passport with the name Karel Dvořák to travel to Czechoslovakia,[19] but it's unlikely that anyone in the States was paying close attention to the Koechers' travels. That spring US intelligence—and pretty much everyone else— was consumed by the fall of South Vietnam. After North Vietnam invaded the South, South Vietnam's capital of Saigon fell on April 20. Images of American helicopters taking off from the embassy roof beamed around the world. By then, many Americans wanted nothing more than to forget about Vietnam, but news at home wasn't any more cheerful. "Our domestic drama," Nixon's national security advisor, Henry Kissinger, reflected, referring to the Watergate scandal that led to Nixon's resignation, "first paralyzed then overwhelmed us."[20]

On May 26, 1975, Hana—who by now also had a new code name of her own, Adrid—had another handover meeting in New York, again organized by the Soviets, who had taken the initiative planning meetings with the Koechers on American soil. Karel's notes again recommended taking a closer look at Soviet diplomat Fedjanin as the possible double agent in Bogotá. The Tehran offices of Aeroflot, the Soviet Union's flagship air carrier, were also tapped, he revealed.[21]

Karel was providing valuable information, but for his handlers, there was a problem fast approaching: his contract with the AE Screen unit was due to expire. On July 9, an StB report speculated on Karel's future prospects. Though Karel never made it clear whether anything close to concrete had ever been discussed with his CIA supervisors, he told the StB that the CIA might consider deploying him as a field agent in Europe. If nothing else, he might consider a return to RFE and a job in Munich. So the StB began to make contingency plans, "looking to transport Rino and Adrid to Europe where it is highly likely they could keep working for the CIA." By this point the StB was no longer directing events; rather, it was reacting to decisions made by the Koechers or in Moscow. Should the Koechers simply return to Czechoslovakia, the StB planned to purchase a Prague apartment for them. Regardless, the StB handed the Koechers another $3,000 in cash for their efforts.

Back in Washington, Karel had been lobbying Vukasin for help finding another job, and it paid off. Later in July, Karel sent word that he would be staying on with the CIA. He would not go back to Europe and instead would remain in the States: "They gave me a contract job to work for the Office of Political Research. They had access to almost anything. The idea was to paint a picture of the Soviet mind, the decision-making process and so forth."

It seemed an unobtrusive contract worker at the CIA could pass almost completely unnoticed. At minimum that would seem a symptom, if not a cause, of the turmoil engulfing the American intelligence community at the time. There were multiple major congressional investigations of the CIA underway, including the famed—and feared—bipartisan Church Committee led by Idaho senator Frank Church. Among other shocking disclosures, public hearings exposed American intelligence agencies plotting the assassination of foreign leaders; spying on civil rights leaders, including Martin Luther King Jr.; and monitoring the political activities of everyday citizens.

In a strong rebuke to virtually every national security directive issued since the end of World War II—the aforementioned NSC-68 and Doolittle Report among them—the committee's final report insisted "there is no inherent constitutional authority for the President or any intelligence agency to violate the law."[22]

The committee went on to conclude that "intelligence agencies have undermined the constitutional rights of citizens . . . primarily because checks and balances designed by the framers of the Constitution to assure accountability have not been applied."[23] After reviewing 110,000 documents and interviewing eight hundred witnesses that detailed CIA-directed coups and assassinations, the committee issued ninety-six recommendations "to place intelligence activities within the constitutional scheme for controlling government power." Among other things, the hearings would lead to the 1978 passing of the Foreign Intelligence Surveillance Act.

Along with the Church Commission, and with the country still reeling from defeat in Vietnam, an insurgency from within the Republican Party had started shaking up America's approach to global affairs. In Southeast Asia, a group that would come to call themselves neoconservatives began to argue, the United States had not been mistaken to wade into a regional postcolonial quagmire. Rather, the error had been to do so without fully committing itself.

The lesson they learned from Vietnam was not that land wars in Asia were unwinnable or that foreign intervention in a civil war was foolish. Rather, they viewed war as a moral crusade for remaking the world and a single country, the United States, as a force for carrying out divine justice. America had failed in Vietnam because it had hesitated to use its full military might, and a lack of public resolve at home had undermined the war effort. Evangelism of every sort would be the antidote.

Amid a challenge in the Republican primary from Ronald Reagan, Nixon's hapless and hastily appointed successor, Gerald Ford, moved to massage this bulked-up arm of his own party. In November 1975, Ford's chief of staff, Donald Rumsfeld, orchestrated the so-called Halloween Massacre. William Colby was out as head of the CIA and replaced by George H. W. Bush. Rumsfeld nominated himself to replace Secretary of Defense James Schlesinger and filled his old job with an ambitious lad named Dick Cheney.

In his memoirs Ford acknowledges that all these personnel changes came in response to "the growing strength of the GOP's right wing."[24] Instead of giving the impression he was in control, the turmoil furthered the public impression of a weak and rudderless president. "Ford's shakeup fails to attain its goal of showing strong leadership," read the *Wall Street Journal*'s Washington Wire column.[25] That military-industrial complex that Eisenhower had warned about as he exited office had been accelerated by wars in Korea and Vietnam and had really started to look like a permanent fixture of American life.

On October 11, a new satirical television show debuted: *Saturday Night Live*.[26] Comedian George Carlin hosted in a navy three-piece suit, and his opening monologue expressed his own concerns about the country's unconscious martial drift in a humorous commentary on how football was displacing baseball as America's pastime. Even leisure activities, once casual and carefree, were becoming rigid and aggressive.

"Football is a land-acquisition game," Carlin joked. "You knock the crap out of eleven guys and take their land away."

He continued:

Football is technological. Baseball is pastoral. Football is played in a stadium. Baseball is played in a park. In football you wear a helmet. In baseball you wear a cap. Football is played on an enclosed rectangular grid and every one of them is the same size. Baseball is played on an ever-widening angle that reaches to infinity and every park is different. Football is rigidly timed. Baseball has no time limit, we don't know when it is going to end. We might even have extra innings. In football you get a penalty. Baseball you make an error—whoops! The object in football is to march downfield and penetrate enemy territory, and get into the end zone. In baseball the object is to go home. I'm going home. And in football we have the clip, the hit, the block, the tackle, the blitz, the bomb, the offense, and the defense. In baseball, they have the sacrifice.[27]

Ford looked intent on following up battles at Korea's Choison Reservoir and the Vietnamese city of Hué by sending American troops to Angola. Much to his chagrin, just eight months after the fall of Saigon, the Democrat-controlled Congress was hesitant to sacrifice still more American youth. In December 1975, the US Senate refused to approve finances for a covert war in Angola. President Ford insisted that the decision represented an "abdication of responsibility" and predicted that it would have "the gravest consequences for the long-term position of the United States and for international order in general."[28] That prediction did not hold, and instead, Cubans, Soviets, and South African mercenaries found themselves bogged down in a messy civil war that lasted twenty-six years.

The Senate had stopped the Ford administration from embroiling the country in the first of an impending tally of neoconservative foreign policy boondoggles. But the respite was brief, and anyway, the prevailing currents were clear. As a new breed of war hawks took flight and Eastern Bloc observers puzzled over the implications, Karel Koecher had his work cut out for him.

9

HIGHS AND LOWS

"Life is nothing but a competition to be the criminal rather than the victim."
—BERTRAND RUSSELL

As Karel talked with his StB supervisor, Václav Kralík, in Vienna's Donaupark on October 2, 1975, he told Kralík about one of his unhappy CIA colleagues, Sergei Kazakov. Perhaps, Karel posited, Kazakov was disgruntled enough to consider cooperating with the KGB. But Kralík had other priorities. He kept turning the conversation back to Karel's work monitoring the Soviet embassy in Bogotá. It was clear the Soviets were growing worried about a possible turncoat in their diplomatic ranks. Kralík had been tasked with getting real answers.

"None of those Soviets seem breakable to me, not really," Karel told Kralík. After listening to months of wiretaps, Karel had doubts that any of the Soviet diplomats had agreed to collaborate with the CIA. "They seemed to me to be pretty good people," he said. "Capable of professionalism anyway."

Karel knew the CIA was "doing something to Fedjanin, that they were tapping the phone somehow," but he didn't know why. For months, Karel had pointed to Viktor V. Fedjanin as the most likely Bogotá embassy official to be collaborating with the CIA—but without concrete proof, he hesitated to say more than he knew. The intelligence game had a way of punishing inaccurate predictions. There were no accidents, the industry's paranoid reasoning went. Mistakes were assumed to be misinformation, and misinformation implied motives. If Karel was wrong, the blowback could be fierce.

After months of prevarication, though, it was clear Kralík really wanted something more concrete: "But you have already written about how you were listening," Kralík said. "If you could venture a guess as to who they might be targeting, it could help." Karel deflected: rather than Fedjanin, Karel now suggested it was better to focus on Alexandr Ogorodnik, a charismatic embassy secretary. "He went to all the cocktail parties. He was so charming. He liked women. He had a car. He was just the most in contact with Americans," Karel pointed out.

As he continued, Karel was also careful to temper his statement. While he thought the Americans would more likely target a flashy character like Ogorodnik for recruitment, Karel did not mean to say Ogorodnik would necessarily agree to work with the CIA. "I don't know him personally, but I would be willing to put my hands in the fire for Ogorodnik. He really is a hot shot. He can handle his shit. It would be logical that they tried on him, because he would have absolutely been really interesting for them."[1]

When Karel began his own new job with the CIA, the Soviets also pressed for more information about the agency's new director, George Bush. A former congressman, ambassador to the UN, and chairman of the Republican Party, he was considered a contender for the presidency as early as the 1980 election. Karel was willing to do his part, but first, just for a moment, he allowed himself to bask in the excitement of having a day job that actually called on him to harness intellect to make complicated analytical judgments.

His new contract for six months' work with the CIA was worth $10,000. Best of all, he could work remotely, so he and Hana were able to live together in New York again. "It was a think tank within the CIA, a great hub of analysis, and they have access to absolutely everything,"

Karel recalled. "They paid you for the work you had done. They paid me well. I did not need to live in Virginia, I would drive down, go to Langley, present whatever, discuss, go back." Eventually he would produce a lengthy report titled "Pragmatic and Ideological Factors in Soviet Decision Making."

Karel had not only penetrated the CIA, but now he was moving about within it. Surely this was worthy of some recognition from the bosses in Prague, but as far as Karel could tell, his supervisors in Czechoslovak intelligence remained unimpressed with his work. If the CIA was willing to pay him well, why shouldn't the StB? Even with his new contract, he and Hana were still pinching pennies while trying to blend in with an elite American milieu.

Fed up, Karel wrote a letter and "suggested a change in how we do things." Never lacking in confidence, Karel addressed his correspondence to Yuri Andropov, the head of the KGB, and sent it in August 1975. He was clear about what he hoped to achieve: "It was not an emotional reaction; it was a deliberate provocation. I thought I would really make them mad, tell the StB that you don't know what you are doing. That's not the way you do intelligence." He also asked for money, telling the KGB that if he was to be effective in the US, he needed to be able to afford decent clothes and a car. He needed to look the part, essentially.

Karel's brashness was rewarded. A month later Andropov authorized a payment of $20,000 to Karel. The Soviets, who never thought much of the StB leadership themselves, were impressed with Karel's initiative and informed the StB that they wanted to start organizing their own dead drops—so the information Karel gleaned from the CIA would go straight to them rather than passing through Prague first. As far as Karel could tell, it no longer mattered whether the StB was unimpressed with his work. The KGB, it seemed, was more than ready to jump in. For the first time in a long while, Karel felt he was in a position of power. After years of struggle, he had managed to carve out something close to an autonomous area of operation for himself. He had a direct link to important people; he was talking to "the leadership of a superpower.

I mean, my God, after all the drifting, suddenly intellectually you realize your potential."

Thrilling as it was to deal directly with Soviets, Karel was now spying in the big leagues, and this came with the concomitant uptick in anxiety. Around this time, StB files started referring to Karel's mounting health problems, largely the result of stress. The next time the Koechers returned to Czechoslovakia, he would need to undergo a thorough health exam, the StB agreed.

In December 1975, as Karel packed up his apartment in Virginia, the first dead drop of the new era occurred. Directions for making future contact were hidden in an empty Coke can and placed under a tree marked with white tape in the woods nearby. At a January 1976 handoff meeting, Andropov's little sweetener arrived. Hana received an envelope. Inside, there were two hundred $100 bills. Karel used $10,000 for the down payment on a $40,000 two-bedroom apartment on the eleventh floor of the Park Regis building on East 89th Street. The building was brand new and thirty-three stories high, and it sat just a block and a half from Central Park and the Guggenheim Museum. In what had to be one of the most bizarre real estate deals of all time, the KGB funded the down payment while the CIA served as a guarantor on the mortgage.

The apartment was small, but the Koechers' living room looked out on St. Thomas More, a pretty sandstone Gothic Catholic church, where Jackie Kennedy Onassis was a regular parishioner. Once furnished, a collection of two thousand books lined one wall—fiction, philosophy, history, the selection ran the gamut. Most of the texts were Karel's, but some of Hana's favorites included D. H. Lawrence's *Women in Love*, the 1961 sci-fi novel *Stranger in a Strange Land*, and *Oppenheimer and Son*, a dual biography of the diamond magnates Ernest and Harry Oppenheimer.

A Smith Corona typewriter sat on a corner shelf, and recent issues of *National Geographic* magazine often lingered on the living room end table. With the sliding wooden accordion door ajar, the bedroom opened up on the main room. From the couch, visitors could see a painting of a reclining nude woman hanging over the low-rise bed.

The apartment complex came with a doorman reception and an underground parking garage. Anne Bancroft and Mel Brooks lived in the building. Robert Redford had a flat nearby and parked his Jaguar in the Park Regis garage. Central Park's Engineers' Gate was two minutes' walk away and the reservoir's cinder running path another forty yards from that. The elite Dalton School was a couple of blocks away. The move transformed the Koechers' lives, not only because of their starry neighbors but because everyone wanted to visit: "Socially it placed me at a much higher level, because indeed I could invite people to come to New York—and they loved to come to New York. People would come to see you and stay over."

This era of overnight guests coincided, perhaps not coincidentally, with the most notorious phase of the Koechers' time in New York. Indeed, if the general public has ever heard anything about Karel and Hana's life in the United States, it almost certainly has to do with the fact that by the mid-1970s, they had become regular attendees at New York swingers parties. Among a certain set of espionage aficionados, the legend of the "swinging spies" has taken on a life of its own. Even the otherwise sober-minded intelligence historian Christopher Andrew can't help but refer to the Koechers as the most "sexually athletic illegals in the history of Soviet Bloc intelligence."

True enough, Manhattan in the late 1970s offered plenty of action. The 21 Club, Toots Shor's, and the Stork were hot spots. Maxwell's Plum on 64th and 1st Avenue was a hopping club. By early 1978, the *New York Times* was calling McMullen's, on 3rd Avenue between 76th and 77th, not far from Karel's apartment, one of the "swingingest and most popular pub-restaurants on the East Side."[2] It was frequented by supermodel Cheryl Tiegs, a young prosecutor named Rudy Giuliani, and a real estate developer's son named Donald Trump, among others. At around 1:00 a.m., limos would line up outside McMullen's to take revelers on to another night spot—Studio 54, which had opened just the year before.[3]

The Koechers weren't big disco fans, but they did like a good party. "If you come for dinner, the host has joints rolled in a cup," Karel said, and cocaine was already prominent on the Upper East Side. "I would say it was standard among affluent people, and I guess it still is."

While Karel readily admits that he and Hana engaged in swinging, he insisted the tales of their exploits are greatly exaggerated. In February 1987, an article in the *Washingtonian* magazine expounded on the Koechers' sex lives, as did a portion of Ronald Kessler's 1988 book *Spy vs. Spy*, which otherwise focuses on FBI efforts to track Eastern Bloc intelligence agents.

In both texts the bulk of the anecdotes amount to secondhand stories of the Koechers' swinging activities more than a decade after they are said to occur. None were possible to verify. For example, the Koechers are said to have frequented a swingers club in Washington, DC—the Capitol Couples club—for about eighteen months starting in mid-1973, just after Karel had started working at the CIA.

"Ah yes," the organizer of that club told the *Washingtonian*. "I remember them quite well. I found them an interesting couple. He was a professor. She was a diamond merchant. Strikingly beautiful. Warm, sweet, ingratiating. Incredibly orgasmic. I went to bed with her several times.

"But I thought Karl"—the Americanized name that Karel often went by during his years in the States—"Koecher was a bit strange. He was always naked at the parties. Usually people keep their clothes on at least some of the time, but he was always walking around naked. And he always had an erection. The women he was with said he was a terrible lover, very insensitive. His wife was everything he wasn't."

As the story goes, the Koechers also hung around a twice-a-week swinger gathering called the Virginia In-Place that was organized by a suburban realtor. Acolytes gathered in a Fairfax, Virginia, home on Union Mill Road between the fall of 1974 and the summer of 1976. The seven-bedroom house had a large circular driveway and a colonnaded porch. One of the main rooms included two mattresses on the floor. The owners of the house worked for the State Department and were away on a posting in Mexico. Unbeknownst to them, their rental house was being used for what were effectively orgies.

Membership cost $1,000 plus $20 at the door. More than two hundred couples joined. They brought their own alcohol but stowed it with a bartender. Drugs were banned. At least one US senator, an assistant secretary of commerce, reporters from the *Washington Post* and *New York Times*, and a top official from the Smithsonian Museum were regulars—as were Karel and Hana Koecher.

"Of course, you usually knew everybody by just their first names," the realtor who organized the parties told the *Washingtonian*. "But there was definitely a Karl, a good-looking fellow who spoke English quite well, but with a slight Czech accent."

For his part Kessler went to great pains to portray the Koechers as sexual daredevils. "At least once or twice a week, Koecher and Hana had one or two couples over for dinner, or went to their homes, to swap spouses for sex," he wrote. "On the side, they each had separate affairs going, and [Karel] dabbled as well in answering personal ads placed by single women."

One economist at the Treasury Department, who asked to remain anonymous, told the *Washingtonian* that he and his wife continued swinging with the Koechers even after Karel moved back to New York, occasionally meeting with them at Plato's Retreat—the famed New York City swingers club at 509 West 34th Street that owner Larry Levenson touted as promoting "social intercourse and sexual intercourse"—or visiting a nearby nudist colony with them.

So had the Koechers' otherwise pedestrian, somewhat strained marriage transformed into a kind of carnal circus? How had the shy and provincial Hana recast herself as Mata Hari and Karel as Casanova? Karel and Hana do not deny taking part in the swinger scene, but Karel insisted the the vast majority of stories that have circulated over the years were exaggerations—little more than a concerted effort to embarrass him and distract from the fact that he had burrowed into the heart of the American intelligence apparatus.

By the time the tales of the Koechers' swinging seventies emerged, Karel was indeed an embarrassment to the US. So it stood to reason that officialdom might do their best to belittle and denigrate him any way possible. Kessler's key sources—anonymous FBI agents who ultimately failed to produce evidence sufficient to prosecute Karel—are problematic. And so is his syntax.

To take but one example, Kessler quoted Hana as saying, "It was just the thing to do at that time. All our friends somehow went to a little club or something. . . . That atmosphere in those years just somehow elicited that."[4] Though Hana spoke fine, if heavily accented English, it seems near impossible to imagine her using the word *elicited*.

Questioned about their sex life later, Hana grew angry. "It's private," she said before outright denying Kessler's story or ever having talked with him about it. Karel also takes direct issue with Kessler's version of events. "He puts me into some sex clubs I have never been to in my life, that I have never heard of," Karel said.

Speaking decades after his book came out, Kessler has no patience for these denials and stood by his original reporting: "I think of them as criminals, and criminals do have a tenuous relationship with the truth."

So which version of the Koechers' lives in 1970s Manhattan and DC is best believed? Were they manipulative erotic adventurers or amiable road-tripping sexual tourists? Though the odd overzealous 1980s wordsmith, and indeed the Koechers themselves, may well have fantasized about the former role, the reality looks to have been closer to the latter.

Karel rightly pointed out that thousands of pages of StB files did not once mention his and Hana's extracurricular activities. "At that time it was kind of loose, I mean, you know, the situation. People don't do it anymore; at that time it was more or less normal."

Loneliness, escapism, and the desire to belong to some sort of community look more decisive in pushing the Koechers toward the swinger scene than any desire to take advantage of those contacts as part of their espionage work. Though their marriage endured plenty of tension, and it's hard to say what might have happened had they lived more conventional lives, Karel and Hana stayed together.

As illegals working for a foreign intelligence agency, they had no choice but to rely on one another. And there is a sense that by seeking companionship elsewhere, they tasted liberation without straying too far from the mission. America would experience a puritanical backlash to the sexual liberation of the 1960s, but sex and promiscuity were not nearly as taboo in continental Europe or Czechoslovakia. As a character in Philip Roth's novella *The Prague Orgy*, set in 1976, puts it, "To be fucked is the only freedom left in this country. To fuck and to be fucked is all we have left that they cannot stop."[5]

For the Koechers, partying was an escape from stress. Alcohol and adultery can paper over alienation—and even the Big Apple itself was in the midst of its own identity crisis at this time.

In the fiscal year 1974–1975, 15 percent of New York City's budget was dedicated to paying interest on debt—twice the money dedicated to firefighters and police.[6] By early 1975, an SEC investigation concluded that banks were still willing to loan the city money, but instead of holding the debt on their own books, they grew ever more likely to market it as a safe investment and pass the risk on to other investors.[7] On March 6, 1975, nobody was willing to buy New York City bonds at an auction. In May, New York had requested the federal government's help in the form of a short-term loan on revenues that were meant to come in by July. In June, a New York state senator suggested the city sell the Brooklyn Bridge. As New York looked to Washington for help, President Ford's chief of staff, Donald Rumsfeld, and the chairman of his Council of Economic Advisors, Alan Greenspan, vehemently opposed a federal bailout.[8]

"Going along with New York would be a disaster," Rumsfeld wrote in a memo to Ford. "First, for N.Y., since they would delay cleaning up their mess. Second for the precedent it would set. In my view the request is outrageous."[9]

Amid the city's fiscal crisis, thirteen thousand teachers (out of a total of fifty-six thousand) had been laid off.[10] In 1976, the South Bronx alone lost ten square blocks, with five thousand housing units, to arson.[11] From 1973 to 1976, the city lost 340,000 jobs.[12]

The Koechers may have used sex as a release from the tedium of daily life, but the data shows plenty of other New Yorkers did too. By 1977, according to the New York Planning Commission, there were 245 pornographic theaters in the city, up from 9 in 1965. Some four thousand people visited Show World—a twenty-two-thousand-square-foot adult film, book, and performance emporium in Times Square—every single day.[13]

That same year, the aforementioned Larry Levenson, who had previously worked as a manager at McDonald's, opened Plato's Retreat in the basement of the former Ansonia Hotel at 270 West 74th Street in what used to be a gay bathhouse. Three years later the club would move downtown to 34th Street. "We're the eighth wonder of the world. It is the biggest thing to hit New York City since the World's Fair," Levenson said of the club on an episode of the *Phil Donahue Show*.[14]

Men could only enter Plato's Retreat if they came with a female date. Entry cost twenty-five dollars per couple, plus a five-dollar membership fee. Much like the beach, a so-called lifeguard sat perched on a high chair to monitor activities.[15] Amid the revelry, the scene also emanated its own special brand of 1970s mediocrity. On some nights, there was a buffet with chicken, ribs, chow mein, meatballs, and potato salad.

"It's a couples movement. Couples that want to be free thinking, free living adult couples," Levenson said. "They don't believe in monogamous relationships. They would rather get involved with other people, but together with their spouses instead of cheating on them."[16]

The Koechers were intrigued by what Levenson was offering and visited the club a few times, but their tastes trended pastoral. As New

York was beset by filth and crime, the Koechers liked to get out of town. "We were members of a nudist club," Karel recalled. "There was in New York State a very small place called Stockholm. It took us about an hour to get there. There were sort of buildings or bungalows. We were renting a room, and there were other people as well, who were renting permanently, staying there over the weekend to escape from New York City. There was a pool, a lake. It was a nice place."

When Karel talked about the Koechers' time in the swinging scene, it came across as casual, friendly, and less aggressively promiscuous: "Occasionally, we would be close with a couple," he said. "We took a motorhome and went to Nova Scotia. Next time we go to Florida, stay there for two weeks for Christmas." Time and again, during interviews, Karel emphasized that social nature of such engagements and that they had nothing to do with espionage work. "There is no way you can obtain secrets this way," he insisted. "As a matter of fact, once I was propositioned by a man. We met socially, he was gay, and he had incredible access. I warned him that he might get into trouble should I be a spy, ha ha ha. That was the end of it."

Around 1976 Karel started working out at the Young Men's Hebrew Association (YMHA) on 92nd Street. He lifted weights, jogged in Central Park, and wrote his reports for the CIA. His occasional bouts of stress-related health troubles—blood pressure, arthritic pain—began to subside. This, coupled with the vibrant social scene, meant that he at last, for a brief period, was enjoying life.

"You are somehow taking part. You might be making a difference," was how Karel put it, though it is not entirely clear whether he considered his main contribution to be on behalf of the CIA, the StB, the KGB, or perhaps simply himself.

Karel's relationship with the Soviet Union was conflicted: they had invaded his country and repressed their own people, and yet, they showed him respect and paid him for a job well done. "They listen to what you are saying. They would not necessarily agree with me, but they would listen," he recalled. Karel liked America and Americans, but he still considered the United States to be the primary Cold War aggressor. His loyalties were shallow, and neither of his paymasters was a shining example to the world or to him. America and the Soviet Union screwed around; why shouldn't he? And so he did. It was getting harder to see any larger objective in working for either of these flawed superpowers.

In Hana's letters home, and during multiple StB interrogations, she made it clear that she wanted to have a child—and yet the swinger's life seemed anathema to that. In April 1976, Hana made a dead drop at a mall parking lot in Queens. Later that month she flew to Mumbai on her diamond-buying business. During a stopover in Vienna, she met the StB handler Zítek. According to one report, Hana kissed Zítek goodbye. Though no one ever quite said that the two of them had an affair, it became clear that the StB began to worry that their relationship was more than professional. "The frequency of [Zítek's] contact with Hanka is quite high," another StB agent, Havlík, wrote, unable to conceal his excitement.

In May 1976, Captain Jan Fila took over the handover meetings with Hana. Fila met her at Brentano's bookstore on 5th Avenue, close to her office in the Diamond District. They exchanged notes in cigarette packs—Dunhills and Kents. The StB was expecting a report on changes at the CIA under its new head, George Bush.

In practice, not much had changed. Meddling in Latin America remained a priority. The myth that the Soviet Union was looking to form alliances throughout the region had become gospel truth on the American Right. Under Bush's leadership, the CIA launched Operation Condor, a vast program that used American intelligence capabilities to back right-wing dictatorships in Latin America. Under the guise of combating Communism, the CIA backed dictators in Argentina, Bolivia, Brazil, Chile, Paraguay, and Uruguay.

All told, some sixty thousand deaths and hundreds of thousands of political prisoners are attributed to the operation, which a now declassified CIA document described as "a cooperative effort by the intelligence/security services of several South American countries to combat terrorism and subversion."[17]

Boosted by the feeling that his insights were being taken seriously, Karel's ambitions grew. He asked for more responsibilities from the StB and suggested they give him information he might include in his reports to the CIA so as to impress his American bosses. His intention was to develop a profitable feedback loop, whereby his reports impressed the CIA and they, in turn, would be willing to share ever more secretive information with him. The StB stood to benefit from this, but not nearly as much as Karel's career prospects.

The suggestion prompted another of the StB's collective mood swings. Their suspicions of Karel returned. Perhaps his renewed enthusiasm signified something else. The higher-ups in Prague wondered whether his loyalties had changed. Maybe Karel was now using his StB connections to serve the CIA. Could the StB's double agent have gone triple? Karel's private life was plenty promiscuous; why not his professional life too?

Amid growing mistrust, the StB wanted the Koechers to return to Czechoslovakia over the summer. While a more standard debriefing in Austria had already been scheduled, the StB decided Karel's new job called for a more thorough vetting.

Ever wary of making major decisions without KGB clearance and still more cautious because of Karel's ability to communicate with Moscow directly, in August the StB asked the KGB if they wished to send one of their own people from Moscow to meet with the Koechers personally.

Five days after the bookstore exchange with Fila, Hana Koecher entered a Manhattan phone booth and dialed the number she had written on a piece of paper.

"This is Jack," a male voice said in English.

"This is Alice. Good," she said on the phone in Czech and hung up.[18]

It was Fila on the other end. The coded language signaled that Karel had agreed to a secret meeting to be held in Europe in September.

Though they did not yet know their final destination, the Koechers were going to Czechoslovakia for the second consecutive year. This trip would prove a great deal more hostile than the last, and they would be joined by a Soviet spy whom onetime CIA chief William Colby described as "smooth as silk, the smoothest guy I've seen in years . . . with his own agenda, of course."[19]

10

BEHIND THE CURTAIN

"Hateful to me as the gates of hell,
Is he who, hiding one thing in his heart,
Utters another."
—HOMER

Karel and Hana Koecher had left Manhattan and come to Europe for vacation. After several days on the Adriatic coast, they developed deep tans, and Hana's flowing hair had faded to radiant blond. Along the way, they had planned to meet their handler, Richard Zítek, in Austria. When they finally did, Zítek had a surprise. Like it or not, they were going to cross the Cold War frontier—they were heading to Czechoslovakia.

Zítek had already arranged to send fake postcards to the Koechers' friends back in the States. As far as the Americans were concerned, the couple were sunning themselves on a Mediterranean beach. There was, after all, no call for suspicion. In the Koechers' Upper East Side neighborhood, trips to assorted rivieras were commonplace. Zítek's security service team smuggled the Koechers across the border and took them to a riverside village about twenty miles southeast of Prague. Despite spending the better part of his life living in the nearby Czechoslovak capital, Karel had never heard of Čtyřkoly.

And there were still more surprises in store.

When Oleg Kalugin later joined Karel at the dining room table in the Čtyřkoly villa, Karel didn't know what to make of the imposing Russian. As the interrogation began, Karel knew enough to know he didn't like him. There was something about Kalugin's manner or his pseudo-aristocratic English. They were about the same age, and yet this KGB man carried himself with an off-putting sense of superiority.

Though this was the first time Karel and Kalugin had met in person, their lives would remain inextricably linked in the coming years. Their encounter in September 1976 was far from random. Kalugin had defied the orders of his KGB superiors by turning up in Čtyřkoly. He came with a purpose, and four decades later, ample questions remain about what, and who, really drove Kalugin's thirty-two-year career in espionage. Many still wonder who he was ultimately working for—besides himself, that is.

"He was the most valuable asset the CIA had," Karel contended, insisting that Kalugin used his high-level KGB post to feed information to American intelligence for years. "He became very much afraid of me, because obviously I could, sooner or later, find out."

The novelist John le Carré met Kalugin in 1993 and wrote about him in 1995. He too had suspicions. To le Carré, Kalugin was "one of those former enemies of western democracy who have made a seamless transition from their side to ours. To listen to him you could be forgiven for assuming that we had been on the same side all along."[1]

Kalugin had been born about two weeks before Karel Koecher—on September 6, 1934. His mother had worked at a weaving factory, and baby Oleg was clandestinely christened in the Orthodox Church. Like Karel, he was an only child, with a former soldier turned civil servant for a father. But while the Koecher family's patriarch worked at the post office, Kalugin's dad got a job as a guard at the Leningrad headquarters of the Soviet secret police, then known as the NKVD.

"Later my father would tell me how he used to stand guard outside and listen to the screams of those being tortured and murdered by Stalin's goons," Kalugin wrote in his memoirs.[2] Despite those stories, or perhaps because of them, Kalugin later opted for a career in the KGB.

When Hitler turned on Stalin and the Nazis invaded the Soviet Union on June 22, 1941, Oleg and his mother fled Leningrad for Siberia. His father's official ties ensured they would live out the war in relative comfort—at least compared to the twenty-seven million Soviet citizens who would die from combat and deprivation. After the war, aged fourteen, Oleg joined the Communist youth group.

Papa Kalugin's positioning inside a brutal totalitarian system came with plenty of perks. Oleg attended summer camps for the children of secret policemen and showed an acumen for languages, learning English from books and shortwave radio broadcasts by the BBC—which the Soviets were unable to jam until the early 1950s. At his high school graduation, Kalugin was chosen to deliver a valedictorian's speech: "I am convinced that there will be enough work in my lifetime cleaning out the scum that poisons the existence of the world's first socialist state," he told his classmates with the fervor of a true believer.[3]

At seventeen, Kalugin aced the KGB entrance exams and started attending one of their top training schools, Leningrad's Institute for Foreign Languages. He thrived studying German and English. In June 1956, Kalugin was chosen to continue advanced training in Moscow. Along with the intricacies of spy craft, he learned Arabic and studied the works of Karl Marx. In 1957, he became a full member of the Communist Party.

"[The] KGB was looking for a new generation of bright young officers, untainted by the crimes of the Stalin era," Kalugin wrote in his memoirs. "I was to be one of the new guard."[4]

With the help of the KGB, Kalugin posed as a philology student and won a Fulbright Scholarship to study in the United States. Starting in the fall of 1958, about seven years before Karel would arrive stateside, Kalugin was part of the first postwar class of Soviet students to visit. Like Karel, he also attended Columbia University in New York.

Half of the eighteen students in Kalugin's scholarship class were intelligence agents, but few shared his desire for the spotlight. Kalugin managed to get himself elected to Columbia's student council. He wrote for the university newspaper and impressed enough people to have a short profile piece written about him in the *New York Times* on May 11, 1959.

The page 7 headline read, "A Popular Russian: Oleg Danilovich Kalugin," and a pull quote described him as "a real personality kid." Kalugin's "engaging smile," the paper reported, meant "this blond, slim, jaunty young man has won many friends." Kalugin's father was described as a "clerk in Leningrad's city government."[5]

Kalugin's wife, Ludmilla, was said to be a math teacher who had stayed back in Russia tending their three-year-old daughter, Svetlana. "The United States is exactly what I thought it would be," Kalugin told the paper. "I was afraid it might be boring, but so far it hasn't been."

After a year abroad, Kalugin returned to Moscow and started with the KGB's First Directorate (foreign intelligence) in September 1959. In a matter of months, he learned he would return to New York. Too talented to be kept on the sidelines and brimming with ambition that risked showing up the stodgy apparatchiks working at headquarters, Kalugin was back in the States by June 1960 as part of a team of KGB agents posing as reporters for Radio Moscow. The Soviet equivalent of Radio Free Europe, the station broadcast the Soviet Union's unique take on world events in dozens of languages.

Jaunty Kalugin, code-named Felix, was assigned to develop sources at the United Nations. About two-thirds of Soviet foreign correspondents at the time were secret agents, as were a full third of the three hundred diplomats at the Soviet UN mission. In what one might term a Cold War do-si-do, a dance where two parties repeatedly circle one another with their back turned to their partner, these were spies reporting on spies while looking to convert still more people into spies. Naturally, it was also necessary to spy on all new spies, if only to guarantee they were not secretly spying for someone else—so the refrain repeated.

For his combined work as a journalist and spy, Kalugin made $480 per month. Improbable as it seems, that was apparently enough for him and his family to live on Riverside Drive while renting a summer house in Bayville, on Long Island's north shore. Kalugin even befriended Jay

Rockefeller, a future senator from West Virginia, and vacationed at the famed family's compound in Vermont.

Kalugin also claims to have socialized regularly with actresses Shelly Winters and Natalie Wood; New York's left-leaning glitterati were fascinated with socialism and the taboo of rubbing shoulders with the son of a Stalinist. "After I had been in New York a year or so, the FBI counterintelligence people must have been certain of two things: one, I was KGB; and, two, I was a womanizer," he wrote with a sense of pride.[6]

Back in the big city, with his family in tow, Kalugin contacted old friends from Columbia, including a fellow traveling physics student who shared government nuclear weapons research with him. In his memoirs, Kalugin also described a meeting with Zbigniew Brzezinski, President Jimmy Carter's future national security advisor and Koecher's associate-to-be at Columbia's Russian Institute. According to Kalugin, he saw Brzezinski give a lecture advocating an escalation of America's nascent war in Vietnam.

Oleg and Ludmilla had a second daughter in New York. But in March 1964, the Kalugins were ordered back to Moscow. At home, the old guard were more than satisfied with Kalugin's work and placed him on a fast track for promotion. He was duly elevated to the rank of major. In September 1964, around the time trainee Karel Koecher was just beginning to lay the groundwork for his move to the States, Kalugin began a nine-month course for training future KGB station chiefs. In December, he received the Order of Merit.

With his previous cover apparently intact, in February 1965, Kalugin learned he was going back to the States. This time, the destination was Washington, DC, where he would pose as a foreign ministry press officer, a position that came with diplomatic immunity, while working as deputy head of political intelligence at the embassy.

Kalugin met with KGB chief Alexander Sakharovksy as he set off. "You did a very good job in New York," Sakharovksy told him. "We are putting you in charge of a lot of people now in Washington. You have to show them how to do a good job."[7]

The mid-1960s were simpler times, and the top man at the embassy, Ambassador Anatoly Dobrynin, had arrived in DC just a few years before. Dobrynin traveled without a bodyguard. On the weekends he drove his own car. Along with maintaining global order, one of the biggest challenges of the time was stretching Soviet diplomatic salaries to match American living conditions. But Kalugin, perhaps already awash in additional sources of income, never seemed to have such troubles.

Kalugin's new office was three blocks from the White House. A good deal of his time was spent gleaning information from other foreign diplomats. He oversaw dead drops with KGB informants and sifted through thousands of classified American documents that came across his desk. He helped manage forty spies—a healthy portion of the one hundred diplomats working at the embassy.

Kalugin gained further acclaim in Moscow for how he handled John Anthony Walker, an officer at the US Navy's Atlantic Fleet base in Norfolk, Virginia, who one day in 1967 walked into the Soviet embassy with a set of valuable documents. The papers proved to be authentic, and Walker continued providing the Soviets materials for nearly twenty years in exchange for money. Walker is said to have helped the Soviets decrypt more than one million US Navy messages.

For his efforts Kalugin was decorated yet again, this time with the Order of the Red Star. Later in 1967, Kalugin returned to Moscow for his annual vacation. He noticed that his colleagues showed "coolness" toward him, something the self-declared "wunderkind"[8] attributed to "jealousy."[9] In 1968, Pulitzer Prize–winning investigative reporter Jack Anderson wrote a column exposing Kalugin as a KGB agent, describing him as a "handsome, Lotharian [sic]" spy who was "entangled in a web of espionage and romance."[10]

Anderson's sourcing on the story was unclear, but the core of his reporting was accurate. Kalugin was indeed a KGB spy, so the fallout from the article was all the more confounding. Instead of being deported by the US government—as would normally be the case for a foreign embassy official found to be conducting espionage—Kalugin was allowed to stay. There was no clear explanation why; in fact, nobody has ever bothered to posit one. Kalugin continued working under the guise of a foreign ministry press officer at the Soviet embassy and maintained diplomatic immunity while operating publicly as the KGB's deputy head of political intelligence.

"His undercover activities in this country are known to the FBI. But only the State Department knows the reason he is still here," Anderson wrote. "Other spies caught in the act have been declared persona non grata and have been given 48 hours to leave the country."[11]

A known foreign-intelligence operative, Kalugin was allowed to stay on the job in the States for another two years, and he did not operate quietly. As Anderson wrote of Kalugin's carousing, "He would romance the lady while his wife tended the home fires in their apartment."[12]

Kalugin denied womanizing and insisted that Anderson, a legend whose reporting and commentary later saw the Nixon administration put him on a hit list, was serving as a mouthpiece for the FBI.[13] This accusation, along with the fact that Kalugin was allowed to openly operate as a spy, remains a strange one. Stories like this, and his own interrogation experience in Čtyřkoly, led to Karel's suspicions about Kalugin. There was something strange about this Russian, but Karel could not quite put his finger on it.

It was clear that Kalugin was suspicious of Karel, but that was standard practice among spies. Nobody was to be trusted. But Karel could not shake the feeling that he had entered that country villa as a valuable, highly placed StB asset. By the time he left, he was an outcast. It seemed inconceivable the StB would want to cut themselves off from an asset placed inside the CIA. Why give up on such a unique source? Kalugin must have changed their minds. But how? And why?

Karel and the StB had exchanged their fair share of unpleasantries ever since the shouting match in October 1970, but until Kalugin's intervention, the StB had never fully abandoned him. The prospect of having an asset, no matter how volatile, embedded in the heart of the American intelligence apparatus was simply too tantalizing. Karel was unpredictable, but in penetrating the CIA, he had managed to do something the StB could only have dreamed of a few years earlier. In the four decades since Kalugin falsely denounced Karel in 1976, the latter has had time to refine his opinion of the KGB man's baleful influence further: "Kalugin is scum."[14]

Kalugin's memoirs are a fascinating document, composed of equal parts braggadocio and score settling; he wraps his verbosity in a leaden prose. As he sought a publisher for his life story, not everyone was impressed.

"He tells his story like a bureaucrat, and presents the KGB as a bunch of bureaucrats with some bad guys among them," Ashbel Green, a senior editor of Knopf, told the *New York Times* after turning the memoirs down for publication.[15] "Kalugin wants a lot of money for the book, and if he wants a lot of money, he can't tell a story that is incomplete."

The book often struggles to tell even half-truths. It is obviously duplicitous and leaves one to wonder what Kalugin might be willing to do in matters of life and death if he so casually lies about trivial things. For instance, Kalugin claimed to have only tried a cigarette once in his life. As he tells the tale, Kalugin's father unexpectedly returned to the family apartment just as a young, precocious Oleg fired up a fresh Belo-morkanal. In a panic, as he heard the key turning in the lock, Kalugin tossed the burning butt out the window. But the rancid smoke of the Soviet cigarette lingered. His father, Daniil, smelled it and asked whether Oleg had been smoking. Young Oleg naturally denied everything, but his father walked the three floors down from their communal apartment in a former aristocratic palace to the street—where he was able to retrieve the still-smoldering cigarette. Upon returning to the apartment, he slapped Oleg across the face.

"I have never since put a cigarette to my lips," Kalugin wrote.[16] Lesson learned.

But if there is a moral to the story for readers of Kalugin's book, it's not—as he intended—that young Kalugin understood the importance of respecting authority and staying wary of vice. Rather, in his retelling of the anecdote, Kalugin demonstrates his flexible approach to the truth. A few years later in real life, and just pages later in the memoir, Kalugin describes himself fashionably smoking once more, this time as a globe-trotting international man of mystery visiting India. "I donned sunglasses and began smoking a cigarette, all in an effort to make it hard for the CIA to identify me," he wrote.[17]

Why lie about something so silly? No doubt espionage work itself, by definition, demands inherent dishonesty. But even more so, Kalugin's KGB seniors positively reinforced his duplicity. His early career path, with promotions every few years, was the equivalent of stepping onto an escalator destined for the top of the KGB hierarchy. Lying was a way to get ahead, and there was every indication that it worked. In February 1970, Kalugin returned to Moscow to take the job as deputy head of foreign counterintelligence. In March 1973, he became the chief of foreign counterintelligence. In 1974, he was named the youngest general in KGB history.

Kalugin traveled frequently throughout the Soviet Bloc to coordinate with allied intelligence agencies. He was feted wherever he went in the Warsaw Pact countries, and he held meetings with senior officials in all the Soviet satellite countries. Kalugin described one such visit to Bulgaria, when a group of interior ministry officers invited him for a day of hunting. The story itself, and the fact that Kalugin felt the need to recount it, shows Kalugin's casual disdain for his supposed comrades in arms—not to mention a latent sadism.

Amid a pastoral retreat with some accomplices, a gamekeeper arrived carrying a sack, Kalugin recalled. The host dumped a bunch of baby pheasants on the ground, but the birds were too young to fly. Dazed and confused, the chicks scrambled into a nearby cornfield, and the Bulgarian interior ministry officials shuffled in after them. Amid much foot stomping and rustling of stover, one or two of the birds began flapping their wings in a frantic fit.

Alas, they could only get a few inches off the ground before giving up. "So I took aim at one of the poor creatures on the ground and pulled the trigger," Kalugin wrote. It was, after all, the polite thing to do.[18]

Kalugin, it turned out, also had a taste for killing Bulgarian homi-noids, as he would later admit to John le Carré. In a lengthy piece for the *New York Times Book Review*, le Carré's disdain for Kalugin sweats through every sentence.

"He has a kinetic restlessness, this former golden boy Oleg of KGB counterintelligence. Listening to him I learn with a bit of a jar that he is also a writer who has toured the United States as a celebrity of some kind," le Carré wrote. "With a quick smile of complicity," Kalugin told le Carré that he was now in private business: "East-West contacts, intro-ductions, commissions."[19]

Kalugin looked to impress le Carré further by admitting that he masterminded the KGB's 1978 murder of journalist Georgi Markov, a Bulgarian dissident assassinated on London's Waterloo Bridge. Agents allegedly used an umbrella to inject him with a ricin pellet.

Markov, a playwright, novelist, and journalist, had defected from his native Bulgaria in 1969. Eventually settling in London, he began working for both the BBC and RFE. He had earlier been friends with Bulgarian Communist Party chairman Todor Zhikov, which seemed to have afforded some initial protection from his outspoken instincts. But when Markov's father took ill and the Bulgarian authorities refused to let him return to the country to visit, Markov became bitter. He didn't care to hide his feelings in his broadcasts.

"Georgi was so incensed by his father's death that his broadcasts became absolutely vitriolic," Markov's widow, Annabel, told the *Guard-ian*. "He named the mistresses of the high-ups, really smearing mud on the people in the inner circles."[20]

A death sentence was issued. "We're not children," Kalugin told le Carré as the two sipped scotch in Kalugin's apartment. "I was the head man for all that stuff, for Christ's sake! Nothing operational could be done unless it went across my desk, OK?"[21]

And after a few drams of Glenlivet—"these KGB Western hands are connoisseurs," le Carré wrote—Kalugin grew more candid. "Markov had already been sentenced to death in his absence by a Bulgarian court, but the Bulgarians were terrible," he continued. "They couldn't do a damn thing. We had to do it all for them: train the guy, make the umbrella, fix the poison."[22] The Bulgarians couldn't organize a simple shooting expedition in a cornfield either—for Kalugin at least, the parallels were obvious.

In 1993, Scotland Yard arrested Kalugin at London's Heathrow Airport for his alleged involvement with the Markov murder but then quickly released him, citing a lack of evidence. There are plenty, including Karel, who think American intelligence may have called upon the two countries' so-called special relationship to have him released. Eventually, le Carré and his twenty-year-old son Nick, who tagged along on the trip to Russia, left Kalugin's apartment. Outside, "the fresh Moscow air never tasted so good," le Carré wrote.

But their encounter did not end there. A few months after the *Book Review* piece was published, not only did the *Times* publish a letter from Kalugin complaining about le Carré's article, but in a masterful exhibition of literary jousting, they also allowed le Carré to respond to Kalugin's response.[23]

Kalugin lamented that he "was upset and somewhat perplexed" by le Carré's article and sought to raise doubts about the accuracy of le Carré's account by insisting that he had incorrectly described the features of the apartment building Kalugin lived in. Though le Carré never once accused Kalugin of having done so, the ex-KGB general also saw fit to explicitly deny having ever worked as a CIA agent. Kalugin also refuted any involvement in the Markov incident, all but accused le Carré of having invented the quotes in his article, and directed people to read his own memoirs for the truth of what really happened. For good measure, Kalugin then accused le Carré of taking advantage of Kalugin's hospitality and insulting Russian national honor before taking a swipe at le Carré's age and his reputation as a writer of fiction: "Memories fail people at times and literary plots run dry."[24]

Le Carré was not amused. In his response he noted that as well as his own son, there were two other—Russian—witnesses to their conversation.

Of the Markov discussion, le Carré wrote, "I remember a monologue, singularly free of the remorse that [Kalugin] now claims is his." He then took umbrage at Kalugin's allegation that he had disrespected Russia at large. "I am sorry for the many decent Russian people who grew up as Communists in good faith, and now must accept that their faith was misplaced," he wrote. "And I am sorrier still, not for Communism's winners, among whom I count the general, but its losers."[25]

Le Carré finished with a flourish: "When the general complains that I have abused his hospitality, I am embarrassed. He has my full apology. Perhaps one day he will apologize to Mrs. Markov."[26]

Back in 1976, when Kalugin met with Karel Koecher, he must have felt untouchable and acted still more insufferable. By even appearing in Čtyřkoly, he had flatly defied orders. KGB Central in Moscow had insisted that the StB be allowed to conduct the interrogation on their own. And yet Kalugin inserted himself anyway.

Kalugin's career is pockmarked with many more such strange occurrences. The US government, and two different American presidents, one from each party, allowed Kalugin, a known KGB agent, to continue to operate out of the Soviet embassy in Washington, DC, from 1968 to 1970. This seems an indication that in his prime espionage years, Kalugin was equally untouchable in the US and the USSR. Amid such unassailably bulletproof status, protected by two superpowers, it is noteworthy that Kalugin would go out of his way to intercept Karel in 1976—and show such clear hostility toward him.

"During my five years in Washington, including more than a year as acting station chief, I never learned of a single case of how a Soviet illegal had penetrated the US government," Kalugin wrote in his memoirs.[27] And yet, that is almost exactly what Karel had accomplished—not only penetrating the American government but the CIA itself. Given that Kalugin was the Warsaw Pact man most singularly responsible for infiltrating Western intelligence agencies and that Karel was the only Eastern Bloc illegal ever to penetrate the CIA, Karel should have been a vital partner for Kalugin. Instead, after the Čtyřkoly interrogation, Kalugin accused Karel of working for the CIA against the Communist Bloc and all but ordered the StB cut off cooperation with Karel.

Along with myriad other curiosities in a lengthy life, it's another instance where it feels like Kalugin was hiding something. "As it later turned out, I was wrong in my assessment," Kalugin later wrote of his denouncement of Karel in his memoirs.[28] But at the time, the StB complied with the influential and confident Soviet general even as the report severing their relationship with Karel recognized that the "materials he handed over during the time of the collaboration were highly valued by both us and our Soviet friends.

"Collaboration with RINO was ended in the year 1976 on the instruction of the federal interior minister, which was given on the basis of RINO declining to stay in the ČSSR, appear in mass media with a critique of the work of the CIA and also on the existence of certain unconfirmed evidence, that he could have been recruited by the opposite side," an StB report from the time continued.

Karel recalled the interrogation bitterly: "I am ordered to stay in Prague and in two days appear at a press conference and accuse Havel and company of being paid by the Americans." Backed into yet another corner, he responded with his trademark pugnacity: "I say, 'Fuck you, I won't do it and if you say I am an American agent, the hell I am.' They got so scared that they let me go."

As for Kalugin, Karel was more explicit than le Carré: "The Americans had an agent with the KGB—Kalugin."

Eventually, Kalugin's KGB superiors would draw the very same conclusion. After leaving Čtyřkoly, Kalugin's days as the KGB's head of foreign counterintelligence were already numbered. Three years later he was demoted and made deputy head of the KGB local office in Leningrad. Instead of jet-setting around the world and killing Bulgarian bipeds for sport, he turned his attention to harassing his fellow Russians. Among his subordinates at his new post was a capable cadet named Vladimir Putin.

"While Kalugin was head of foreign counterintelligence we did not expose a single American agent. After we removed Kalugin, we exposed dozens and dozens of our enemies. That fact alone says a lot," Vladimir Kryuchkov, the chairman of the KGB from 1988 to 1991, later told a Canadian documentary film crew.[29]

As the calendar turned to 1977, Karel and Kalugin would find themselves entangled in what would become an infamous spy scandal. Both would bear the brunt of the blowback. As Kryuchkov put it, "The story of Koecher's misfortune, the story of Koecher's suffering is a direct result of Kalugin's actions."[30]

But before Kalugin's fall, more people would have to die.

11

TRIGON

"There are two histories: official history, lying, and then secret history, where you find the real causes of events."
—Honoré de Balzac

By 1975, Oleg Kalugin and the rest of KGB leadership were already convinced there was a mole in the Soviet Union's Bogotá embassy. Moscow pressured Prague, and Karel's StB handlers had in turn pressed him for information that might uncover which Soviet diplomats in Colombia were being targeted by the CIA. He saw a few possibilities but finally ventured to guess that an affable embassy secretary named Ogorodnik seemed a logical choice.

The son of a Soviet naval officer, Alexandr Dmitryevich Ogorodnik also had hoped to make a career on the seven seas. Born in 1939, as a youngster in Sevastopol, home port of the Soviet fleet, Ogorodnik was schooled at an exclusive naval academy. Young Sasha was the eldest of three children and part of what Kalugin called a new generation of Soviet elite. Their fathers, not to mention the twenty-seven million citizens who died, had proven their loyalty to the country during World War II. Now it was their turn.

As Alexandr studied engineering to prep for a naval career, his eyes started giving him trouble. When he failed an eye exam, dreams of following in his father's footsteps blurred and then faded to black. Alexandr would need to find another way to serve the motherland. Ogorodnik's father had a top job, and his early years on the Black Sea coast had only reinforced the merits of Communism: the Soviet model had delivered education and a choice of career paths, not to mention health care and social justice for all. He abandoned engineering and took up economics in hopes of becoming a diplomat. At age twenty he joined the Communist Party.

Ogorodnik had varied interests. Though he would never make a career at sea, he maintained a lifelong love of sailing. He also liked opera and often went to performances alone—so as to better focus on the music. Ogorodnik was smart and personable. Like many a character in this saga, he had a knack for languages, learning fluent English and Spanish.

Ogorodnik finished school in 1970 and worked briefly at a publishing house before taking a job at the foreign ministry. He started out with short trips to Costa Rica and Colombia, where his Spanish was useful. In his early thirties, it was finally time for Ogorodnik to take up a full-time post at an embassy abroad. But there was one problem—he wasn't married. At the time, the Soviets rarely let single men work as diplomats outside the country.

Young, single men are a threat to peace in the best of times, but the Soviet diplomatic corps had additional motives for their rule: people with families to worry about were a lot less likely to defect to the West. Marriage was an easy way to tether that temptation—or so their thinking went.

Ogorodnik was handsome, and there were plenty of Soviet women looking to travel. Alexandra Harutinyan, a slender woman of Armenian descent, was game. So Alexandr and Alexandra, separated by a single vowel, agreed to get hitched. It was from the beginning a marriage of convenience. With the formalities complete, the young couple was deployed to Bogotá, where Ogorodnik took a job as second secretary at the embassy.

The Soviets had only reestablished diplomatic ties with Colombia in 1968, so when Ogorodnik arrived in 1972, he was part of a contingent still trying to reingratiate the Soviet Union with his hosts. In the early 1970s, Latin America was a Cold War hot spot. In 1970, socialist Salvador Allende had won the presidency in Chile, and US president Richard Nixon feared the country would become "another Cuba." A later US Senate investigation found "extensive and continuous" CIA involvement in Chile between 1963 and 1973—the year Augusto Pinochet overthrew Allende in a coup. Allende shot himself before he was captured, and Pinochet's regime banned political opposition, "disappeared" thousands of people, and held power until 1990. "We didn't do it," Secretary of State Henry Kissinger told Nixon in a phone conversation just days after Allende's ouster, before adding a revealing rider to his denial: "I mean we helped them . . . created the conditions as great as possible."[1]

The CIA was plenty active elsewhere in the region too. The agency had successfully bugged Soviet embassies, trade missions, and diplomats' apartments, including in Bogotá. As tapes from the phone taps rolled into a suburban office tower at 200 North Glebe Road in Arlington, Virginia, they landed on Karel Koecher's desk.

Karel listened to and translated Russian conversations into English before sending them for further analysis. Listening in, he got to know Ogorodnik well, finding the diplomat "joyful, pleasant, obviously not the drab Soviet type." Ogorodnik liked American movies and television: "His favorite was the old *Mission Impossible* TV series."

As Ogorodnik's private journals would later show, this newfound taste for Western culture correlated with his souring opinion of the Soviet system. After just a few months abroad, Ogorodnik had realized life could be very different. He had also discovered that his privileged upbringing was far from typical. Even in Colombia, a pleasant enough place but not one offering a lifestyle typically admired internationally, Ogorodnik had a sense that life could feel colorful, better.

"He realized that the Soviet leaders were lying," said Alejandra Suárez Barcala, a daughter that Ogorodnik sired during his Bogotá stay.

Alejandra never met her father, and Ogorodnik never knew she existed, but years later she came across private journals that detailed his evolving worldview during his posting in Bogotá. "Things were not what they told me. They are doing horrible things every day and they are lying about them," he wrote.[2]

KGB officers operating at the embassy tried to recruit Ogorodnik—a legitimate diplomat—to pull double duty as an intelligence agent. He was reluctant, and it's unclear whether he ever agreed to fully join their ranks, but others took an interest in Ogorodnik too. As always, the CIA was also looking for recruits, and Ogorodnik's taste for American culture, nightlife, and women attracted their attention.

At no other time in his career did the duality of Karel's double-agent role appear so acute. He found himself listening in on a man whose loyalties were being tested from all sides and who was struggling to determine where his future lay. Karel was in a similar position: his role as a CIA analyst meant he listened to tapes and advised his CIA colleagues on potential Soviet recruits. At the same time, as an active StB agent, he was tasked with advising the Communist Bloc on potential traitors or American targets. Instead of choosing one or the other, he did both.

Only nominally married, Ogorodnik had a dalliance with another embassy man's wife. Despite a total foreign ministry ban on fraternizing with women from a host country, he also took a shine to a Spanish lady named Pilar Suárez Barcala. Such relationships marked Ogorodnik as a risk-taker and—should it prove necessary—offered the CIA pressure points to compel cooperation. It wouldn't be the first time the CIA put the squeeze on a potential asset when they needed to. Karel had seen it before: "They can go there to recruit him and do all kinds of nasty things, to force him to do it. Run over a child, put him behind the steering wheel and pour some whiskey on him. Sorry to say that, but it's done."

But the CIA played a friendlier game this time and found themselves a willing partner. Pilar had come to Colombia a few years before with a letter of recommendation from an important Spanish clergyman.

Charismatic, beautiful, and with impeccable Catholic credentials, she was quickly drafted into Bogotá high society. She took a series of jobs, working for a time for the global food conglomerate Nestlé before finding work at a cultural center that staged art exhibitions and public events.

"My mother and I had a lot of problems, but she was clever, with a lot of character," her daughter Alejandra said. "She did have a variety of relationships with men." As Ogorodnik and Pilar took to one another, the CIA saw an opportunity. American agents would have a hard time approaching a Soviet diplomat directly, but a woman like Pilar might serve as a bridge. "My mother was never inside the CIA," Alejandra insisted, but she agreed that "it's true that the CIA used my mother to contact my father."

The Soviet diplomatic mission was housed in an old four-story mansion that resembled a castle. It had a large garden full of exotic trees and flowers, a swimming pool, and a fountain. Ogorodnik lived a mile away with his wife in a small two-room apartment in a building that housed other Soviet officials. He would meet with Pilar at the Hilton hotel, where they both relaxed around the pool. The CIA kept close watch. One day, after laying the groundwork, they approached Ogorodnik in the Hilton sauna with an offer, using Pilar as their go-between.

The deal on the table asked Ogorodnik to report on the happenings at the Soviet embassy. In exchange, he and Pilar would later be resettled in the United States. Though Ogorodnik was dissatisfied with the Soviet way of life, he was not prepared to betray his homeland for nothing: he also wanted money. "I don't doubt there was a lot of money," Alejandra said. "They say he was the best-paid agent ever."

In January 1974, Ogorodnik agreed to cooperate and was given the code name Trigon. He earned several times his monthly embassy salary. To avoid attracting attention, he channeled much of it to an escrow account, which he could then later access after defecting to the West. He also bought emeralds, which he gave to his mother so that she might someday exchange them for cash should something happen to him—a prescient move. The CIA also provided Ogorodnik—with his history of poor vision—with contact lenses, lest this ladies' man feel his style was being cramped by clunky Soviet eyeglass frames.

As Karel watched the CIA courting Ogorodnik, he warned the Soviets: "I advised Moscow that they are going after him. That the only thing to do is to recall him as fast as possible. I didn't want to ruin his career or life." But despite the advice, the KGB "never recalled him." Indeed, StB transcripts generally indicate that Karel suggested Ogorodnik as a potential target for American recruitment. But they also show Karel arguing that Ogorodnik appeared a man capable of resisting any CIA approach. Karel was correct on the first point but mistaken on the latter.

In the summer of 1974, Pilar became pregnant with Alejandra by Ogorodnik. The CIA asked her to keep the pregnancy a secret, and she agreed. In December 1974, Ogorodnik was scheduled to finish his rotation at the Bogotá embassy and move back to Moscow. The CIA had a new offer for him: return to Moscow, act as an informer for two years, and then they would extract him, reconnect him with Pilar, and resettle the pair under assumed identities. Better yet, the CIA told him they would pull him out immediately if he thought the KGB was beginning to get suspicious.

It was tempting, but the mission was much riskier than anything he had done so far—he would be operating in Moscow, where the KGB exercised near total control. For a day or two, he thought the risk would be too great, and he considered defecting then and there—walking into the US embassy and requesting political asylum. Perhaps, if he had known that Pilar was expecting a child, he would have done so. But Ogorodnik had an ego and, like Karel, thought he could play a role brokering Cold War peace or changing the situation on the ground in his own country. He wanted to make a difference, so he took the assignment. "My father knew what he was doing," Alejandra affirmed. "He knew it was risky, maybe he was willing to take too much risk, but it was not because he was used by the CIA."

Ogorodnik was trained by Langley in secret writing techniques that allowed him to embed messages in letters and extract messages from mail the CIA sent him. He learned to decode one-way-voice-link radio broadcasts using disposable deciphering pads.[3] Ogorodnik practiced making dead drops using props—like hollowed-out rocks with trap doors—that could hide a message and blend into the terrain of a park or the woods. Most crucially, he learned to take pictures with a T-50, a miniature camera that could be hidden in a pen or cigarette lighter.

Back in Moscow, in February 1975, Ogorodnik started work at the American department of the Foreign Policy Planning Office of the Soviet Ministry of Foreign Affairs. Despite Karel's warning that officials at the Bogotá embassy were CIA targets, the Soviets had given Ogorodnik a job where he had access to some of the most important strategic documents on Soviet-US relations, including cables from the Soviet embassy in Washington, DC.

To Karel, who had given his warning to the KGB, the decision to give Ogorodnik top secret clearance was "crazy." And he seemed to have a point. If the KGB suspected Ogorodnik was passing information to US intelligence or was even a candidate to do so, it would seem the Foreign Policy Planning Office was among the worst possible places for him to work.

One of the people responsible for clearing Ogorodnik was Oleg Kalugin. At the time, Kalugin was charged with uncovering Soviets who had started working with the CIA, meaning Ogorodnik would only have been able to take up his new post at the foreign ministry with Kalugin's approval. Even if Kalugin was personally unaware that Ogorodnik himself was an American spy, as his foreign counterintelligence department continued to search for the Bogotá embassy mole, common sense would dictate taking a cautious approach to anybody returning from duty in Colombia.

Instead, Kalugin's department allowed Ogorodnik to work in an office where he was capable of causing maximum damage. The StB files offer concrete proof that Karel's warnings about the Bogotá documents had been transmitted by mid-1975 at the latest; indeed, it's likely they crossed Kalugin's desk as early as 1974. And yet Ogorodnik continued working unimpeded at the Bogotá embassy for the rest of that year and then moved on to a sensitive position at the foreign ministry in Moscow.

Even if bureaucratic churn meant the case had somehow avoided Kalugin's attention in 1974 and 1975, his interrogation of Karel in September 1976—when Kalugin asked Karel about missing pages from some documents he had sent regarding Ogorodnik—is proof positive that he was aware of Ogorodnik by then. And yet Ogorodnik continued to work in the Soviet foreign ministry with access to top secret files.

The timeline meant that Kalugin had—due to incompetence or neglect—either declined to take action on Karel's report; investigated and concluded Karel was wrong; investigated and concluded Karel was right but chose to do nothing; or investigated, concluded Karel was right, and then decided to use the situation to his own advantage. Kalugin briefly mentioned Ogorodnik in his own unreliable memoirs but bewilderingly asserts he was recruited by the CIA while attending Columbia, the university in New York City, not while he was stationed in Colombia in South America. It is either a ridiculous mistake or yet another absurd attempt at misdirection.

For his part, once back in Moscow, it's clear Ogorodnik did provide information to American intelligence. Using the T-50s the CIA provided, he photographed foreign ministry documents. Marti Peterson, a CIA agent posing as a diplomat at the US embassy in Moscow, arrived in October 1975 and took over as his primary handler not long after.

Marti had married a CIA operative, John Peterson, in 1969 and traveled with him to Laos. She got a job working as a secretary in the CIA's Southeast Asian office, and when John was killed in a helicopter crash in 1972, Marti decided to pursue a full-time career as an operative.

By the mid-1970s, there were more than fifty thousand KGB agents active in Moscow alone, surpassing the worldwide total combined number of FBI and CIA employees.[4] Running American agents in the Soviet capital was almost impossible. Peterson was chosen for the job because the KGB seemed less suspicious of women, and she found that, "during my first month, I had not detected any surveillance coverage."

In a sign of the times, many of Peterson's own CIA colleagues showed similar chauvinism, assuming that Marti was actually being followed by the KGB but lacked the skills to notice. "My male peers in the office doubted my ability since they had all experienced coverage from their first week in Moscow," she wrote in her memoirs.[5]

Peterson became the first female case officer to operate in Moscow.[6] "I acted the double role every day," she recalled. "I had my job I had to do and do it well in the embassy. And I had the other job. I was motivated by the excitement in the moment and the adrenaline and the belief that I was in a boxing match that I had to come out a winner."

Though Peterson never met Ogorodnik face-to-face, she corroborated what others have said. "He had a Western mind in a Soviet body. He had a large ego and believed he could manage his own life and wanted to do that. His behavior was always a man who was writing his own script."

On July 15, 1977, a good six months beyond the two-year mark by which the CIA had pledged to extract Ogorodnik, Marti Peterson left her Moscow apartment to make the latest in a series of dead drops. Inside her brown leather purse, she carried a Soviet driver's license, some spare change for the subway or a pay phone, and a hollowed-out hunk of fake concrete that held materials for Ogorodnik.

As she drove off in her navy-blue Zhiguli, Peterson continued past the US embassy to the industrial outskirts of Moscow. Once there, she circled the streets for the better part of two hours. A bag on the passenger seat slid around with every turn. Inside was a change of clothes and a can of Carlsberg beer—something she routinely brought to privately toast the end of each successful mission.

Eventually Marti doubled back toward the center of town, parked near Gorky Street, and went down the stairs into the nearby metro station. As she looked around to see if she was being followed, she checked people's shoes. Always with the shoes. Experience taught Marti that KGB agents tracking Americans would occasionally change coats or hats to disguise themselves. Rarely—if ever—did those costume changes extend to footwear. On this night, there were plenty of tacky square-toed numbers—so nothing suspicious.

Marti changed trains once before exiting the metro at the Lenin Stadium station. At street level she started walking again, first one block, then another, then back to the first again. Occasionally Marti rested at a bus stop or park bench to see whether anybody was following. She had an SRR-100 stuck to her bra. A wire ran up her shirt to a neck-loop antenna. The white rectangular device, a bit smaller than the original iPod, could detect encrypted conversations on KGB radio and helped tip CIA agents off to KGB activity in their area. As she approached the drop site, she noted three men milling about. The SRR-100 stayed quiet, so she thought little of it.

Although it was already 10:15 p.m., long Moscow summer days meant the sky hovered between darkness and light. Marti crossed the street and ascended the metal staircase to the pedestrian walkway on the railway bridge that served as a regular drop point. The tracks ran down the middle, and there were sidewalks on either side. Four identical turrets, constructed of soot-blackened stone blocks, held the old bridge up. Arched passages made it possible to walk through the center of each tower. Amid a protracted dusk, the shadows in these caverns made for an ideal dead drop spot.

Few people would casually stroll this route, and those who did would move quickly across the bridge to avoid the jarring of a passing freight train. Marti stepped into an alcove that burrowed through one of the bridge's stone towers. She placed her package in a small shelflike opening in the rock and began her retreat. The plan called for strolling the nearby neighborhood for an hour or so. In the meantime, Ogorodnik was meant to pick up the package she had left and drop off materials of his own. As Marti reached the bottom of the stairs, she spotted the three men again.

The SRR-100 was silent, but they were now moving toward her. Before Marti knew what was happening, one man grabbed her from behind while another locked up her arms. A third approached from the front and ripped the SRR-100 from her neck. A rickety van screeched as it pulled up. Another dozen men jumped out. She was surrounded. The KGB had been waiting for her. Marti shouted and struggled, kicking one of her assailants in the shin. But there was no way out.

Marti was arrested and hauled down to Lubyanka Prison for interrogation. As for Ogorodnik, he never showed for the drop—he was already dead and had been for nearly a month already.[7]

Ogorodnik had been arrested on the night of June 22, 1977. Igor Peretruchin, the KGB officer in charge of the arrest, described waiting for Ogorodnik in the courtyard of his apartment building. "As I remember, twilight quickly thickened, and evening came. It became chilly in the yard. The wind blew through the arches of the house," he wrote. "It gave the impression that you were in a wind tunnel."[8]

Two heavies were there to assist Peretruchin, and they waited in the courtyard shadows. Eventually Ogorodnik's black Volga pulled in. Peretruchin told Ogorodnik they needed to talk, and after helping him unload some files from the trunk of the car, he walked alongside Ogorodnik until they reached the door of the building. There the two other agents loomed. Ogorodnik was flustered, but seeing no alternative, he passed through the lobby of the building and entered the elevator. The four went up to Ogorodnik's apartment. As soon as they crossed the threshold of his flat, the KGB agents proceeded to search for weapons, finding multiple pistols, cartridges of compressed gas used to shoot poison needles from a cylinder, and a pen capable of firing live ammunition.

A few minutes later, a set of KGB investigators arrived and presented Ogorodnik with arrest and search warrants. As Peretruchin sat with Ogorodnik on the couch, the investigators picked apart the apartment.

"Tell me, will they shoot me?" Ogorodnik asked Peretruchin.

"Well, I can't say. It's not up to any of us. Everything will be decided by the court. Here, much will depend on you personally, how frank you will be during the investigation and trial. Now you must first of all decide on which side of the barricades you prefer to be on."

"Yes, I understand, but you deceived me! How can I trust you now?"

Ogorodnik was not expressing his distrust for Peretruchin personally; rather, he was implying that the KGB itself had betrayed him. "You" referred to an institution, not a person. In a cloud of confusion and double-dealing, Ogorodnik's words, uttered in resigned terror, hinted that he genuinely had something to feel aggrieved about. If his cries are understood to be saying something similar to "The KGB deceived me! How can I trust the KGB now?"—it sounds a lot like Ogorodnik may have agreed to work for someone at the KGB, perhaps to send disinformation back to the CIA. As he sat there on that June night, he would have realized that this person had set him up.

According to Peretruchin, the KGB search discovered a Chinese flashlight used to conceal a film canister. Hidden in a book was a code sheet for decoding radio messages. There were carbon papers for sending messages and a stack of special paper that could easily dissolve in water. As the search continued, Peretruchin was called away around 1:00 a.m. He was surprised that he was being withdrawn in the middle of an active arrest, but it was late—the middle of the night—and he was tired, so he thought little of it and went home to bed. Ogorodnik was somebody else's problem until morning.

The next day, early, before he headed in to work, Peretruchin called the department officer to "find out how things were." He was staggered to hear that Ogorodnik had been poisoned: "How could this happen in the course of an investigative measure, when everything and everyone is regulated to the limit by the Criminal Procedure Code? For me, a lawyer by training, it simply did not fit into my head. It was impossible to imagine such a thing even in a bad dream!"[9]

At this point in the narrative, both the official KGB and CIA versions of events start to align. In fact, the CIA was unusually transparent about what they say happened next, even posting an article about it on their own website.

As the unified CIA-KGB story goes, Ogorodnik had requested cyanide capsules from the CIA so that he might kill himself in case of capture. After a long debate, the CIA agreed to give him some; a supervisor in Langley named Aldrich Ames—who would later betray his country and, as another double agent, sell American secrets to the Soviets—authorized providing Ogorodnik with the poison pill.[10] In fact, the CIA claimed that Ogorodnik received two such cyanide capsules hidden in Montblanc pens on two separate occasions. Ogorodnik was said to have destroyed the first one out of fear of being discovered before later requesting a second.[11] On June 22, 1977, in the midst of writing out a confession, Ogorodnik asked to use his preferred pen. The KGB saw nothing suspicious in the request—although given that they had already found one pen capable of shooting bullets, they might have shown a little caution—and handed Ogorodnik his poisoned pen. Ogorodnik swallowed the capsule, dying instantly.

Even if the story was true, such a detailed account had to originate from someone who was in the room, making it ever more remarkable how similar the official—oddly transparent and public—CIA and KGB versions of the Ogorodnik story were. "The official report that he committed suicide was issued by Kalugin, and the CIA confirmed it," Karel confirmed.

But why would the CIA validate the KGB's story?

Karel had a ready explanation: "Because Kalugin was their agent."

Several veterans of the KGB and the current Russian government insisted Kalugin was secretly working for the CIA. He was subsequently sentenced in absentia to prison time should he ever return to Russia and has therefore opted to live out his days in the United States.[12] For his part, Kalugin has always denied working for the CIA, insisting he was being slandered and punished for publicly criticizing the Soviet and Russian political systems.

Kalugin's record for candor leaves much to be desired, and if he had been a CIA informant, he would necessarily deny it. However, his behavior, never mind the entire trajectory of his career, makes much more sense if understood as the actions of a CIA double agent.

For instance, it might explain why he received such a glowing 1959 profile in the *New York Times* (the CIA helped place the story) and why he was allowed to continue working in the United States for a full two years after publicly being exposed as a KGB agent in 1968 (the CIA intervened to keep him in the States). Most consequentially for Karel Koecher, it would explain why Kalugin had wrongly accused Karel of being an American spy in 1976. For if Kalugin was working for the CIA, he would have been right to be concerned that Karel, with access to internal CIA information, might discover him and tell the StB or KGB. Though Kalugin was several orders of magnitude more important than Karel to the Eastern Bloc spy apparatus, Karel still had the ability to threaten Kalugin's life and livelihood.

When it came to Ogorodnik, Kalugin's treachery would also account for how somebody already suspected of being a CIA plant got a job in a secretive division of the Soviet foreign ministry. It was Kalugin's job to expose Soviets collaborating with the CIA, and he knew the Bogotá embassy had been targeted. Yet he cleared Ogorodnik for his new post.

It would also explain why Peretruchin's unit was called off the Ogorodnik investigation at the last minute only to find out the next morning that he had died overnight. If Kalugin had used Ogorodnik to interface with the CIA, he would have little choice but to eliminate him for fear Ogorodnik would tell others about their collaboration.

Though much of this story amounts to informed speculation, the very fact that Ogorodnik, a known CIA target, was allowed to work in a top secret branch of the foreign ministry requires that one of three things be true.

The first option was that Kalugin was bad at his job (hence the forth-coming demotion). In this alternative, Kalugin simply failed to investigate Ogorodnik, investigated him poorly, or declined to take action despite whatever his investigation uncovered.

The second possibility is that somebody above Ogorodnik's pay grade decided to look the other way while he shared genuine information with the CIA. In this instance, Kalugin, or a superior, would have known that Ogorodnik was working for the CIA and would have let Ogorodnik continue to do so as part of their own collaboration with the CIA.

A third possibility is that Ogorodnik was used as a channel to feed the CIA disinformation. This could have come about if Ogorodnik had alerted his Soviet superiors that the CIA was trying to recruit him and was then ordered to play along. Or, in an alternative subvariant, Ogorodnik may have genuinely wished to help the CIA only to later be discovered by the KGB. If the KGB knew about Ogorodnik's American connection, they may have only allowed him access to documents that would confuse the Yanks or used him to send disinformation to the CIA.

All three scenarios would implicate Kalugin, and some variation of the third almost certainly happened.

Ogorodnik's last drop included a piece of microfilm containing a memo written by Anatoly Dobrynin, the Soviet ambassador to Washington. That memo claimed that former US national security advisor Henry Kissinger had preemptively briefed him on the American position at the forthcoming SALT II arms control talks. Those talks occurred after Kissinger—and his boss, President Gerald Ford—had left office, so the briefing, if it had occurred, would have been a deliberate collaboration with a foreign power to undermine the American policy under the new US president, Jimmy Carter. Such a briefing could have amounted to treason.

A few years later, on December 16, 1980, investigative reporter Jack Anderson, the same journalist who outed Oleg Kalugin as an active KGB agent back in the 1960s, wrote about the incident. As Anderson told it, Kissinger met with the Soviet ambassador to Washington,

Anatoly Dobrynin, on April 11, 1977. Dobrynin wrote a memo summarizing the meeting and cabled it back to Moscow. A spy with the code name Trigon—that is, Ogorodnik—gave a microfilm copy of Dobrynin's cable to the CIA during his final drop.

"According to Dobrynin's cable, Kissinger told him Carter's SALT II proposal was unacceptable, had misinterpreted the Soviet position and should be rejected by the Russians," Anderson wrote. "Kissinger also told the Soviet ambassador, according to the still secret cable, that Carter's policy on human rights merely showed the naïveté and the weakness of the new president and his national security advisor, Zbigniew Brzezinski."[13]

The Kissinger-Dobrynin meeting did actually occur, and several sources have confirmed the existence of the microfilm. Figuring out whether the reported contents of the memo—and its treasonous implications—are accurate is more difficult. Its veracity was never verified. It seems the cable was most likely a forgery—meaning Ogorodnik was, knowingly or unknowingly, providing disinformation. Adding to the intrigue, in the 1997 book *Confessions of a Spy*, journalist Pete Earley quotes infamous double agent Aldrich Ames and another ex-CIA official as saying the microfilm had since disappeared from the CIA vaults.

An initial CIA review found Ogorodnik's "own actions had brought about [his] downfall,"[14] but the official line has since shifted. Instead, the CIA blamed Karel Koecher, who had been listening to wiretaps at the Bogotá embassy and either intentionally or without his own knowledge provided details that allowed the KGB to figure out Ogorodnik had been collaborating with the CIA. Karel became a convenient way to write off the failure of the Ogorodnik mission.

However, even if Karel's information led to Ogorodnik being identified as a CIA collaborator, it wouldn't explain the many other mishaps the CIA had around this time. The same year Ogorodnik died, in 1977, Colonel Anatoli Filatov was exposed as a CIA informant. His CIA case officer in Moscow was also arrested. Also that year, a suspicious fire broke out in the US embassy in Moscow. The chaos at the time was such that new CIA chief Stansfield Turner actually blocked the CIA's Moscow station from taking part in active espionage for the better part of a year so as to better determine what might be going on.[15] None of these contemporaneous incidents can be connected to Karel Koecher.

And in post-Soviet Russia, new questions arose about how Ogorodnik actually died. In a May 24, 2001, interview with the Russian newspaper *Trud*, Nikolai Kovalev, a former head of the FSB (the security agency successor to the KGB), said that Ogorodnik had not died from poisoning but from natural causes—a heart attack.

"I saw the autopsy report," Kovalev told the paper. "The conclusion of the doctors was acute cardiac failure caused by the arrest. . . . Neither investigators nor doctors found traces of poison in the body, although that myth is still alive."

The same article went on to quote the KGB medical report, which concludes that "Citizen Ogorodnik A.D." had heart problems and that "against the background of emotionally mental stress, an attack of acute coronary insufficiency developed, leading to acute heart (left heart with pulmonary edema) failure, cardiogenic shock, cerebral coma, fatal." The medical team "did not find poisoning with any poisonous substance" and found "no other morphological changes indicating that death arose from another cause.

"All of the above gives grounds come to the conclusion that the death of Ogorodnik Alexander Dmitrievich came from an acute coronary and cardiovascular insufficiency, which developed on the background previous heart disease (small focal diffuse myocardial sclerosis, incomplete blockage of the leg of the bundle of hepatitis C—violation of intra-atrial conduction)," they concluded emphatically.[16]

How Ogorodnik died does not alter the fact that he spied for the CIA. But the two very different accounts of his death are suggestive—and have become part of Cold War mythology. At the center of the puzzle is the question of how or why a fake cause of death was explicitly endorsed by both the KGB and the CIA. If the intelligence services of the world's two superpowers got their story wrong, why did they get it wrong in exactly the same way? We might expect spy services to lie—it's part of the job—but it's rare for two competing services to lie identically.

Even Ogorodnik's onetime CIA handler, Marti Peterson, acknowledged that she still has trouble making sense of everything that happened. Though she stuck to the story that Karel, working for the KGB while employed at the CIA, exposed Ogorodnik, she also conceded it is only a theory. "I have some of the same gaps," Peterson admitted before concluding, "I am going to have to wait another thirty years" until the related files are declassified.

But the CIA, otherwise reluctant to comment on most operations, has taken a suspiciously outspoken stand on the Trigon case. In an article published on their own website, they blame Karel Koecher for outing Ogorodnik as a CIA collaborator and, ultimately, causing his death. Of all the incidents in the agency's secretive seventy-five years, it remains unclear why they would choose to be so transparent on this one.

Karel has his own theory. When Ogorodnik returned to Moscow, Kalugin ordered him to continue cooperating with the CIA, and Kalugin used Trigon as a channel to communicate with the CIA. Kalugin could help Ogorodnik provide genuine material to the CIA, look the other way while he did, or use him to send disinformation. Whenever Ogorodnik ceased to be useful, Kalugin had the option of exposing him. In this way Kalugin could justify his position as chief of foreign counterintelligence while covering up his own duplicity. The only possible witness to an arrangement like this would have been Ogorodnik, and once he was dead, nobody would be the wiser. "Mind you, I am not saying this is a CIA operation as such; this is Kalugin's operation," Karel said. "The CIA's position would be, Kalugin is scum, but he's our scum."

The Ogorodnik case was revelatory and obscure all at once. Three apparent double agents—Ogorodnik, Kalugin, and Koecher—collided as a fourth, Ames, hovered in the background. It's no wonder that reliable testimony was hard to find. But teasing out details of a strange death in Moscow cannot overshadow one abiding lesson from the murky escapade: none of the intelligence services were pure; all were damaged.

By 1977, human beings were being treated like poker chips at a penny-ante card game. Individual lives were mere tokens to bluff, fold, or raise the stakes in a struggle between great powers. Whatever was left of a Cold War contest based on principles had devolved into a foggy morass of dissimulation and deceit.

12

THE BEGINNING OF THE END

"This planetary challenge to the position of human beings in the world is, of course, also taking place in the Western world, the only difference being the social and political forms it takes. It may even be said that the more room there is in the Western democracies (compared to our world) for the genuine aims of life, the better the crisis is hidden from people and the more deeply they become immersed in it."
—VÁCLAV HAVEL

On January 31, 1977, the StB issued a document titled "A Report on the Termination of the Rino Case." It was the latest denunciation of Karel, and this time it seemed there would be no turning back. The report referred to Karel's "negative personality traits," listing "unhealthy ambition, Westernism, lust for money, desire for a flamboyant way of life, political liability." It was clear that the Czechoslovak intelligence service had accepted Kalugin's advice that Karel was "obviously working for the Americans and that they have to do away with [him]." Karel thought that Kalugin "probably meant that literally because he himself killed several people," but the StB did not pull the trigger.

The final straw had come when Karel refused to appear live on Czechoslovak television to denounce the CIA. He was "ordered to stay in Prague and in two days appear at a press conference and accuse Václav Havel and other intellectual dissidents of being paid by the

Americans." He would be a convincing prosecution witness. As Karel said, "I was in the dirty tricks section of the CIA."

The StB tried to convince Karel before finally giving up in the face of his typical pugnacity: "Fuck you," Karel said. "I won't do it, and if you say I am an American agent, the hell I am. If you don't want to let me go, they'll be looking for me—so, okay, start a war."

The fact that he "fundamentally rejected any appearance in Czechoslovakian mass media criticizing the CIA" was taken by the StB as showing "a clear stance not only about the ČSSR and Czechoslovak counterintelligence, but also documenting the dishonesty of his position to both the ČSSR and the [Communist Party]." A handwritten addendum to a document dated February 3, 1977, insisted that Kalugin's interrogation of September 1976 proved that Karel "was and is an enemy and an instrument of the American intelligence agency. Rino is a provocateur, Adrid [Hana's code name] took part with him in the provocation."

The StB had good reason for wanting to paint Václav Havel and his friends as American lackeys. The postwar boom was long over, and economic growth was slowing throughout the world. In Eastern Europe living conditions were falling ever further behind Western European norms. In 1963, the so-called Comecon countries—the Soviet-led economic bloc composed of the Eastern European countries—controlled 12 percent of world trade, but by 1979 that number had fallen to 9 percent. Over the course of the 1970s, Czechoslovakia's hard currency debt grew by a factor of twelve,[1] and growth slowed each year. By 1980, the economy was actually shrinking.[2]

Immediately following the 1968 Prague Spring, the Czechoslovak Communists had reimposed censorship, purged the party of internal dissenters, and successfully silenced any external opposition. *Normalizace*, as both the process and the period came to be known, counted on improved standards of living counteracting any desire for political expression. So long as everyone had a TV—and by 1975 some 90 percent of Czechoslovak households did[3]—and enough to eat, the regime figured it might just muddle along. For a few years, the strategy worked; a good portion of society was content to keep their opinions quiet so long as they could spend weekends sipping beer at a *chata*—the ubiquitous basic rural cottages that Czech city dwellers all seemed to have access to. Nobody believed in the system any longer, but the general sense of resignation meant that disappointment was kept at a low simmer and not an agitated boil.

As a character in Philip Roth's novel *The Prague Orgy* put it, "Only writers and intellectuals continue to be persecuted, only writing and thinking are suppressed; everybody else is content, content even with their hatred of the Russians, and mostly they live better than they ever have."[4]

But with the economy stalling and full-fledged dissidents adopting innovative rabble-rousing techniques, cracks in the system started to appear.

In 1975, thirty-five countries—with Eastern Bloc countries like the Soviet Union, East Germany, and Czechoslovakia joining the United States, Canada, and much of Western Europe—signed the so-called Helsinki Accords. The agreement codified the postwar borders in Europe and outlawed changing these borders by force. The Soviets were happy to sign as they finally saw it as confirming the country's postwar expansion. East Germany was also ready to oblige since it meant all other signatories recognized the disputed partition of Germany.

Though the Eastern Bloc had no intention of honoring all the provisions of the accords, some of the details, albeit technically unenforceable, proved hugely disruptive. Principle VII of the agreement, for example, demanded all signatory states to "respect human rights and fundamental freedoms, including freedom of thought, conscience, religion or belief, for all without distinction as to race, sex, language or religion."[5]

Much to the Soviets' chagrin, this section of the accords led to a flowering of groups in the Soviet Union and elsewhere in Eastern Europe through which citizens—quite unexpectedly—demanded that governments adhere to their own pledges. The first such group in Moscow was founded in May 1976, and among the eleven original members was a Jewish dissident named Anatoly Shcharansky.

In Czechoslovakia, similar mischief was afoot. On January 6, 1977, what came to be known as Charter 77 was published in a West German newspaper and the next day in *Le Monde*, the *New York Times*, and elsewhere. Signed by a "loose, informal, and open association of people . . . united by the will to strive individually and collectively for respect for human and civil rights,"[6] the signatories demanded that the Czechoslovak authorities live up to their own promises. Rather than confront the Communist regime by forming a competing political party or movement, the charter sought to avoid direct confrontation.

The Czechoslovak president, Gustáv Husák, didn't get the message and responded with a crackdown anyway. Václav Havel was among the spokesmen for the Charter 77 movement. He and two others were arrested for trying to bring the document to the parliament. Just 243 people signed the original document, and 1,621 joined in over the next decade—a minuscule portion of the fifteen million people living in Czechoslovakia at the time.[7] Authorities took away signatories' driver's licenses, had them fired from jobs, removed their children from school, forced them into exile, and jailed them.

"The latest thing is to let people go, people who want to leave the country," Philip Roth wrote after convening with many of the intellectuals who signed Charter 77. "Those who don't want to leave, they must keep silent. And those who don't want to leave, and who don't wish to keep silent, they finish up in jail."[8]

Though Husák was reluctant to repeat the 1950s show trials, he wasn't averse to reviving the rhetoric of those times, and the official press branded the Chartists "traitor[s] and renegade[s]" or "loyal servant[s] and agent[s] of imperialism."[9]

Though neither East nor West admitted it, or even perhaps realized it, their two systems were confronting remarkably similar problems— stalled growth, collective disappointment, and malaise. In a twisted way, Husák's ploy to placate Czechoslovaks with consumer goods very much mimicked the consumption-driven engine of capitalism. In a landmark 1978 essay called "The Power of the Powerless," Havel started out analyzing the inherent weakness of Husák's governing philosophy before going on to point out the similar contradictions in the West.

The essay centered on the story of a "greengrocer," a vegetable seller, who displayed the regime-friendly slogan "Workers of the World Unite" on a sign in his shop window. The greengrocer does not believe in the slogan; in fact, nobody does. But displaying the slogan is a means of avoiding hassle from the authorities. As the saying has lost all meaning, the authorities don't believe the greengrocer sympathizes with the slogan, and they also don't care whether he does. They only insist that he participate in the ritual of displaying the slogan to demonstrate his acquiescence.

"Individuals need not believe all these mystifications, but they must behave as though they did, or they must at least tolerate them in silence, or get along well with those who work with them," Havel wrote. "For this reason, however, they must live within a lie. They need not accept the lie. It is enough for them to have accepted their life with it and in it. For by this very fact, individuals confirm the system, fulfill the system, make the system, are the system."[10]

Havel argued that this example illustrated how Czechoslovakia had already reached a "post-totalitarian" state. The government no longer ruled by fear or terror, as it had during the Stalinist purges of the 1950s. Furthermore, it was incapable of totally dominating all aspects of public and private life in the way it once did. By the 1970s, methods of control were more prosaic, propped up by people, like the greengrocer, who reflexively engaged in the unthinking obeisance that granted the system its legitimacy. Havel believed that if the greengrocers of the world simply stopped going through the motions, the system would wither away.

"It can be said, therefore, that the inner aim of the post-totalitarian system is not mere preservation of power in the hands of a ruling clique, as appears to be the case at first sight," Havel continued. "Rather, the social phenomenon of self-preservation is subordinated to something higher, to a kind of blind automatism which drives the system."[11]

As an antidote, Havel encouraged people to carve out autonomous spaces for themselves, metaphorical places where they could "live in truth." He was convinced that the bankruptcy of the system would become obvious as people ceased pretending that the abnormal was normal. *Normalizace* was not normal. The sooner everyone admitted this to one another, the sooner it would end. In an interesting turn, Havel went on to note similar dynamics in the West.

"It would appear that the traditional parliamentary democracies can offer no fundamental opposition to the automatism of technological civilization and the industrial-consumer society, for they, too, are being dragged helplessly along by it. People are manipulated in ways that are infinitely more subtle and refined than the brutal methods used in the post-totalitarian societies," he wrote. "But this static complex of rigid, conceptually sloppy, and politically pragmatic mass political parties run by professional apparatuses and releasing the citizen from all forms of concrete and personal responsibility; and those complex focuses of capital accumulation engaged in secret manipulations and expansion; the omnipresent dictatorship of consumption, production, advertising, commerce, consumer culture, and all that flood of information: all of it, so often analyzed and described, can only with great difficulty be imagined as the source of humanity's rediscovery of itself."[12]

Havel's analysis of the West was largely ignored by the West, even though it was becoming increasingly hard to deny the stagnation and resignation on either side of the Cold War divide. At the same time, in both the Soviet Union and America, astringent voices were prevailing over those who had argued in favor of superpower détente.

Pressure in the Republican primary for the 1976 US presidential nomination from the ascendant neoconservative wing of the party had moved Ford away from Kissinger-style negotiation in the direction of a more confrontational posture. Brezhnev noticed and squared his shoulders. On April 16, 1976, Brezhnev wrote to Ford that the American leadership "says and does a lot of things which can only be viewed as the opposite" of strengthening relations, and he wondered if the rhetoric leading up to the 1976 presidential election didn't "constitute grounds for endangering everything of significance and value that was so hard to achieve in Soviet-American relations."[13]

Ford ultimately won the Republican nomination for the presidency, but by a closer than expected 1,187 votes to 1,070 for Ronald Reagan. Just a few weeks before Ford faced Democrat Jimmy Carter in the November 1976 election, a Soviet foreign ministry analysis worried that the campaign debate had "produced a number of points unfavorable for us . . . in particular . . . the general tone of the statements by both candidates who insist upon maintaining military might of the United States as a basic prerequisite for dealing with the Soviet side." Even Carter's positions couldn't help but be influenced by "certain rightist tendencies in US public opinion on issues of Soviet-American relations."[14]

Although Carter beat Ford, a major shift in how Americans were perceiving the Cold War was underway. Though he held no formal office, Reagan and his followers were winning the public debate. Rumsfeld, Cheney, and others had maneuvered themselves into positions of influence during the late Ford administration, and Reagan continued his public assault on peaceful coexistence with the Soviet Union from offstage, mocking the very concept of détente. "Isn't that what a farmer has with his turkey until Thanksgiving Day?" he mused on the radio in 1978.[15] In the Soviet Union, there was no such public shift, perhaps because the Soviet president was having trouble responding to anything at all: Brezhnev's health was failing. "So let me make it clear," his personal doctor would later tell the BBC. "Leonid Ilyich Brezhnev was taking sedatives and tranquilizers, but in such huge quantities that he was effectively a drug addict."[16]

Carter's victory ought to have delivered Karel Koecher's greatest reward for the StB. Karel's former professor Zbigniew Brzezinski was the new national security advisor. The StB had a man who knew a man who sat in the most secret counsels of the enemy as they discussed national security. But there was a problem: in their infinite wisdom, the StB had decommissioned Karel just when he could have been most valuable to them. By the time Carter took office, Karel was no longer an active intelligence operative. By trusting Kalugin over Karel, the StB—and by proxy the KGB—had sabotaged one of their best chances to anticipate American foreign policy. Instead, the StB kept Karel out of the loop for the entirety of the Carter years.

After leaving Čtyřkoly and flying back to New York via Vienna, Karel technically remained a part of the CIA's stable of external contractors. He still held a security clearance, but he stopped taking assignments from Langley. After the StB's threats, including the possibility of being assassinated if he continued cooperating with the CIA, Karel had little reason to stay involved in intelligence work. So he quit both the StB and the CIA—"I thought I was off the hook"—and for a good while, he really believed that he would be able to live like a normal American citizen. The double agent was no agent at all.

In search of their next adventure, the Koechers did something even Ronald Reagan would have approved of—they started a business. Their firm, Novissa, specialized in wholesale jewelry. Karel was chairman, and Hana handled the day-to-day business. The Koechers invested $20,000; Hana's boss, Savion, and a third partner (named Portnoy) kicked in $20,000 each as well. International diamond dealing is almost always done on credit, and the Savion name carried some weight with the banks; their lengthy record in the precious stone trade served as a sort of collateral.

"Hana would go to Israel or Antwerp and buy diamonds. You had to negotiate with the banks, so I did this kind of thing. Savion was a Jew from Bratislava," Karel said. "I have an accent myself but looked a little more acceptable, having gone to school in the US. Of course, the finances are not so complicated. They trust you if you show the right numbers."

For a brief period, it looked like a potentially lucrative career change. Starting in 1976, there was a three-year boom in the diamond market as inflation pushed investors with cash on hand toward diamonds, gold, and other commodities.[17] Hana continued her day job with Savion too, even earning herself another raise.

Karel wasn't exactly taxing his philosophy PhD, and the new work did not feel world changing, but he was hopeful about alleviating some long-running financial concerns: "It is a little frustrating, because I spent so much time trying to get educated to the highest possible level, but there is no way to apply it to anything serious."

The jewelry trade allowed the Koechers to ensconce themselves in their Upper East Side neighborhood. The New York Yankees' new slugger Reggie Jackson had moved in just a few blocks away, at 80th Street and 5th Avenue, and the Koechers socialized in high society. They went to parties and took weekend trips with other swinging couples. "We were spending a lot of time in Europe," Karel said.

The Koechers' onetime handler Jan Fila took passing note of these changes from the Czechoslovak mission at the UN. He and his wife, Marie, had a son named Marian in 1977, and Jan continued supervising other assets from the New York residency. He had little contact with Karel, although the StB issued occasional reports on their ex-operative. Karel had become an afterthought.

The StB praised Fila's work, giving him marks of "excellent" in the categories of business, party involvement and morality, and personal commitment to counterintelligence. It recommended he be given a promotion and even a "company car."

As one evaluation stated, "Comrade Šturma is an educated and talented spy. He perfectly manages most counterintelligence work. He manages the agency with extreme discretion, he thoroughly prepares for information extraction and briefings, perfectly organizes and precisely carries out plans, which were many times valued even by our Soviet friends. He fully understood the new focus of the concept of work against the main enemy on his own territory." Fila was deemed "politically mature and class-aware."

And yet it started becoming clear that the StB also had a growing sense of paranoia about Fila—not to mention plenty of other things. "The FBI expressed an unusual interest in Šturma," read an April 21, 1979, report. "It is necessary to speculate whether the agent did not leak any information." A few months later, the files expressed further fears, describing a phone call Fila made and questions that turned up in an FBI interrogation that indicated the American government may have been listening in on the call. "The resident discloses that Šturma has not yet changed sides, but the dangerous circumstances regarding him still prevail," the report read. The StB still wondered if their operation had a leak, and since it could not be the deactivated Karel, they had no choice but to direct their suspicions elsewhere.

Instead of plugging a leak, cutting out Karel seemed to have exposed StB operations to even greater American scrutiny. Perhaps they had made a mistake. Maybe they were trusting the wrong people. If Fila wasn't the problem, could it be someone else? And what ever became of that KGB General Kalugin? He was the one who had advised ousting Karel to begin with. It was time for the StB to look in the proverbial mirror.

In 1979, *The Culture of Narcissism* by historian Christopher Lasch was an unexpected best seller. The book declared that it would analyze "American Life in an Age of Diminishing Expectations." Lasch took what until then appeared a clinical term directed toward individuals and applied it to society as a whole. Though Lasch's focus was firmly rooted in the United States, like Havel's essay from the year before, the book seemed to address a wider human crisis of modernity.

"Storm warnings, portents, hints of catastrophe haunt our times," Lasch wrote. "Long-term social changes," according to Lasch, led to "a scarcity of jobs, devalued the wisdom of the ages and brought all forms of authority (including the authority of experience) into disrepute. . . . In a society in which the dream of success has been drained of any meaning beyond itself, men have nothing against which to measure their achievements except the achievements of others."[18] It was a dog-eat-dog worldview not at all limited to society's so-called have-nots.

"Much of what is euphemistically known as the middle class, merely because it dresses up to go to work, is now reduced to proletarian conditions of existence," Lasch believed. "Many white-collar jobs require no more skill and pay even less than blue-collar jobs, conferring little status or security."[19]

It was a description that could be applied exactly to Karel's own world-weariness—his high ideals having been exchanged for more immediate and glittering gratifications. Many people would accuse Karel Koecher of being a narcissist. If Lasch was to be believed, he was just one of many, a man of his times.

Karel was not only adrift from the spy world but also falling from favor in the world of academia. "Karel just got a notification from [Columbia University], that the commission couldn't assign him a position for next year, because they have an age limit of 40 and Karel is older," Hana wrote in a letter to Karel's mother, Irena, in July 1977. "Considering that we don't want to go to Washington, it is hard for Karel to get a good position. And we don't want to go to some American 'hick town' either. Thank god that I make enough money in New York for both of us."

Hana's work in the diamond industry kept the Koechers afloat and was enough for them to maintain appearances, shopping for clothes at the likes of Saks Fifth Avenue. In fact, a good deal of their money went to keeping up with the fashions of the Upper East Side, and the Koechers' cash flow struggled to match that of their friends and neighbors—many of whom came from multigenerational wealth. Karel applied for a fellowship with West Germany's Humboldt Foundation, which would have granted him a two-year stay at the University of Munich, but that failed to materialize.

"Karel was supposed to go at the end of October to Germany, but because it was nothing stable, we made up our minds and we will keep living here. We have good income here, knock on wood. So at this moment we are not missing anything," Hana wrote before going on to say how much she wished to visit her family in Czechoslovakia. Hana also revealed that the Koechers' own diamond business was struggling: "In my employment in the recent months, there have also been changes"—the Novissa company was failing, and the overall diamond market was heading toward recession—"which means I am no longer going shopping. And I doubt that I will be able to visit Europe this year. What a pity."

In November 1977, Hana wrote to Karel's mother again: "I still don't have the visa for Czechoslovakia, that won't work out this year." And later that month, she reached out to her own parents. She wrote, "I still don't have any response regarding my request for a visa. I think I made a mistake when I asked the same company. Other travel agencies at least tell you when the request is denied. I don't have any response."

In the spring of 1978, the Koechers again applied for visas to travel to Czechoslovakia. This time, Hana got one, but Karel's request was denied—he was being snubbed by his former employers: "Rino submits yearly requests for a visa to Czechoslovakia," the StB admitted. "Thanks to our intervention this remains fruitless. He is fully aware, and he was told, that in the case he 'dropped' collaboration, all compromising materials will be used against him." Hana made use of her visa and dropped in to visit her family in Prague on the way back from a diamond run to Jerusalem. The StB monitored her every movement.

Karel, who had dreamed of being at the center of world events, temporarily found himself on the sidelines. The Cold War continued apace without him. On October 16, 1978, the fifty-eight-year-old Pole Karol Wojtyla was elected pope. The youngest pope in more than a century and the first non-Italian to hold the office in 455 years, he chose the name John Paul II. On June 2, 1979, Pope John Paul II dropped to his knees and kissed the ground at Warsaw's airport on his first return to his homeland since becoming pontiff. That same month, at Vienna's Hofburg palace, Carter and Brezhnev signed the SALT II agreement to further limit nuclear arms. Though the United States would keep to the agreement through 1986, Carter withdrew it from Senate consideration in January 1980, and the treaty was never formally ratified. In January 1979, Shah Reza Khan Pahlavi, a staunch American ally, fled Iran, and Islamic extremists soon took over and stormed the US embassy in Tehran, taking fifty-two American diplomats hostage. The US felt itself pulled further into Middle Eastern politics.

By the end of the 1970s, the Soviet Union's international entanglements meant their defense burden was proportionally three times greater than that of the United States but was propped up by an economy just one-sixth the size.[20] That was compounded on Christmas Day 1979, when the Soviet Union invaded Afghanistan. Foreign Minister Andrei Gromyko told fellow members of the politburo that the war would be over "in three or four weeks."[21] The Soviet troops would, in fact, be in Afghanistan for a decade. By the time the Red Army extracted itself, fifteen thousand troops would be dead, as would three Soviet leaders.

In September 1979, far from the center of events shaping the times, Karel began teaching philosophy at Old Westbury College, a four-year undergraduate college in the bottom quarter of American college rankings that was situated a mile off the Long Island Expressway in suburban New York: "I taught for some time. SUNY had a campus on Long Island, but they had an experimental department which was called comparable ideas and cultures or something like that. It was dominated by religionists, but anyway what they didn't have was somebody with a scientific background, who could introduce science as a cultural phenomenon, so I taught classical logic, and I taught the history of science." Still, he was restless. The dean of the school, Philip Camponeschi, told the *New York Times* in 1984 that Koecher often argued with colleagues about the curriculum. Because he was unable to contain his frustration, Karel's contract was not renewed.

"Certainly it was a pleasant life, but unfulfilling, professionally unfulfilling. I was qualified to do professionally meaningful things," Karel insisted, but he found himself having to teach "kids that had problems reading," which limited the depth of any discussions.

Karel was drifting. As he looked to transition back into academic life—what choice did he have?—Karel reached out to his old PhD advisor, Charles Frankel, who was in the midst of creating an advanced research center focused on the humanities. Frankel promised to help Karel find work, but in May 1979, Frankel and his wife were shot and killed during a robbery at their home in suburban Westchester County.[22] The local acting district attorney, Thomas A. Facelle, said the "execution-style killings" were "the most bizarre he had ever witnessed."[23]

This was but another incident that contributed to the general feeling that a way of life—indeed, the American dream—was veering off course. As Kay Tyler, one of Frankel's neighbors, told the *Times*, "People are trusting. They don't lock their doors," but after the murders, "people will become skeptical."

Apprehensions like Mrs. Tyler's were becoming the norm. In a 1980 Gallup poll, just 27 percent of Americans said they trusted the government. In January 1981, 78 percent of Americans said they were dissatisfied with the direction of the country.[24] Attitudes toward postwar liberalism—and its foundations in robust public services, secure employment, and low-cost education—had transitioned from an emerging consensus in the 1960s through the indifference of the 1970s and hardened into outright antipathy.

"The Seventies was the decade in which people put the emphasis on the skin, on the surface, rather than on the root of things," novelist Norman Mailer said in 1979. "It was the decade in which image became preeminent because nothing deeper was going on."[25]

The new age found its avatar in Ronald Reagan, a onetime mediocre movie star and minor celebrity who defeated Jimmy Carter in the 1980 US presidential election. While Reagan's genial style appealed to the shallow 1970s, his divisive identity politics—the model for Republicans to come—and combative foreign policy reinvigorated American politics and reheated the Cold War.

Reagan was the oldest president in US history as he took office. He had opposed the Civil Rights Act, the Voting Rights Act, and the creation of Medicare. Meanwhile, his foreign policy team set off alarm bells in Moscow, where an ailing and aging politburo was running out of steam, control, and time. For the past five or so years, Reagan had publicly attacked any accommodation with the Soviets. In his January 1981 inaugural address, there was no mistaking whom he was referring to:

> Our forbearance should never be misunderstood. Our reluctance for conflict should not be misjudged as a failure of will. When action is required to preserve our national security, we will act. We will maintain sufficient strength to prevail if need be, knowing that if we do so we have the best chance of never having to use that strength. Above all, we must realize that no arsenal, or no weapon in the arsenals of the world, is so formidable as the will and moral courage of free men and women. It is a weapon our adversaries in today's world do not have. It is a weapon that we as Americans do have.[26]

The Soviets didn't know what to make of Reagan's evangelical speaking style. Taken literally, the words amounted to a mix of fanciful nonsense and ignorant aggression. They scrambled to learn more about the hawkish team he had surrounded himself with—Alexander Haig, George Shultz, Richard Perle, Jeanne Kirkpatrick, and former CIA chief George Bush. They reached out to their allies in Prague, and in November 1981, the StB thought they might ask Karel Koecher for help.

Oleg Kalugin—who had stoked suspicions that Karel was, in fact, working for the CIA against the Communist Bloc—had seen his once-promising career enter a death spiral. As Kalugin's star dimmed, Karel's started twinkling back to life. In fact, the StB tacitly acknowledged they had misinterpreted Karel's motives and began internal discussions considering how best to apologize to the Koechers and perhaps try to convince them that Karel's shabby treatment was all part of some larger plan. The "terminal" interview in 1976 was rebranded as brilliant subterfuge.

The commanding officer "will state that the interrogation in the year 1976 was part of a complicated and hard combination leading to strengthening Rino's backstory and his cover," one report read. "Damage, emotional and otherwise, which was done to him were fully outweighed by the need to guarantee his security and besides we are fully prepared to compensate for these consequences in a different way, if Rino will understand us."

Even the StB had trouble believing such fiction, and documents recognize that Karel might not have a thick enough skin to forgive them. They would need something else to tempt him back into action. As the StB debated how best to reactivate Karel, they changed tack and instead tried appealing to his ego: "Rino will in the end be encouraged by an emphasis on the counterintelligence department's desire that he be allowed to reach the pinnacle of his career as a high-level counterintelligence spy." It was a long way up from a discarded all-but traitor.

Desperate for information about Reagan's intentions and with few active assets as adept at mingling with elite American intelligence officers as Karel, the Soviets had also reevaluated their opinions of him. Desperation has a way of spurring action, and Moscow pledged to bankroll a new operation. "From preliminary negotiations with friends their willingness to take part in the costs of the contact is clear. The willingness comes from trust in him and an appreciation of the merits he has in his counterintelligence work," the StB reported. "The current situation in the United States under the Reagan administration and Rino's potential and current options fully justify us to renew the collaboration."

Jan Fila was tasked with drafting Rino back into action, but this process came with its own complications. A May 1980 StB memo had repeated earlier concerns that Fila might be cooperating with the FBI. It advised moving forward with the "planned withdrawal of Šturma at the beginning of 1981 to headquarters" and urged "inspection of the state of the subjects that a comrade Mjr. Šturma is responsible for." In a twist that would have major implications for the Koechers, the results of that StB inspection ultimately led to Fila getting promoted. He was given yet more responsibilities for handling StB agents operating in the United States.

This dizzying series of reversals unfolded over a matter of months. One official (Fila) on the cusp of being withdrawn was reempowered to activate a spy (Karel) who had been utterly discredited. The Soviet and Czechoslovak intelligence agencies hoped to belatedly catch up to the changes in American politics. In the background, another spy (Kalugin) was plummeting from KGB crowned prince to a stained pariah. The chaos was indicative of a Warsaw Pact in terminal decline—not to mention the fickle nature of loyalty, trust, and truth in the Cold War.

13

OUT OF THE WILDERNESS

"It is symptomatic of the underlying tenor of American life that vulgar terms for sexual intercourse also convey the sense of getting the better of someone, working him over, taking him in, imposing your will through guile, deception, or superior force."
—CHRISTOPHER LASCH

As Hana was working in her 47th Street office on the morning of March 3, 1982, she heard a knock and looked up. Through the glass pane on the door, she recognized a familiar face from handover meetings at Brentano's bookstore just a few years before. It was Jan Fila. She was surprised to see him.

The StB had promoted Fila, and he was now in charge of managing both the Washington and New York StB residencies. Just over a year into Ronald Reagan's presidency, Fila decided he needed to reactivate Karel Koecher.

By 1981, the Soviet intelligence services were on high alert. "While still head of the KGB, Andropov did believe the Reagan administration was actively preparing for war, and he was joined in this belief by [Dmitriy] Ustinov, the defense minister," Anatoly Dobrynin, the Soviet ambassador to the United States, wrote. "They persuaded the Politburo to approve the largest peacetime military intelligence operation in Soviet history."[1]

A 1981 internal KGB study showed the global balance of forces tilting in America's direction, and the bombast emanating from Reagan and his advisors only added to Soviet worries. In the reckoning of most Cold War historians, the early 1980s were the most dangerous time since the Cuban Missile Crisis. George Kennan opined that the atmosphere at this time had "familiar characteristics, the unfailing characteristics, of a march toward war—that and nothing else."[2]

The United States was in the process of altering the Single Integrated Operational Plan, its general plan for a possible nuclear war. Previous thinking on nuclear combat assumed any nuclear exchange between the United States and Soviet Union would be catastrophic—at a minimum obliterating both countries if not the human race. But "mutually assured destruction" had, for the first time in decades, given way to a growing belief in Washington that the US might emerge victorious from an atomic clash.

Amid these heightened anxieties, the Soviets launched project RYAN,[3] which called for mobilizing every possible asset in response to the perceived American threat. KGB field offices in embassies around the world received their first directions on RYAN in November 1981. Satellite agencies, like the Czechoslovak StB, were drafted into the effort too. A memo dated January 15, 1982, recommended Fila take a "business trip" to New York in February for the purposes of "carrying out contact with Rino." Fila traveled under the guise of attending a special meeting at the United Nations about "UNIFIL troops." He was authorized to make the trip with "a first class travel allowance."

The StB hoped Karel, or perhaps his social contacts, would offer insight into what felt like an American administration hell-bent on war. "At the meeting Rino should get long-term tasks related to the Reagan administration and its politics with emphasis on signaling a possible global or local conflict," the StB directed Fila.

But for that to happen, Karel would have to agree to cooperate with the StB again. It was not at all obvious that he would. Quite apart from Karel's ordinary orneriness, the StB had falsely accused him of being an

American agent, fired him, and ordered him to quit his job with the CIA. They had also threatened to ruin his life, or have him killed, if he ever made any trouble for them. Asking Karel for a favor at this point was not going to be easy. So, unsurprisingly, Fila felt Hana to be a safer person to approach. She was calmer, and they had worked together before when Hana had served as a courier during the mid-1970s.

Fila pretended to be a Swiss businessman in town for work and told Hana he had brought her a message from her sister, Petra. He handed her a letter and left. Hana called Karel and told him that the letter suggested a meeting later in the day. Karel was curious and couldn't help but feel he had nothing to lose from meeting Fila. In fact, it was clear that Fila wanted something from Karel, so he would arrive at the meeting with something of an advantage. When Karel met Fila "on some corner somewhere," the StB agent "apologize[d] in the name of the Czech intelligence services," Karel recalled. It wasn't enough to flatter Karel. He held the Czechoslovak intelligence services in very low regard, and he took the occasion to remind Fila of that: "They could go fuck themselves as far as I'm concerned."

But Fila presented himself as speaking for Moscow Center too. That was different. The two men agreed to meet again the next night at a Chinese restaurant on 23rd Street, and Karel returned home to talk over his options with Hana.

Karel was having trouble finding work—he had applied for a job at the Organisation for Economic Co-operation and Development in Paris, where he hoped to work as a political analyst. He didn't get the position, and he missed out on a series of corporate positions too. Not only had the American economy not bounced back from its malaise, but things were getting worse. By June 1982, the prime interest rate was 21.5 percent, and forty-two banks failed over the course of the year. The unemployment rate in the United States topped 10.8 percent.

In the early 1980s, Novissa, the Koechers' business, also struggled through diamond trading's worst ever recession.[4] "The firm is in a state of continued decline, Rino and Adrid manage to delay bankruptcy only by the fact that many other similar firms are in a similar situation and because of their good references and record, the crediting bank is liberal in its approach to their debts," read an StB report at the time.

On the one hand, Karel had managed to somehow extricate himself from having any obligation to the StB or the KGB. He and Hana were American citizens, and if they wanted to, they probably could have gone on living in the United States with no further obligation to spy for anybody. On the other, Karel was once again intrigued by the idea of being needed. It was not a feeling he often had. Karel regretted his skills had never been used to their fullest and still hoped to play a role defining world events. "Hana left it to me," Karel recalled. "Probably knowing also, obviously I had expressed that finally, maybe, I would do something meaningful."

Even as he made his way to the second meeting with Fila, Karel was undecided. He considered turning Fila down, but his curiosity got the better of him. And he had an exit strategy if he didn't like what he heard: "If I don't like it, I'll just report it to the FBI."

Over moo shu pork, the pair began talking over the details. Karel recalled, "I asked what he wanted me to do. He said, 'You have many contacts in Washington. More or less just socialize,' which I did, and you still learn a hell of a lot of things, especially if you have a security clearance, which I did." According to Karel, the StB said they would be content with little more than gossip, albeit informed gossip. "It didn't amount to obtaining some hard-core intelligence, but rumors."

Bored, unfulfilled, and yet still infused with self-confidence, Karel accepted Fila's offer on the spot. He would socialize for socialism. He could readily revive his old contacts. Besides, it was good to be back in the game: "It felt like I was getting a break," Karel realized.

Karel and his old boss at the CIA—Milos Vukasin—had remained on good terms. But even more interesting than Milos was his wife, Maria, a wealthy hotel heiress: "She was financing Reagan already when he was governor of California, contributing huge amounts of money to his campaign. So he was president, and she got a job at the White House."

Maria was the perfect person from whom to learn the inside scoop about the Reagan White House. "Gossip won't help you strike the United States with ballistic missiles, but it will tell you who is in favor and who's not and whether Reagan is sincere when he says he is ready to bomb and nuke somebody or whether it is just rhetoric," Karel said. "You can't get documents or something, but you get a pretty good idea of the thinking in Langley or the White House." Karel would check in with Moscow every two months.

On March 30, 1982, Fila reported on his meeting with Koecher. "The scope for operations in the United States is deteriorating under the influence of ideological propaganda from the Reagan administration and the radical right. This shows itself in the fear from some of the people who are interesting to us as contacts," he wrote of the blend of nationalist fervor and stepped-up surveillance under the new White House regime. And yet Fila was also careful to note—by way of insisting their work might continue—that he saw "gaps in capacity of the offices of the FBI in New York, which still enable contact and agency work."

In April 1982, Fila was promoted again, this time to superintendent of the 52nd division of the interior ministry. Any concerns about Fila's loyalties from the late 1970s appear to have been allayed. The documents explaining his promotion yet again praised his willingness, a dozen years ago, to "stand by the official Marxist-Leninist position" during and after the 1968 Warsaw Pact invasion of Czechoslovakia.

In May 1982, the Koechers went to Vienna and were smuggled across the border. They returned to the villa at Čtyřkoly, and this time the reception was more welcoming. They were back in Prague's good graces and again viewed as promising informants on the inner workings of the Main Enemy. Hana and Karel also visited their parents in Prague, though Karel's father had died by then. The StB gave Karel $2,000 and agreed to pay him $500 per month. He was worth keeping close, and there was no need to reignite old disputes over money.

Hana was meant to meet Miroslav Plášek, a New York–based agent, in July. Although Plášek had to cancel that meeting, he met Hana in September, October, and November. Karel was a font of rumor, innuendo, and more. At the November 18 meeting, the StB gave Hana $1,500 to finance another trip to Vienna. And Hana had something for Plášek: "Rino handed over political information about the preelection campaign in the USA," an StB report read, going on to note that he also managed to obtain "Pentagon document nb. 313 from the Department of Navy, which describes plans for the construction of navy ships."

Hana began working as a regular courier again, to the satisfaction of the StB: "She has matured and she is aware of her contribution for them to maintain their existence. She is open to practical reasoning; she is proud of her husband's knowledge and his counterintelligence work. In terms of orientation and a skillful approach to the work, she functions at a high level."

The year 1982 was a midterm election year, and to stay in political circles, Karel got himself a job working on the campaign team for millionaire banker and New York gubernatorial candidate Lewis Lehrman. A Republican former president of the Rite Aid chain of pharmacies, Lehrman narrowly lost the November election to Mario Cuomo, who was the strong favorite. Still, being part of the campaign was useful for Karel. "Rino is gaining trust in Republican circles—that is the neoconservative wing from which he could move on to gain a position that corresponds with our goals (as an advisor, a publicist, etc.)," the StB noted, concluding that Karel had "proved that he is capable of being creative in solving tasks."

November also brought momentous change to the Soviet Union; Leonid Brezhnev, the second-longest-serving leader of the Communist Party to date, finally died. He was succeeded by Yuri Andropov, the head of the KGB and Karel's former benefactor. Few in the United States knew it at the time, but Andropov was already sick with a terminal kidney disease. He would last just eighteen months in office before dying; Konstantin Chernenko would succeed him before succumbing to a combination of liver cirrhosis, heart failure, and emphysema a year after that. Amid the turnover in leadership, not to mention the pompous funerals and power struggles that followed each successive death, the Kremlin consensus on Reagan remained constant: he and his advisors were zealots thirsting for confrontation.

So Moscow pushed Prague, and Prague pushed Karel, to find out what the Reagan administration was plotting. All of a sudden, cash was plentiful: the StB paid Karel like it never had before. Though he officially struggled to find work, Karel was spending freely—so much so that he may have drawn unwanted attention, for around this time, the FBI started following the Koechers.

The Reagan administration was placing renewed emphasis on tracking down spies in general. In 1982, Congress approved a 20 percent increase in the FBI's counterintelligence budget over the next five years. Though Karel insisted he could detect whenever he was being followed, even the StB sensed increased danger and decided they should exclusively pass information through Hana. They could contact her less conspicuously: "There is a smaller chance of attention from the special services and a significantly bigger possibility of meeting with Adrid on the regular route to and from work."

The Reagan administration tried to ratchet up pressure on the Soviet-led Eastern Bloc in any number of other ways too. Despite economic troubles, or perhaps because of them, the Reagan administration started pouring money into defense. By 1985, Reagan had doubled the defense budget compared to what it was when he came into office.

"The main result of the first years of the Reagan presidency, and of our contacts with him, was his refusal to pursue a constructive dialogue while he aimed for military superiority and he launched an uncompromising new ideological offensive against the Soviet Union," the Soviet ambassador to Washington, DC, Dobrynin, concluded.[5]

Ahead of another meeting with Fila in Vienna in December, Karel complained of the "psychological strain" he and Hana were experiencing. In the first of a series of Vienna meetings, Karel met Fila on December 15 on the steps of the Central Post Office, just off Schwedenplatz a few blocks from the Donaukanal. From there they walked a few hundred yards to the Altes Rathaus restaurant, where Fila gave Karel $2,500, plus another $500 for his regular December stipend. It was enough to ease the stress, and Karel agreed to return to New York and keep listening in on the Reaganites.

Around the turn of the year, Karel made a new friend while working out at the YMHA on 92nd Street. Joseph Downs had recently joined up at the "Jewish Y," as he called it, and the two men started chatting. "I went there to play racquetball," Downs remembered. "I would just run into him in the weight room. He would be running on the track."

Karel still had an eye for the ladies. Though he and Hana had slowed down since their mid-1970s swinging heyday, they continued spouse swapping on the weekends. "He was a particularly strange guy. He would sidle up to a nice-looking woman," Downs continued. "You could watch his eyes and mannerisms. If he got rebuffed, he would be frustrated."

Not only was Downs an FBI agent, but he was a counterintelligence agent charged with tracking suspected spies from Bulgaria. His initial meetings with Karel were pure coincidence. "I would see him at the steam room and have casual conversations," Downs continued. "I suspect that he knew I was an FBI agent, but I never disclosed that."

Initially, Downs had no idea who Karel was. But one day, Downs's supervisor asked to tag along with him to the gym. Downs recalled, "Only then did I learn that Karel was a spy" and that the FBI was already following this resurrected StB agent. "I took the supervisor a few times. He wanted to size him up."

In February 1983, Plášek gave Hana a note to pass on to Karel. It contained a rather obvious instruction: "Pay special attention to the question of the possible preparation for a nuclear war." So

Karel dutifully went to the FEMA office in New York City and told them he was an academic researcher. Then he asked for a copy of the emergency plan for the city should there be a nuclear war. They handed him what amounted to the city's existing evacuation plan. "It's almost unbelievable, but NYC does not currently have a viable civil defense system in case of nuclear war," Karel reported back.

With the ripe, low-hanging gossip already harvested, Karel reverted to type and started writing lengthy analyses of American politics and sending them back to Prague. He still believed his views would be valued. His conclusions, however, were not popular in Prague. Even as he argued Reagan's brinksmanship was dangerous and irresponsible, Karel's writings came off as insufficiently damning of the US: "When you want to curtail civil rights, there has to be an enemy. The enemy has to be very bad, and I wasn't painting the enemy as such a bogeyman." The bureaucratically inclined StB would have preferred any official paper stamped with a serial number—"some worthless, stupid document," as Karel put it—to his informed but intricate judgments.

After several such deliveries, the StB ordered Karel to concentrate on economic matters. He was incensed at being slighted and again recalled what had led to his split from Czechoslovak intelligence in 1976. Additionally, and of much greater concern to Karel than the StB's incompetence, there was mounting evidence that he was being followed by the FBI: "I said, hell, I want to leave the US and move to Austria and quit. I want to retire." Karel was convinced the FBI had installed some kind of listening or tracking device in his car. He experienced a bizarre incident on a New Jersey highway. While Karel was driving, a passing motorist waved him down and indicated that his tires were flat. When Karel pulled over, he found identical holes in two of his tires.

These strange occurrences were just beginning. Most curious was a man with binoculars who seemed to be watching the Koechers' apartment from across the street. Karel recalled, "We lived on the twelfth floor; it was a good view, and there was a church tower on 89th Street.

There was a space, there were some apartment buildings, and there was a guy with binoculars. Obviously, if they had anything, I would have been picked up already." So Karel concluded that the surveillance team was a message: they were happy for Karel to know that he was being watched and that his movements were tracked. Karel was spooked but not panicked: "I think, I will take care of it, I will just leave. Nothing can stop me. I was worried, sure, but not very worried."

Days before a Christmas 1983 trip to Austria (again), Hana and Karel had been to the Museum of Natural History, and they were convinced somebody was following them. As they set out on their journey and waited to board a plane at JFK Airport, a thief—or a professional—swiped Karel's briefcase.[6]

On the ground in Vienna, Karel met with Fila again—and told him all about the surveillance. He also spoke with Stanislav Ulík, the StB man overseeing all operations targeting the United States. As was the case in so many of these meetings, everybody worried that everybody else was wearing some kind of bug, so they spoke in a sauna inside the Czechoslovak embassy. Ulík expressed his dissatisfaction with Karel's recent deliveries, and the StB canceled Karel's $500 monthly stipend, insisting that from now on they would only pay when he delivered intelligence they considered valuable.

For her part, Hana grew alarmed. The shadowy man with binoculars was particularly disquieting, and she stepped back from acting as a courier altogether. "In October 1983 Adrid stopped fulfilling her role of the messenger and to a certain extent Rino began to take charge of the connection in 1984," the StB noted. But as far as Karel was concerned, his existence as a spy had been compromised. It was time to move on. New York was dangerous, so as soon as he got back from Vienna, he prepared to sell the apartment and move. Karel was partial to life in Austria.

In January 1984, Karel sent a message back to Prague confirming that he planned to stop further cooperation. It was just a few weeks before his former sponsor, Yuri Andropov, also stopped cooperating—with anybody. The ex-KGB chief turned Communist Party general secretary died in February, having led the Soviet Union for just fifteen months. By the middle of the year, Fila was reporting to his superiors that Karel's output was "zero." In July 1984, the two men met in Zurich. Karel again insisted he was going to leave the US altogether. Their next rendezvous was scheduled for March 1985. It would never happen.

On November 15, 1984, the Koechers left an appointment at a bank on West 57th Street. They had sold their apartment for $218,000 and, in preparation for their departure, had just wired the money to a bank account in Zurich. As Karel walked Hana to her office, he carried a black Samsonite suitcase. They went east to 5th Avenue and then turned south toward the Diamond District. One group of FBI agents followed their progress by car; meanwhile, FBI agent Kenneth Geide and two others trailed the Koechers on foot.

Past the pawn shops and cash-advance places on 47th Street, Karel and Hana made their way up to Hana's fourth-floor office in the Diamond Club building. A pair of agents pulled up and parked outside in a black Chevy Impala, and a Pontiac Bonneville full of G-men moved in behind them. In the meantime, the agents who had trailed the Koechers by foot milled around on the sidewalk, smoking cigarettes and pretending to window shop in a jewelry store across the street. Karel escorted Hana into her office. By the time he came out alone at 11:15 a.m., Special Agent Joseph Downs was waiting there on the sidewalk. Karel immediately recognized him from the YMHA.[7]

"I extend my hand, say I haven't seen him at the club lately, that I have some friends that I would like him to speak to," Downs recalled. "A car pulls up. He voluntarily got in the car. The driver was really excited, speeding along. I am trying to be casual, keep Karel calm, and we are bouncing up 7th Avenue."

Karel's memory of events corresponds with Downs: "They say, 'Will you kindly come with us, we have an offer for you.' Nobody arrested me or anything. I didn't feel like I had a choice. But they were friendly. So obviously they want to discuss something. I was about ready to go to Austria, so it even would make sense that they would want to speak to me before I leave."

As the group traveled to the Barbizon Plaza Hotel at 58th Street and 6th Avenue, Karel thought—or hoped—the FBI just wanted to have a chat. He knew they had been following him for months, and they knew he had been working for the StB. At last, it was all out in the open. Karel told himself that he had been in worse situations before and that, if he handled this right, he could make his way to Austria with no one the wiser. That assessment wasn't far off, either. "If he had not come voluntarily, we did not have enough evidence to arrest him," Downs admitted.

They entered the Barbizon Plaza via the back service entrance and went up to room 2640, a two-bedroom suite with a balcony that overlooked Central Park. The CIA's Jerry Brown was waiting for Karel, smoking a pipe. A video recording shows what happened next. Agent Geide began:

> I think we should establish one thing. We know who you are and what you've done since you arrived in this country. Um, in other words, your association with the, as we would term it, the opposition, hostile intelligence services, and we don't want to sit and discuss that. We, we just want to establish right away that we do know who you and who your wife are, and your activities on behalf of those folks over the years. With that established, what we want to do is talk about a proposition for you, and talk about your future—your future and your wife's future—and that future I think is gonna depend on what we accomplish today in our conversation with you. Umm, we think we have some things that will be interesting to consider as time goes on.

"Yes, yes," Koecher muttered.

"We appreciate who you are, and your abilities, and we would look at this as where we will mutually help one another and, uh, hopefully, as they say, as we go on, we will be able to make certain proposals to you that I think you will find very, very attractive."

Geide promised Karel that the Koechers could continue with their planned trip to Europe and that their lives would stay the same.

"Okay," Koecher deadpanned.

Then Brown chimed in. "Now what can you gain out of this? Ah, you can gain just, right at the present time—which would be very much in your favor—would be just a continuation of your life as it is."

"Uh huh," a noncommittal Karel grunted.

"Now, and I think under the circumstances, I think you would probably be elated with just that," Brown said.

"Correct," Karel said, sounding not at all elated.

"And I think you can look forward to a harmonious relationship, and we are not going to try to do anything which will harm you or Hana in any way."

The interrogation continued. At around 2:30 p.m., the FBI had lunch brought in. Geide told Karel that Hana had been picked up and was being interrogated in a nearby room. In fact, she was refusing to say anything and had immediately requested a lawyer. Karel was asked to take a lie detector test; his answers to questions about how much information he had given to the StB and KGB suggested to the FBI agents that he was lying. Until this moment the FBI had assumed Karel had exaggerated his importance, but the FBI agents in the room surmised from the polygraph that Koecher was underplaying his impact and that he was a more important spy than they had appreciated or he had admitted.[8]

Thus far the FBI was treating Karel to the proverbial "good cop" routine, and after a few hours of relatively friendly dialogue, they let Karel and Hana go home. But the conversations with US intelligence had only just begun.

"For about a week, we met several times, kind of every day I went to the hotel, and we talked. They wanted to know what I did for the Russians, and they offered to turn me," Karel said. "In exchange for cooperation, immunity. So I was trying to kind of accommodate them as much as I could without putting anybody in danger. The basic information they already had, but they needed some details. But mostly I was establishing some ties."

Up to this point, Karel felt he was able to control the direction of the conversation reasonably well, but "then something happened. Suddenly, the CIA guy, Jerry [Brown], is not there. I asked what happened to Jerry, and they tell me Jerry had a near-fatal accident. He is in intensive care. Somebody hit him in the head when he went hunting."

Once a foreign spy is caught, the CIA's main priority is to find out how much they know and what possible damage they could have done. The FBI, in contrast, is looking to investigate crimes on US soil or against US citizens. More dangerous for a man in Karel's position were the people in the Justice Department, who started to circle the Koecher case. Many, if not all, of the people working at Justice had political ambitions, so a headline-grabbing prosecution was becoming a priority. The US attorney in the Southern District of New York, the very jurisdiction where Karel was being interrogated, was future New York City mayor and US presidential candidate Rudolph Giuliani. And Giuliani loved seeing his name in the papers.

With the CIA's Jerry Brown out of the picture, the approach toward Karel shifted, and he found himself "caught in this internecine fight between the CIA and the FBI."

On November 22, the Koechers went to Hewitt, New Jersey, for a Thanksgiving celebration at the home of George Kukla, a Czech immigrant and climate scientist who spent his career arguing that global warming was a natural phenomenon rather than man-made.[9] By this time, the FBI was keeping close to the Koechers at all times. Two agents gave Hana and Karel a ride to the party. On November 26, 1984, the Koechers met up with a couple they had been swinging with since 1981. They went to dinner and later returned to the Koechers' apartment to pair off. On their last night of freedom in the United States, FBI wiretaps confirm that Karel and Hana went down swinging.[10]

The next day, on November 27, 1984, the Koechers were scheduled to depart on the overnight flight to Vienna. The FBI man, Geide, again offered to drive the Koechers—this time to the airport. He suggested they come to the Barbizon Plaza Hotel, where he promised he would have a car waiting to take them to JFK. But instead, on their arrival, Karel was arrested for espionage and Hana detained as a material witness. He faced the death penalty.

14

EXCHANGE

"The truth of history crowds out the truth of fiction—as if one were obliged to choose between them."
—SUSAN SONTAG

After just a few days on the inside, Karel had already made a friend. Sandy Alexander pulled Karel aside during exercise hour on the roof. Sandy had a new cellmate, Tim, who had managed to smuggle a knife into New York's Metropolitan Correctional Center (MCC). When Tim wasn't babbling on about Cuba and Communists, he was talking about attacking Karel, Sandy confided.

The so-called Guantanamo of New York, the MCC is a twelve-story concrete fortress a short walk from New York's City Hall and the Court House of the Southern District of New York in Foley Square. Later, it would hold 1993 World Trade Center bombers Ramzi Yousef and Omar Abdel Rahman, Mexican drug lord "El Chapo," and Bernie Madoff, perpetrator of the biggest financial fraud in American history. In August 2019, convicted sex offender Jeffrey Epstein killed himself in MCC's special housing unit.

In January 1985, there were plenty of sinister villains boarding in the southern cellblock on the ninth floor. Mafia crime boss John Gotti slept a few steel doors down from Karel. The "Teflon Don" had just orchestrated the assassination of his predecessor, Big Paul Castellano, outside a steakhouse and was awaiting trial on a separate charge. Karel, as he recalled, had the distinction of being "the only prisoner facing capital punishment" at that time. He had spent some twenty days in solitary confinement since arriving.

Karel's new pal—big, bearded, tattooed Sandy Alexander—was no saint either. The founder of the New York chapter of the Hells Angels, he was doing sixteen years for slinging cocaine. On top of this, Karel had read that he had "killed some kind of FBI informant, cut the guy in half with a chainsaw." Somehow Karel and Sandy got along: "We developed a rapport though. He was almost like a puppy."

Light snuck into the cell through slit windows, but the frosted glass made it impossible for Karel to see what was happening outside on the streets. Aluminum sheeting had been drilled into the walls. It made it easier to wipe off vomit, blood, or urine but made Karel's prison cell feel like a refrigerator. In this cement citadel, just a few blocks north of Wall Street's sharp-dressing swagger, Karel found himself keeping company with rapists, murderers, and gangsters.

Two months had passed since the FBI sting at the Barbizon Hotel. Karel would spend another year at MCC without a trial. While US attorney Rudolph Giuliani made plenty of headlines—"Infiltrating the CIA was easy . . . getting on the board of directors of a Manhattan co-op . . . now that was something else," read the punchline of a comic featuring Koecher in the November 30, 1984, *New York Post*—he just couldn't make a case stick. The only evidence Giuliani had against Karel were the things Karel had admitted.

Karel had been faced with a choice to either agree to cooperate with the FBI and CIA—telling investigators everything he had done as a spy thus far and promising to cooperate further—or go to jail. Karel had accepted the deal and found himself incarcerated anyway. The CIA offer to turn Karel and have him return to Europe to inform them on the StB had been an intriguing one. As Karel sat in his MCC cell, he thought back to what he might have done differently.

It's hard to know what the FBI and CIA were thinking. Flipping Karel would have made him, in industry parlance, a turnaround double agent. In other words, after posing as a defector to get a job with the CIA and then funneling information to the Czechs and Russians, the CIA wanted to turn him back to spy on the Eastern Bloc instead. Notoriously unreliable, turnaround double agents generally demonstrate a predilection for shifting personae and loyalties to fit their needs.

"It has never been successfully done," said David Major, the member of President Ronald Reagan's National Security Council who took charge of the Koecher file. "We use this case as a study for how you do things wrong."

Once Giuliani and Justice reneged on that deal, their case was doomed. Karel's self-incriminations were inadmissible. "That was their case, the statements he gave them was their whole case," said Robert Fierer, Koecher's attorney. "There was tremendous political pressure to get him convicted."

But Giuliani charged Karel with espionage anyway because he didn't want to be seen not to. Ambitious to a fault, Giuliani wouldn't quit. He was tough on crime. He had prosecuted the mob. Giuliani just didn't have the goods on Karel, so he scrambled to come up with something, anything, that might help convict Koecher. As an inexhaustible series of legal motions played out, Karel shivered away in his cell. The only thing that consoled him was the thought, "They can't use anything I told them; it's the fruit of the poison tree."

The Justice Department pressured Hana to make her testify, but it was slow going. She too had been detained at the Barbizon. After the FBI had separated her from Karel, she had refused to speak, demanding an attorney. As an American citizen, she had that right, and no matter what Giuliani tried, the Constitution kept getting in the way.

"After being advised of her constitutional rights, Mrs. Koecher was asked a number of questions concerning her activities which were plainly material to the investigation of which her husband was the target," a grand jury subpoena from December 1984 read. "She steadfastly refused to answer any of the questions asserting, after consulting with counsel, her marital privileges against disclosure of confidential communications with her husband and the giving of testimony potentially adverse to the interests of her husband."[1]

The authorities contended that Hana was an accessory to espionage and that, as such, they could make her forfeit spousal privilege rights. "They were thinking they could squeeze her," Fierer said. "She was not squeezable." They needed her to testify against her husband in open court, but Hana wouldn't crack. So they upped the ante by holding her in contempt of court, throwing her in lockup, and setting her bail at $1.5 million.

Hana kept her cool and stayed quiet. "I preferred to be like Mrs. Columbo," she later said with a smirk, referring to the wife of the popular television detective who is often mentioned but never seen. With an appeal of her contempt charge pending, wealthy friends from their Upper East Side neighborhood posted Hana's bond. Once she was out, she returned to her job as a Manhattan diamond dealer. Somebody had to make some money to cover the mounting legal fees.

Karel's case stalled while Hana's contempt case played out for the better part of a year. "There was tremendous political pressure to get him convicted," Fierer recalled, "and people at the Justice Department never, ever think they have made a mistake."

Eventually Gerard Lynch, an attorney who took up Hana's case on behalf of the American Civil Liberties Union and later became a federal judge, argued Hana's case before the Supreme Court. "But by that time, I began to hear indirectly that a trade was in the works," Lynch said.

Karel was growing frustrated, and he blamed Fierer, his lawyer, who wasn't particularly impressed with his client's motives. As Fierer put it, "My view of him at the time was that his approach to life had nothing to do with being a patriot of Czechoslovakia or any other entity. He was in it for Karel Koecher."

Perhaps inevitably, Karel had selected his lawyer from among the people he had met while partying. Their relationship was now less than civil. Karel didn't trust Fierer, while Fierer thought Karel arrogant and megalomaniacal.

Locked up with no sense of an imminent trial date, Karel's mind began to race: "It is pretty unusual to be kept in custody without trial for such a long time. You start to allow for the possibility that you might never get out." Like Hana, he was by now an American citizen entitled to constitutional protections—the right to a speedy trial among them. And yet no trial was forthcoming. "I suspected there was collusion with the Justice Department," Karel reflected. "For [Fierer], it was a good deal, because he could just charge me more money."

Fierer also recalled tensions growing between lawyer and client: "He and I, I would say, did not get along."

But Karel was all the more tense about the prospect of running into that armed lunatic named Tim somewhere along the corridor. Amid the other pressures, Sandy Alexander's news was enough to make Karel physically sick.

All indications were that Tim was "a real psychopath," Karel recalled, "a maniac murderer." Karel was afraid to let this madman out of his purview. He took Sandy's warning seriously: an attack could come at any time. Besides, Karel knew that it was not standard practice to allow violent offenders to carry weapons. That made him suspicious, which may have saved his life: the day after Sandy's warning, in the spring of 1985, as the prisoners made their way to pick up lunch, Tim lunged at Karel with a blade. Karel shouted, "He's trying to murder me!" and was fortunate that Sandy, who was standing next to him, was also anticipating the attack: "I grabbed him around his neck and knocked him to his knees, punched him and kicked the knife," Sandy, an ex-marine, recalled years later. "And I said to [Karel], 'Don't worry. No one will hurt you!'"[2]

Amid the commotion, the attacker picked up the knife, "ran down the stairs, and disappeared, not far from the cells of Sicilian boss

[Gaetano] Badalamenti and John Gotti." Soon, "the guards shouted: 'Everyone back to their cells! We are locking up,'" Sandy continued. "I went back to the cell, and my roommate never returned. It was incredible. Then they began counting."

Prison guards made the rounds, tallying up prisoners like schoolteachers taking roll in homeroom. Tim did not come back. "It was just me in my cell," said Sandy, who died in 2007. "Then they yelled: 'Okay! The numbers are fine.'" But Tim was nowhere to be seen.

Who was Tim? Had someone sent him? Where did he go? If he had been sent to attack Karel—as Karel believed—the prison guards had to have been in on the plot. Karel started to panic, convinced that somebody was trying to kill him. He could endure a few months in prison but not the thought that at any moment, a lurking assassin might kill him in cold blood, with the chilly indifference of the authorities. He wouldn't allow it, not after all he had been through. Instead of waiting for the legal process to play out, something that could take years, Karel "opted for a rather risky move." He called his attorney. They met at MCC. Karel wrote a single name on Fierer's yellow legal pad: "Anatoly Shcharansky."[3]

By 1985, Natan Sharansky—as he would later call himself after Hebraizing his name—was the world's most famous political prisoner. Ronald Reagan had campaigned for the presidency in 1980 on the platform of facilitating Jewish emigration from the Soviet Union. Appealing to aggressive anti-Communism and freedom of religious expression, Reagan had promised, "The long agony of Jews in the Soviet Union is never far from our minds and hearts. All these suffering people ask is that their families get the chance to work where they choose, in freedom and peace. They will not be forgotten in a Reagan Administration."[4] Sharansky was the most famous imprisoned Soviet Jew and had spent nine years in prison including long periods of solitary confinement. He had been arrested by the KGB on the order of Yuri Andropov.

"I didn't think that the Justice Department would agree to me being swapped for anyone. I thought they really wanted to finish me off, but if

the Russians offered Sharansky," Koecher reasoned, it would be an "offer you cannot refuse. To do so would be a political scandal."

Karel grabbed a second piece of paper from Fierer's pad and began handwriting a letter—in Russian. He addressed it to Vladimir Kryuchkov, the head of the KGB in Moscow. Karel asked Fierer to relay the note to the Czechoslovaks, who would then pass it on to the Soviets. "He came up with the idea, and it made perfect sense to me," Fierer said. "Reagan is a TV president, Gorbachev is a TV chairman. If I win this case, it's a huge embarrassment to the United States. Karel can do damage, and Sharansky is already doing damage."

When Sharansky had attempted to immigrate to Israel in 1973, the Soviets denied him an exit visa. The official explanation for preventing Sharansky's travel was that his experience, working with computers at an oil and gas facility, meant he harbored state secrets that were too valuable to share with the outside world. But it was obvious that Sharansky's regular acts of civil disobedience had provoked the Soviet government. He was an irritant to the politburo, and he joined the ranks of the *refuseniks*, an unofficial group of mostly Jewish Soviet citizens who were blocked from leaving the country.

Along with working as a translator for Andrei Sakharov, winner of the 1975 Nobel Peace Prize and perennial thorn in the Kremlin's side, Sharansky became the spokesman for the Moscow Helsinki Group, the most important human rights organization in the country and a regular source of embarrassment for the Soviet regime.

Sharansky's defiance, wit, and communication skills made him an international symbol of resistance, and he was skilled at shedding light on the perverse cruelty of the Soviet regime. Eventually, the authorities had enough, and on March 5, 1977, the propagandist newspaper *Izvestia* accused Sharansky of handing over secrets to the United States. A few days later, on the Ides of March, he was arrested on charges of high treason, a crime that carried a potential death sentence. Just minutes before his arrest, Sharansky was, as had become commonplace for him, holding court in his home with a group of American journalists.

At his July 1978 trial, Sharansky, a brilliant logical thinker, served as his own attorney, but few were surprised when the judge found him guilty. "For more than 2,000 years, my people have been dispersed," Sharansky said to a silent courtroom after learning his sentence. "But wherever they are, wherever Jews are found, every year they have repeated 'next year in Jerusalem.' Now, when I am further than ever from my people, from [his wife] Avital, facing many arduous years of imprisonment, I say, turning to my people, my Avital: Next year in Jerusalem. Now I turn to you, the court, who were required to confirm a predetermined sentence: To you I have nothing to say."[5]

Along with Reagan's explicit support, such theatrics made Sharansky a cause célèbre in the United States. Just months into his first term, in May 1981, Reagan met with Sharansky's wife in the White House and assured her he would personally pursue her husband's release. Avital had successfully fled the Soviet Union for Israel, with the understanding that Sharansky would join her later. She had gotten the visa Sharansky had been denied, and the pair had married just before her departure. Avital's casting as an "Israeli Audrey Hepburn," as one newspaper called her, intensified media interest.

When Karel first suggested that Fierer should broker a trade for Sharansky, the lawyer was far from impressed: "I thought he was crazy. I said to him, and this is something I probably shouldn't have said, I said, 'You're a second-rate spy'—because at that point I didn't know all that he had done—'Why would one of the foremost dissidents in the world be swapped for you?' He said, 'I am telling you. They know my work, and they will swap Sharansky for Koecher.'"[6]

Koecher may have known that Sharansky's imprisonment was badly affecting his health. While MCC may have felt cold, Sharansky, some five thousand miles away, fought off hypothermia every night in Perm 35, a gulag work camp nine hundred miles east of Moscow. About half his eight years of incarceration up to that point had been in solitary confinement. The novelist Aleksandr Solzhenitsyn once lamented how

Soviet work camps led to a "narrowing of man's mental and intellectual horizon," spurring the "decline of a man to the level of an animal and his process of dying alive."[7]

Sharansky's body was suffering. To obtain the highest level of food rations, he was required to stitch together 345 burlap sacks per day, an unachievable number. There were no beds; he slept on the ground. He spent his time alternating between solitary and stints in the hospital. Still, Sharansky did what he could to keep his mind sharp. A former teenage chess prodigy in his hometown of Donetsk, Ukraine (then known as Stalino), Sharansky had once defeated world champion Gary Kasparov. To keep sane in prison, Sharansky played game after game of chess inside his own head. "Thousands of games—I won them all," he said. "The KGB hoped that I would feel weaker and weaker mentally. Actually I felt stronger and stronger."[8]

As Karel and Sharansky defied death in their respective prisons, the grim reaper came to collect another moribund Soviet leader. Konstantin Chernenko had been ill ever since he had succeeded Yuri Andropov. By the end of 1984, Chernenko was rarely seen outside of the Central Clinical Hospital, and he routinely was dependent on a wheelchair to get around. Officials used a facsimile of his signature on documents, as he could no longer lift a pen. By February 1985, when the Soviet public was first informed that their leader was in poor health, he had started to resemble an "enfeebled geriatric-like zombie" waiting at death's door, in historian John Lewis Gaddis's memorable phrase.[9]

Chernenko crossed that threshold on March 10, 1985. The last of the World War II–era leaders of the Soviet Union, he was also the last chairman of the Communist Party to have been a member during the Stalinist purges of the 1930s. He was replaced by a much younger, bolder leader with new ideas—fifty-four-year-old Mikhail Gorbachev, whose first public appearance was at Chernenko's funeral four days later. Gorbachev was the first college-educated leader of the Soviet Union since Lenin. His relationship with Reagan, after a frosty start, would eventually reach a point where both were able to find common ground.

In November 1985, Reagan and Gorbachev met face-to-face for the first time in Geneva, where they discussed whether and how relations between their countries could be improved, the future of the Strategic Defense Initiative, and some human rights issues, including easing emigration restrictions from the Soviet Union. Though neither leader expected much from the first meeting, each reacted positively—the direct conversations between the two leaders exceeded their allotted time—and they agreed to reciprocal visits to the US and Russia over the following two years. What the summit needed to lock in the positive momentum was a symbolic gesture of good faith from both sides, something that could begin the process of building mutual trust.

Fierer had been dispatched to Prague with Karel's letter. "I told him, 'Take this letter; go to Prague. Somebody will surely be waiting for you at the airport. You give them the letter, and they pass it on to Moscow,'" Karel recalled. "It simply said that my life is threatened. They can't convict me. I suggested that they trade me for Sharansky."

Despite his doubts, Fierer went—it was a free first-class ticket to Europe, after all. "My feeling was, nothing ventured, nothing gained, and besides, I'd never been to Prague." The StB archives include a bevy of surveillance pictures from Fierer's arrival on the tarmac. His shock of blond hair, his exotic boots, and his trench coat with a bizarre outer cowl made him look rather like Andy Warhol—if the artist had dressed like a nineteenth-century lord.

In early July, the first meeting to discuss the exchange took place at the massive, brutalist Intercontinental Hotel, near Prague's famed Old Town Square. Fierer spoke with Jan Fila, the same StB agent who had reactivated Karel in 1981.

Fila's report from the meeting summarized Fierer's argument for the Sharansky exchange: "The top heads of the Jewish lobby, in particular the United Jewish Appeal and B'nai B'rith, assured him that the Republicans were taking big money from them for their 1986 campaign.

If Sharansky is offered, nobody will refuse an exchange. Reagan and every Jew in the USA will support it."

On a second visit to Prague later in July—this time Fierer brought his wife along to see the sights—Fierer had another meeting with StB officials at Karel's mother's apartment. Those discussions took place four months before the Geneva summit between Reagan and Soviet leader Mikhail Gorbachev, where the exchange agreement was finalized. After a brief talk, Fila and Fierer parted, but Fila returned the next morning. They talked for several hours more, and Fila's report on the meeting revealed growing trust in Fierer. "If we go through Sharansky, it will go quick. We are only at the beginning; in the second and final phase, we will need diplomatic agreements."

On the third day—July 21—Fila returned and said that his superiors had agreed to pursue the deal.

Plenty of hurdles remained. "The exchange of Rino and Adrid for Sharansky is impossible," the Prague central office of the StB wrote in an August 22 report. The real decision, of course, would be made in Moscow, and Soviet leaders had flat-out refused to consider trading Sharansky. KGB chief Kryuchkov—who compared Karel's turbulent and precarious experience as a spy to "falling into a meat grinder"—set out to convince the rest of the Soviet hierarchy they should make the deal. "We would have exchanged three Sharanskys for Koecher," the late Kryuchkov said by way of emphasizing the value he placed on Karel.[10]

With no chance of convicting Karel and facing the real possibility that they might have to cut him loose, the American government was eager to get something from a trade. "Sharansky was always on the planner, always on the agenda," said John Martin, a former Justice Department official who was key to brokering the deal. "It was important to the Russians; it was important to the United States and its allies."[11]

On January 23, 1986, Fierer was awaiting the latest in an interminable string of legal procedural rulings, this time yet another motion to suppress Karel's confessions to the FBI. The phone rang. It was Bruce

Green, an assistant US attorney working the case. "There's going to be a trade," he said.

Karel first got wind of the deal from a conversation with Hana: "She says, 'Guess what? I am here with this German lawyer, sitting in my office. Out of the blue, like lightning, he is sitting next to me and says you will be home in two weeks.' The next day the warden asks me to his office, offers me coffee. There is a Czech consul sitting there asking me how I want my stuff sent back."

The lawyer with Hana was Wolfgang Vogel, personal emissary for East German leader Erich Honecker and the same man who had brokered the 1962 prisoner exchange involving downed American U2 pilot Gary Powers and KGB spy Rudolf Abel.

A snazzy dresser and, by the mid-1980s, the proud owner of a gold Mercedes, Vogel collected royalties and loyalties on both sides of the Iron Curtain. The West Germans gave him an annual retainer of more than $200,000, and Chancellor Helmut Schmidt had once referred to him as "our mailman." All told, Vogel traded some 150 spies from twenty-three countries. As well as spy exchanges, Vogel helped sell political dissidents for hard currency—33,755 East German prisoners to the West and 215,019 others were part of family reunifications that Vogel facilitated. In addition to his own small fortune, Vogel's efforts earned an estimated $2.4 billion for the East German government—money that kept the faltering regime afloat.

"My paths were not white and not black; they had to be gray," he once said in court.[12]

At first, the Justice Department had scoffed at Fierer's suggestion of trading Koecher for Sharansky. But amid realizations no conviction was forthcoming, and with Vogel on the case, the calculus had changed. Karel agreed to plead guilty to the espionage charges, accept a life sentence that was commuted to time served, and renounce his US citizenship. On February 3, 1986, Karel Koecher formally accepted his legal guilt. At 11:00 a.m. on February 9, Hana turned herself in to the FBI, and the couple were taken to JFK Airport. She also agreed to forfeit her

American passport. After more than twenty years living in the States, the Koechers were personae non gratae. They could never return to the country they had just started to consider home.

When the FBI busted Karel at the Barbizon Hotel, he had been wearing a simple sweater, which was returned to him when he left court. But his return to Prague called for a flourish. Going quietly was not his style: "I had Hana buy me a pair of shoes, Gucci. I told her to go to Saks Fifth Avenue. We had an account there." Hana told the shopkeeper that her husband was in the hospital and needed to try the shoes. Saks let her borrow the left loafer. "She couldn't go to the jail, so they took me to the prosecutor's office, and they were just looking on as I was trying on these very expensive loafers." The shoe fit. Hana went back to Saks to get the other one and also bought Karel a new Brooks Brothers suit.

When the Koechers boarded a commercial Pan Am flight from New York's JFK to Frankfurt, Karel was flanked by seven FBI officers. They were the first on the plane and the last off. Hana sat across the aisle from her husband. Neither was handcuffed. As the plane took off, Karel still had trouble grasping that he was about to be free. He wondered what life in Czechoslovakia was like: it had been more than two decades, after all. Even if it was no different, he was different. The flight attendant, in her powder-blue uniform, rolled by with the drinks cart, but the FBI officers insisted they stay dry.

Once in Frankfurt, the Koechers were taken from the commercial airport to a nearby military facility. Hana bunked in an officer's empty room for the night. Reluctantly sober, Koecher was forced to sleep in the base drunk tank anyway: "The Justice Department had them treat me as rough as possible."

John Martin from Justice recalled events much the same way. "Here [the Koechers] have been forced to renounce their US citizenship, to guarantee that they would not return to the United States," he said. "All of this is pretty rigid and demeaning. It was not a pleasant experience for them; it was not intended to be."[13]

Back in the Soviet Union, Sharansky's experience was even tougher. He had been hospitalized with chest pains and was emaciated. But he began to receive better treatment, more food, and regular visits by doctors. He gained eighteen pounds in a single month. In an attempt to cover up years of abuse and neglect, Sharansky was being fattened up so that he would look as healthy as possible for the coming exchange.

As Sharansky recounts in his memoir, *Fear No Evil*, on January 22, 1986, he was suddenly taken from the hospital to the guardhouse. The abrupt change in his rigid routine confused him. With no idea what was in store, he hoped he might have a visitor. Perhaps his mother, he thought, whom he had not seen for more than a year. "The corridor to the right led to the meeting room, while straight ahead was a heavy iron door and bars—the exit from the zone," Sharansky wrote. "They led me straight ahead. Before I knew it, the door had shut behind me, and I found myself in the custody of four men in civilian dress."[14]

Sharansky was bundled into a car, which set off across the snowy taiga. In the first village they reached, he was transferred to another car, a black Volga—the stylish if unreliable vehicle of choice for top Soviet officials. Like a shipwreck survivor returning to civilization from a deserted island, Sharansky was fascinated with the car's cassette tape deck. He watched with amazement as a KGB man "took some kind of gadget in his hand and stuck it into a box in front of him; a moment later the car was filled with music," Sharansky wrote. "I wondered: Did everyone now have tape decks in their cars, or only the KGB?"[15]

Traveling in a two-car convoy with a police escort, local police officers along the way saluted as he passed—mistakenly believing Sharansky to be a high-ranking official. Where were they going? Sharansky asked plenty of questions but was met with silence. Four hours later, Sharansky got his first clue—a road sign marking a turn to the airport.

Sharansky was ordered onto a TU-114 commercial plane. Then it took off—almost empty. Sharansky did not see any other passengers. High above the frozen forest, Sharansky's KGB handlers stayed silent.

For a man accustomed to the drudgery of the gulag, the action was disorienting. "When I probed my feelings, I found to my astonishment that my dominant emotion was sorrow," Sharansky wrote. "Below me was a world I knew so well, where I was familiar with every detail, every sound, where they couldn't pull any dirty tricks on me, where I knew how to help a friend and deal with an enemy."[16]

He watched out the airplane window. "Suddenly I no longer felt in control," Sharansky continued. "I lost my self-confidence."[17] As the plane traversed the landscape, with no drink cart to bolster morale or calm his nerves, he couldn't help but worry the world had passed him by. Two hours or so passed before he saw they were approaching a large city. It was Moscow.

Another Volga motorcade followed, and police officers on the side of the road again saluted. Just as Sharansky began to allow himself to feel a little optimistic, he recognized that the car was pulling into Lefortovo prison, a facility familiar to him from a lengthy stay nine years earlier. Back in a holding cell, the perverse comfort of prison routine returned. Identical days passed without explanation. On the morning of February 10, Sharansky was reading books by Schiller and Goethe when the cell door swung open.[18]

The guard gave Sharansky some civilian clothes—a blue shirt and gray suit. Unlike Koecher's tailored department store attire, the clothes didn't fit. They were several sizes too big. Denied a belt, Sharansky used string to hold his pants up. Outside, he was greeted by the same four KGB officers who had met him at the gulag. Sharansky noticed film crews and photographers nearby. "The last time I saw cameras was at my trial. Why were they here now?" he wondered.[19] Again, Sharansky was taken to a plane. Sometime after takeoff, a senior bureaucrat emerged from the back: "Shcharansky, Anatoly Borisovich. I am authorized to declare to you by order of the Presidium of the Supreme Soviet of the USSR, for conduct unworthy of a Soviet citizen, you have been stripped of Soviet citizenship and as an American spy you are being expelled from the Soviet Union."[20]

They must have just crossed the border, Sharansky decided. Once the plane started its descent, Sharansky looked down and on the runway saw some initials—DDR, for Deutsche Demokratische Republik. He was in Communist East Germany. After a short drive from the airport, Sharansky entered a house and was greeted by a man who introduced himself in English as "lawyer, Wolfgang Vogel."

The exchange itself was set to take place across the Glienicke Bridge, a MASH green scaffold spanning the Havel River that linked West Berlin with the East German city of Potsdam. "I never believed it was going to occur," Koecher's lawyer, Fierer, said. "I mean, I did not believe it was going to occur when I was standing on the Glienicke Bridge. I still thought, This is *Alice in Wonderland*, and I am in Never Never Land [*sic*]."[21]

The rumor of Sharansky's imminent release had led international television crews to set up mobile studios on the West Berlin side of the Bridge of Spies a full week before the exchange happened. A *New York Times* report described February 11, 1986, as an "elaborately synchronized East-West prisoner exchange that appeared to be one of the most concrete, and dramatic, results of the meeting in November [1985] between President Reagan and Mikhail S. Gorbachev, the Soviet leader."[22]

American officials and Sharansky remain wary of conceding he was traded for Koecher. To do so, they believe, inflates Koecher's importance and risks portraying Sharansky as a spy himself—the latter narrative a mainstay of mid-1980s Soviet propaganda. "To a degree, they have a point. I wouldn't consider Sharansky a spy," Koecher conceded. "But it was a trade, of course. They even had a formal agreement about what was going to happen, and we were the two people involved."

To blur the reality of the swap, an assortment of low-level operatives were traded on the same day. Returning to the Eastern Bloc were Polish intelligence officer Jerzy Kaczmarek; Yevgeni Zemlyakov, a former Soviet trade official jailed for industrial espionage; and Detlef Scharfenorth, an East German agent charged with recruiting spies in West Germany. Coming westward with Sharansky were Wolf-Georg Frohn, an Austrian working for the CIA; Czechoslovak Jaroslav Javorsky; and West German Dietrich Nistroy.

Sharansky contended that he never knew whom he would be traded for. He did not have much cause to care. He was getting out, that was the important thing. After a breakfast of coffee and cake, he got on a minibus. "When we reached the bridge," Sharansky wrote, "I saw the Soviet flag up ahead. 'How symbolic,' I said. 'This isn't really the border of East Germany but the boundary of the Soviet empire.'"[23]

"On our side it was quiet and deserted, but a dull roar could be heard on the other side of the bridge," Sharansky continued.[24] Though the American military had pushed the TV crews back and instituted a thirty-hour ban on civilians coming within several square miles of the bridge, more than two hundred reporters were nonetheless on the scene. Anticipation was high.

February 1986 would be the most frigid month in Berlin for the next twenty-six years. The high that day was thirty degrees Fahrenheit. There was a seventeen-mile-per-hour wind. Chunks of ice flowed in the water below. Officials had to shovel snow to clear the white line on the bridge indicating the border. Karel Koecher was, literally, a spy coming in from the cold. He and Hana had to wait, handcuffed, in the back of a van until Sharansky had first made the crossing.

Dressed in a black overcoat and those sagging pants, the five-foot-three Sharansky wore a Russian *ushanka* on his head. John Martin from the Justice Department and Francis Meehan, US ambassador to East Germany, accompanied him. He was ordered to walk straight across the bridge, but in a final act of defiance, Sharansky instead zigzagged back and forth en route to the demarcation line. "The American ambassador to East Germany introduced me to the American ambassador to West Germany, who took me by the hand," he wrote. "'Where's the border?' I asked.

"'Right there, that thick line,'" Richard Burth, the US ambassador to West Germany, replied.[25]

Then it was the Koechers' turn. Karel was uncuffed. He wore a full-length coat with fur collar, a plaid scarf, and a tilted fedora. Not to be outdone, Hana wore fur head to toe—black hat, white full-length coat. Karel not so much walked as strutted, his new thin-soled loafers already caked with slush and snow. But they looked good.

Once they had crossed the border line, he and Hana got into a waiting car. Vogel's wife, Helga, sat behind the wheel of their gold Mercedes. Vogel compared his feeling at the time to "that of a surgeon after a successful, complicated operation."[26]

Sharansky reunited with Avital for the first time in twelve years. He flew to Israel later that same day. Meanwhile, the Koechers were headed back to the Eastern Bloc. The excesses of 1970s New York City were a far cry from what waited for them back home. In the mid-1980s, Czechoslovakia remained among the most suffocating of Warsaw Pact states—lacking the glasnost or perestroika in the wind elsewhere. There would be no more Guccis, no coke, no swinger parties.

The Koechers were trading their apartment at 50 East 89th Street, a block from the Guggenheim and leafy Central Park, for the drab grays of prefabricated concrete. But compared to the cold of an MCC prison cell, it wasn't all bad. Despite that, Karel felt that "I am superman, not only because I overcame all this, but I am going back to this Communist world, particularly back to Prague, where I am untouchable."

EPILOGUE

"When time surges on at breakneck speed, those who can fling themselves into its torrential waves without hesitation have a head start."
—STEFAN ZWEIG

NOVEMBER 30, 2016
Dolní Břežany, Czech Republic

I drive past the old Communist-era tower blocks on the outskirts of town. The open-air wholesale Vietnamese SAPA market that supplies produce to Prague's restaurants is buzzing with activity. A minute or so later, I cross a highway overpass, and the city just stops. I'm immediately in the countryside. No urban sprawl here—yet.

After another kilometer I enter a small village, pass a bus stop, then make a left on to a small dead-end street. It's the last house on the right. I park, get out of the car, and jiggle the lever handle on the gate to the low-rise brown picket fence. Locked, but there is a buzzer with an intercom. So I ring and wait. It takes a few minutes for an eighty-two-year-old man to shuffle around from the back of the house. He is bald on top, and his white hair is buzzed close on the sides. Karel Koecher greets me in a gravelly voice.

I tell him I'm doing fine. Karel and Hana had been on vacation in Austria a few weeks before. He likes Austria and always dreamed of settling there but never did quite make it. Holidays will have to do. Austria has the Central European feel of Prague, but Karel likes its additional polish. It's foreign and familiar all at once; the nature is amazing.

We enter a small vestibule from a side door on the house. A cat curls around my legs as I take off my shoes. Much like in Japan, Czechs always remove their footwear before entering a home. Once you're used to the custom, as I now am, it indeed feels a barbarous affront to track the grime of the outside world into someone's private space.

Karel gives me a pair of *pantofle*—slippers. He asks if I want coffee and invites me to a seat in the living room. A TV guide, an encyclopedia of wine, a dictionary, and a Lands' End catalogue cover the coffee table. The paintings hanging on the walls run the gamut from abstract to nature scenes, and a VHS player and an older—but good quality—hi-fi adorn the shelves. Over near the kitchen is a fish tank. Karel returns with coffee and poppy seed cake.

Hana is, as usual, at work—she arranges seminars that bring together construction professionals and professors from technical schools. So we again have the house to ourselves, Karel says. He sits in a chair and I on the couch—just as we have at four previous meetings, most of which lasted several hours.

"What can I do for you?" Karel asks.

I tell him how much I have enjoyed our talks over the past year or so. We drift into a brief discussion about the forthcoming American election. It's about a week before Donald Trump defeats Hillary Clinton; disconcerting and unpleasant as the campaign has been up to this point, it's all anyone wants to talk about with an American abroad. Like a car accident, everybody pumps the brakes to gawk at the scene before moving on with their day.

Karel starts talking about societal chaos in the United States—and there is plenty to talk about. He assumes that Donald Trump will win. He tells me he wrote an article for a Czech website explaining why this will definitely be the case. I'm not so sure about that, I say.

"Wanna bet?" he asks, with a tinge of annoyance.

I don't. I want to talk more about his life and less about Trump. So I steer away from the election, turn on my iPad's recording app, and place it on the table. Karel takes note, and we revert to where we had left off a few weeks ago.

After hours conversing with Karel, I feel less sure about what it was all for. I don't mean his mission specifically, but the Cold War itself. At just under a third of American GDP, the 1990 Soviet economy was proportionately the same size it had been in 1950.[1] By this and many other metrics, forty years of struggle had left a lot of people where they were when it started, save for the innocent dead and untold capital squandered on weapons, war, and lies.

Karel has thoughts: "For years I have been thinking about intelligence services as institutions. What I learned from my experience, and my own research, is that the history of intelligence services is more or less a history of failures. American intelligence has been dismal, in Iraq and so forth, even Vietnam. The world is really fucked up, and intelligence services have a lot to do with it."

After months of research, I tend to agree. Across thousands of pages of archive files, the StB looks a lot like a hyper-empowered mutation of the DMV. Though Western intelligence agencies like MI6 and the CIA do a better job of branding—by keeping files classified—I am starting to wonder whether geopolitical decisions might better be made by just flipping coins.

"Do you mean to say that the whole Cold War was unnecessary?" I ask.

"It was artificial. From the Soviet side, there was no aggressive intention whatever. That was simply a myth."

Karel blames not the CIA but the Pentagon: "The generals really wanted new resources and troops."

I am certainly interested in exploring the idea that American behavior exacerbated tensions during the Cold War. It was by no means the prevailing dictum during my late Cold War childhood, and that makes it a provocative strand to pull at. Why have these conversations at all if not to attempt to see this history through a new lens?

But still, it seems to me that the Soviets did plenty to stoke the insanity. They were funding guerrilla movements, supplying weapons that drove war, and overthrowing unfriendly governments. They invaded Karel's homeland of Czechoslovakia, I point out: that would seem pretty aggressive.

But Karel makes a distinction: Soviet aggression was not directed at the United States. He views the Soviet interventions as defensive. As far as the primary Cold War rivalry, Karel still views the United States as the main antagonist.

"So in your view, the American aggression was ideologically driven or the result of something like the classic military-industrial complex?" I ask.

"Military-industrial complex," he says. "I am sorry that we had to have that fucking Cold War, because I see so many opportunities, or even desires on both sides to just not feud. The people are very similar. The chief of KGB counterintelligence, for example, and CIA chief of counterintelligence, I knew both. Same guys. Excellent education, perfect command of languages, like twins. Why the hell should we stab each other in the back?"

After hours of talks, and as I hear Karel out, I can't help but feel that pretty much every metanarrative—good versus evil, the relative peace and stability of a bipolar global order, the inextricable link between free markets and political liberty—still circulating about the Cold War amounts to nonsense. Even eminent historians such as John Lewis Gaddis interpret the Cold War in ways that confound me. "The Cold War experience showed," Gaddis wrote, "that it is not easy to keep markets open and ideas constrained at the same time."[2] And yet China has spent much of the past fifty years—a period of time approaching the entirety of the Cold War—going a long way toward demonstrating the opposite.

To me the most preposterous interpretations, and perhaps the most popular in the United States, are stories that simultaneously paint the Soviet Union and its leaders as both comically inept and ingenious supervillains. All at once, Western myth imagines Communist institutions as lumbering, inefficient, incompetent, and—simultaneously—an existential threat to global order and the survival of the human species. Those same buffoons that couldn't figure out how to manufacture shoes in children's sizes almost talked your grandmother into betraying her country.

Through sleight of hand, such arguments assert two incompatible ideas at once. While the Soviet system was inherently flawed and doomed to implode, the United States' supposed victory in the Cold War is also said to demonstrate American superiority.

More troubling, it feels like that sort of victory-lap euphoria has driven economics, politics, and international affairs ever since. To me, it's akin to a professional football team playing a group of high schoolers and then concluding their winning game plan was the difference. Only when both teams are evenly matched are tactics and strategy decisive factors. Either the opponent presented a real challenge and thus had some merit, or they didn't, and the game plan remains untested.

In practice, losing teams often learn more about what works and what does not. Drunk on self-satisfaction, the winning team has trouble pinpointing which factors contributed to victory. The victory alone is proof enough that each tactic used and every play called were both prudent and necessary.

When Karel was traded on the Bridge of Spies and returned to Czechoslovakia, he hoped to be feted as a hero. But that never did happen. By the time he returned in 1986, the system had been so hollowed out, and the Communist Party so wary of being exposed as a paper tiger, that anybody coming in from the outside was suspect. So Karel met up again with old intellectuals, many of whom had since turned against the regime. After 1989's Velvet Revolution, he briefly toyed with politics, hoping a reformed Communist Party—including him—might play a role in the country's democratic future.

"After the collapse of Communism," I ask, "how do you think things went? I mean, let's say we can go back to 1989, could things have ended up better?"

"To give a very fast answer, the Communist regime more or less destroyed the elite," Karel says. "Some of them emigrated after the [Warsaw Pact] invasion, and the rest that stayed were prevented from taking part in public life to such an extent that they never assumed any positions from which they could lead the nation. So the political and economic elite after the Velvet Revolution were amateurs—like Havel and company with absolutely no knowledge whatsoever and no ability to learn—and criminals. The only people who had money at that point were those who stole. The elite was a mixture of idiots and thieves, and that totally destroys the fabric of society."

Though Havel and his cohorts are still revered by many—myself included—there are few Czechs who still argue that they were canny politicians fully up to the task of guiding the country through the choppy post-Communist era. Karel's views on Czechoslovakia's transition years are not exactly controversial. Right or wrong, they more or less amount to conventional wisdom on the country's evolutions during the 1990s and 2000s. The peaceful division of Czechoslovakia into two countries was very much driven by rival factions carving up the economic spoils. Today, the 1993 split into separate Czech and Slovak republics feels like it was inevitable, but at the time, majorities in both countries preferred to stay together. Kleptocracy, regretfully, proved more powerful than Havelian idealism, and the former playwright resigned the presidency to avoid presiding over the divorce.

"Communism is not something you can reform, but you can transform it," Karel says.

I don't understand what he means. This feels like a distinction without a difference, I say. I challenge him: while a place like Prague boasts an extensive public transportation system, good schools, and other remnants of a socialist welfare state, that doesn't justify repression that was at worst violent and, even at its best, dehumanizing.

"If you try to dismantle that oppressive apparatus, everything comes down. They had to go very slowly; it just went too fast," Karel says. "It could have worked if the American side had cooperated, providing loans and so forth."

Unlike in the rest of the former Eastern Bloc, in Czechoslovakia, and then in the successor Czech Republic, the Communist Party has remained a political player. In fact, up until the elections of 2021, the Communist Party had won seats in the country's parliament for its entire democratic history. Even today, there are still Communist officials at the municipal level throughout the country. Karel long ago ceased to be interested in their brand of politics, which now largely amounts to busing pensioners to polling stations, clientelism, and strategic dealmaking to funnel government or European Union subsidies to loyalists.

"Isn't life better now, though?" I ask.

"Are people better off? It depends. People like me are better off. My friends are better off. You can travel and so forth. But most people are not interested in that. Most people want to have a job, want to feed their children, et cetera, et cetera. They don't go to Italy and Lake Como. They are not better off."

We take a short break, and Karel offers to lend me some books he had mentioned earlier. So we head upstairs to his study. There is a menorah on the shelf, a collection of hefty tomes on the history of espionage, and texts on philosophy and logic, among other topics. Eventually he decides to send me bootlegged digital versions of the books, one about the rise of China and the other weighing the likelihood of a future clash between the United States and China.[3] Even in his eighties, Karel sees things like copyright law more as a suggestion than a rule. And he still has superpower struggles on his mind.

Karel reads the *New York Times* every day—the same paper that he once used to give the all-clear signal during meetings with his StB handlers. He takes daily exercise in the nearby forest. Though he is starting to look a little frail, he moves well—not bad for his age, anyway. A decade younger than Karel, Hana has yet to retire. I have met her a few times, but she is not much interested in talking to me or about the past. Karel purposely invites me over when she is at work. I can tell she doesn't trust me.

"I need to ask more about how you were eventually caught," I say.

Though Karel likes to blame his rival, Oleg Kalugin, and I share his general distaste for the ex-KGB general, quite a lot of circumstantial evidence indicates it was Jan Fila, the man who recruited Karel to rejoin the StB in 1982, who eventually informed the Americans about Karel's espionage work. Not only does the FBI claim they started following Karel and Hana early in 1982, almost the exact time that Fila reached out to reactivate the couple, but Fila later abruptly quit the StB and disappeared from the face of the earth—leaving behind a wife and son.

It seems all but assured that Fila continued living under an assumed name in the United States. When I talked with some ex-FBI guys involved with Karel's case, they refuse to cite Fila by name but claim they did have their own source in Czechoslovak intelligence at that time. While Karel agrees that Fila ultimately defected to the American side, he resists the idea that Fila was the one who turned him in.

But I point to an StB document I found, dated October 13, 1986, where there is an underlined note: "Rino suspected a betrayal. He listed Rak"—Fila's latter-day code name—"as a potential traitor." Back in the 1980s, even Karel thought Fila had fingered him to the FBI.

But Karel isn't budging now. He insists Fila was a good guy and would never have betrayed him. I am having trouble understanding why, but then I realize it absolves Karel from having to consider, or admit, that his entire reactivation might have been part of some kind of elaborate sting.

Indeed, the StB files indicate that they worried about Fila's connection to the FBI starting in the mid-1970s. If Fila had been working with the FBI when he reactivated Karel, it would detract from Karel's own superspy mythology and perhaps force him to admit—something I think true—that impatience and ego made him too eager to involve himself again with the StB. That would mean Karel let his emotions get the best of him. That he left himself vulnerable, and that the FBI managed to take advantage of this.

"It would be standard that they would have some contact," Karel says of Fila and the FBI. "They may be looking for ways to find some common ground."

So I ask whether he has any idea what happened to Fila later.

"No. And as far as his defection is concerned, I absolutely approve," Karel says. The Czechoslovak government "would have locked him up. Because he was basically accused of turning me in. Which I doubt."

To me, it's clear it must have been Fila. But Karel is not interested in talking about this any further. So I turn to the morality of spying: "The job requires you to lie pretty much all day every day. That's hard for the average person to understand. Do you just accept that as part of the job? I mean, do you ever really get used to all the lying?"

"No, you don't. You feel bad. You are ashamed. Even if you think you are doing the right thing, you are deceiving your friends or people that trust you."

"How do you characterize your own moral performance?"

"Once you are in intelligence, you have to suspend certain moral beliefs, there is lying and so forth," he says. "But when it comes to really cutting the mustard, I believe I was utterly moral. If you lie in the framework of your assignment, that is one thing, but it doesn't mean you lie to your wife or whatever. There are many decent people in the CIA. I just wish we were on the same side, let's put it that way."

I wonder, though, once you are out of espionage, does it become apparent that your morals somehow got thrown out of whack? I continue. "In the midst of it, was there anything you could do to recenter yourself, or does amorality become the norm?"

"You do get inured," he says. "It's a very hard thing to be moral in those situations sometimes. You don't expect the regime will change and it will all be declassified. You have to decide yourself that there is some moral obligation to maintain. You don't have to believe what I am saying, but when you are talented, you are capable, and you are not exactly a coward, there are moments when you believe you can come up with ideas that others cannot. So you try doing what you can. In this case, it's true nothing came out of it."

"Is there any sense that some of the people you deceived deserve an apology?"

"I am not against saying I'm sorry. I'm sorry that I lied, but I'm not sorry that I tried to make a difference," Karel says. "That, I think, is honorable. So in general, it is very hard to say I'm sorry because it would be interpreted as apologizing for things I did not do."

I ask whether Karel has any regrets.

"Yes, I do," he says. "Well, I . . . it was certainly an adventure, and it was thrilling, but what kind of accomplishment is there? Nothing except an adventurous life. Maybe a quiet life somewhere in a small town teaching math would be more fulfilling. But you cannot avoid it. If you are really bumped up against ambitions, dreams that you want to accomplish. . . . So this is the wisdom of an old man."

We lapse into a discussion about Karel as a youngster. My thoughts drift back to his unpleasant upbringing, to the letter his father wrote hoping to sabotage Karel's application to film school. I have a young daughter myself and find it hard to comprehend a parent knowingly harming his or her child.

"My father was a believer, in God, the Church. I guess that is what he disliked most about me, because he was a man of authorities and respect," Karel says. "I just wasn't going to do that. It was very much reinforced in the US; the culture is certainly founded on questioning authority."

Every time I bring up his father, Jaroslav, Karel's face contorts, his voice turns sharp, and he moves to change the subject. But I can't help myself.

"This is a little abstract and, I admit, somewhat manufactured," I say. "But your father was a soldier, and in your own way you were a soldier. He served a country that ceased to exist and probably never got his due because of it. I am not sure how to say this, but there seem to be some parallels."

Karel does not like this. His response is stern. A second ago, we were friends. Now, we are adversaries. He does not wish to be associated with his father. A Freudian might argue that he made a good many life choices intent on demonstrating how different he really was.

"The parallel is, I worked for a state that existed at the time when I worked for it. Certainly, I was not like him. He went to military school since the age of eleven, so you are brainwashed forever. He was a bigoted Catholic, which I am not. He doesn't understand a thing about the world. That is not my case, I am very realistic," Karel pushes back. "Taking sides, I am taking sides as a rational choice, not opportunistic, but because that is the side that offers me, goddamn it, a meaningful path, meaningful in a moral sense, because I am not duped. I am telling them how things are, goddamn it. I went to Brzezinski's school, and I am just giving back what I learned. The StB didn't have anyone like that."

Karel's brow is now furrowed. He is angry. We keep talking, but now he's more intent on proving points than having a discussion. Still, I am interested in how Karel sees the world today.

"At this point it's the Russians who are defending the basic Western values, in my opinion," Karel tells me. "Family values. Possibly you could even say it about fighting terrorism and so forth too."

It is a narrative popular among Europe's far right, and though I won't know it until after the coming American election result, it appeals to a shocking proportion of the American electorate too.

"You mean prevailing liberal ideology is flawed?" I ask.

"It's very flawed. It's not even liberal, it's . . ." he trails off, catching himself. "It's a myth that Russia threatens other countries. I never saw any of that."

"But just to go back to the other point you made, and family values, if you say Russia is the one defending those things, that implies Western Europe and the United States are not."

"Yes, I do imply that."

"And so in your analysis, the prevailing ideology in Western Europe and the United States is what?"

"Political correctness," Karel says. "The certain homogeneity of Western cultures that was essential is ruined. You will have ghettos; you will have no-go zones. It totally destroys civilized life. The whole gender thing. I am very liberal, but the whole transgender thing is a bit too much."

I don't agree, but apart for the emphasis on Russia, I wonder how much Karel's views diverge from an octogenarian living in Ohio, for example. "And so what does that mean?" I ask. "The persistence of those things. What are the consequences?"

"The consequences are, you will get more and more people moving away from, I don't know, call it spiritual life, to materialism."

"So relativism will destroy everything?"

"Yes, and it opens the doors to all kinds of extremism. It means the end to civilized relations. You are in danger if you are not fairly aggressive yourself. It's a jungle mentality instead of civilized."

Like many others who spent a good part of their lives in the Cold War, Karel considers that highly unusual set of circumstances as the norm. Everything else is a sort of deviation from that norm. As I sit there, I think of the books and pseudo-intellectuals now touting some variation of a "new Cold War" between the US and China or US and Russia. I was a child during the late Cold War, but the further it recedes into history, the more anomalous it feels. With a bit of distance, most of the stories I encounter in my research make it seem as delusional, nihilistic, and uncivilized as the plot of a dystopian sci-fi novel.

"I don't think people can sort out these problems; it will go on forever. I just don't think we can live in peace," Karel says. "The clandestine services are a questionable tool in every sense of the word. You have no real way of verifying the predictions they make. Then you have all kinds of people who try to sneak in and use intelligence agencies to further their own personal cause. It's just a disaster."

Karel says he tried to make a difference, and it's clear as ever he still has tremendous belief in his own abilities. If exceptional people—even those driven by supposedly pure motives—who try as hard as they can are not able to change the course of events, what hope is there? "So is it that the wrong kind of people are drawn to intelligence work? The very nature of the job attracts the wrong element?" I ask.

"In the seventies, it was almost a gentleman's battle. Even violence, sure there was violence, but both sides were very realistic; violence was not really necessary. Vietnam, that really destroyed the profession. It's too bad. I was really quite often sorry. When you speak about the CIA, it's like you are speaking about a person. That's not so. There are many people there, and not everybody is of the same mind. I liked some guys in the CIA.

"In my case, becoming a spy was a choice of last resort," he continues. "I was pushed that way because I couldn't just do what they wanted me to do when I was younger. Any philosopher worth anything, you question authority. You question authority, and that is the only way to live a dignified life."

"And you feel like that defined you in your years as a spy too?" I ask. "Do you consider it a defining characteristic of your personality even now?"

"Absolutely," he says, "there is no difference. Even to the point of being willing to switch sides if one side becomes reasonable and the other side doesn't. Simply, I am not going to be a supporter just to be a supporter. It is about loyalty to yourself. . . . I don't give a fuck about belonging. Sure, I would like to belong, but there is nothing to belong to."

ACKNOWLEDGMENTS

While my language skills were sufficient to get this project going, they were not nearly polished enough for me to fully grasp nuance nor accurately quote the many archival documents cited in this book. I need to thank Bibiána Cunningham, Kirill Fedotov, Natalie Emma Johnsonová, Julie Mahlerová, and Yulia Pokhorova for their help translating documents from Czech, Slovak, and Russian. Without their work, this book could not exist. Any mistakes in the text are my own.

I am also much obliged to the staff at the Institute for the Study for Totalitarian Regimes and the Security Forces Archive in Prague—especially Jan Makovička, whose help tracking down documents and photos was invaluable. To me, it is still mystifying that so many of the documents that went into forming the backbone of this book even exist. I thank the people who work to organize, preserve, and research these materials for a living.

I need to thank my parents, James and Arleen Cunningham, who forced me to write a school report on the fall of the Berlin Wall when I was nine years old—no doubt sparking an unhealthy interest in Cold War lore and provoking the lengthy and precarious journey to write this book.

And finally, it would be professional malpractice not to mention my wife, Bibiána, and daughter, Eva, for their patience and kindness while I was writing. Thanks, girls.

BIBLIOGRAPHY

BOOKS

Addison, Angus. *The World Economy*. Paris: OECD, 2006.

Allison, Graham, and Philip Zelikow. *Essence of Decision: Explaining the Cuban Missile Crisis*. New York: Addison Wesley Longman, 1999.

Andrew, Christopher. *The Secret World: A History of Intelligence*. New Haven, Connecticut: Yale University Press, 2019.

Andrew, Christopher, and Vasili Mitrokhin. *The Mitrokhin Archive: The KGB in Europe and the West*. London: Penguin, 2018.

August, Frantisek, and David Rees. *Red Star over Prague*. London: Sherwood, 1984.

Bearden, Milt, and James Risen. *The Main Enemy: The Inside Story of the CIA's Final Showdown with the KGB*. Toronto: Presidio Press, 2004.

Bevins, Vincent. *The Jakarta Method: Washington's Anticommunist Crusade and the Mass Murder Program That Shaped Our World*. New York: PublicAffairs, 2020.

Bren, Paulina. *The Greengrocer and His TV: The Culture of Communism After the 1968 Prague Spring*. Ithaca, New York: Cornell University Press, 2010.

Camus, Albert. *The Myth of Sisyphus and Other Essays*. Translated by Justin O'Brien. New York: Vintage Books, 1991.

Clarridge, Duane R. *A Spy for All Seasons: My Life in the CIA*. New York: Scribner, 1997.

Cohen, Adam, and Elizabeth Taylor. *American Pharaoh: Mayor Richard J. Daley, His Battle for Chicago and the Nation*. New York: Back Bay Books, 2000.

Demetz, Peter. *Prague in Black and Gold: Scenes in the Life of a European City*. New York: Hill and Wang, 1997.

Dobrynin, Anatoly. *In Confidence: Moscow's Ambassador to Six Cold War Presidents*. London: University of Washington Press, 2001.

Earley, Pete. *Confessions of a Spy: The Real Story of Aldrich Ames*. New York: Berkley Books, 1998.

Fischer, Benjamin B. *A Cold War Conundrum: The 1983 Soviet War Scare*. Washington, DC: CIA, 2007.

Frankel, Charles. *The Case for Modern Man*. New York: Harper & Brothers, 1956.

Frei, Norbert. *Adenauer's Germany and the Nazi Past: The Politics of Amnesty and Integration*. Translated by Joel Gold. New York: Columbia University Press, 2002.

Gaddis, John Lewis. *The Cold War: The Deals. The Lies. The Truth*. New York: Penguin, 2005.

Galeano, Eduardo. *The Open Veins of Latin America*. New York: NYU Press, 1991.

Gleason, Abbot. *Totalitarianism: The Inner History of the Cold War*. New York: Oxford University Press, 1995.

Golan, Galia. *The Czechoslovak Reform Movement: Communism in Crisis 1962–1968*. London: Cambridge University Press, 1971.

Goldman, Jan, ed. *The Central Intelligence Agency: An Encyclopedia of Covert Ops, Intelligence Gathering and Spies, Volume 1*. Santa Barbara, California: ABC-CLIO, 2016.

Harward, Brian M. *Presidential Power: Documents Decoded*. Santa Barbara: ABC-CLIO, 2016.

Hašek, Jaroslav. *The Good Solder Švejk*. New York: Penguin, 2000.

Heimann, Mary. *Czechoslovakia: The State That Failed*. London: Yale University Press, 2009.

Hoffman, David E. *The Billion Dollar Spy: A True Story of Cold War Espionage and Betrayal*. London: Anchor, 2016.

Hrabal, Bohumil. *Mr. Kafka and Other Tales from the Time of the Cult*. Translated by Paul Wilson. New York: New Directions, 2015.

Immerman, Richard H. *The CIA in Guatemala: The Foreign Policy of Intervention*. Austin: University of Texas Press, 1982.

Judt, Tony. *Postwar: A History of Europe Since 1945*. London: Vintage, 2010.

Kafka, Franz. *The Trial*. Translated by D. Wyllie. New York: Echo Library, 2007.

Kalugin, Oleg. *Spymaster: My Thirty-Two Years in Intelligence and Espionage Against the West*. New York: Basic Books, 2009.

Kennan, George F. *Memoirs 1925–1950*. New York: Pantheon, 1983.

Kennan, George F. "The Sources of Soviet Conduct." In *American Diplomacy*, 113–134. Chicago: University of Chicago Press, 2012.

Kennan, George F. "The State of U.S. Soviet Relations." In *At a Century's Ending: Reflections, 1982–1995*, 82–92. New York: W. W. Norton, 1996.

Kessler, Ronald. *Spy vs. Spy: Stalking Soviet Spies in America.* New York: Charles Scribner's Sons, 1988.

KGB. *The Official KGB Handbook: English Translation.* London: Industrial Information Index, 1991.

Khrushchev, Nikita, and Sergei Khrushchev, ed. *Memoirs of Nikita Khrushchev, Volume 2: Reformer.* State College: Pennsylvania State University Press, 2006.

Koecher, Karel. "Ideology, Philosophy and Science." PhD diss., Columbia University, 1970.

Lasch, Christopher. *The Culture of Narcissism: American Life in the Age of Diminishing Expectations.* New York: W. W. Norton, 1979.

Le Carré, John. *The Pigeon Tunnel: Stories from My Life.* London: Penguin, 2017.

Maddison, Angus. *The World Economy.* Paris: OECD, 2006.

Mahler, Jonathan. *Ladies and Gentlemen, the Bronx Is Burning: 1977, Baseball, Politics, and the Battle for the Soul of a City.* New York: Picador, 2005.

Olson, James M. *Fairplay: The Moral Dilemmas of Spying.* Lincoln, Nebraska: Potomac, 2010.

Peretruchin, Igor K. О чем не заявил ТАСС: Подлинная история "Трианона" [What TASS didn't say: The true story of Trianon]. Moscow: Algorithm, 2017.

Perlstein, Rick. *Nixonland: The Rise of a President and the Fracturing of America.* New York: Scribner, 2009.

Peterson, Martha D. *The Widow Spy: My CIA Journey from the Jungles of Laos to Prison in Moscow.* Wilmington, North Carolina: Red Canary Press, 2012.

Phillips-Fein, Kim. *Fear City: New York's Fiscal Crisis and the Rise of Austerity Politics.* New York: Picador, 2018.

Roberts, Priscilla, ed. *The Cold War: Interpreting Conflict Through Primary Documents, Volume 1.* Santa Barbara: ABC-CLIO, 2019.

Rosenblatt, Josh. *Why We Fight: One Man's Search for Meaning Inside the Ring.* New York: Ecco, 2019.

Roth, Philip. *The Prague Orgy.* London: Vintage, 2016.

Rozell, Mark J. *The Press and the Ford Presidency.* Ann Arbor: University of Michigan Press, 1992.

Schulman, Bruce J. *The Seventies: The Great Shift in American Culture, Society and Politics.* Boston: Da Capo Press, 2002.

Ševela, Vladimír. *Český krtek v CIA* [Czech mole in the CIA]. Prague: Prostor, 2015.

Sharansky, Natan. *Fear No Evil: The Classic Memoir of One Man's Triumph over a Police State*. New York: PublicAffairs, 1998.

Suárez Barcala, Alejandra. *Nombre en clavé: Trigon: La historia de cómo cubrí que me padre era un agente de CIA* [Code name: Trigon: The story of how I discovered my father was a CIA agent]. Madrid: Punta de Vista, 2019.

Tuckerova, Veronika. "Reading Kafka in Prague: The Reception of Franz Kafka Between the East and the West During the Cold War." PhD diss., Columbia University, 2012.

Ward, Richard H., K. L. Kiernan, and D. Mabrey. *Homeland Security: An Introduction*. Newark, NJ: Matthew Bender, 2006.

Westad, Odd Arne. *The Cold War: A World History*. London: Penguin, 2018.

White, Duncan. *Cold Warriors: Writers Who Waged the Literary Cold War*. London: Little, Brown, 2019.

Wolf, Markus, and Anne McElvoy. *Man Without a Face: The Autobiography of Communism's Greatest Spymaster*. New York: PublicAffairs, 1999.

Žantovsky, Michael. *Havel: A Life*. New York: Grove Atlantic, 2014.

Zweig, Stefan. *The World of Yesterday*. Translated by A. Bell. London: Pushkin, 2014.

ARTICLES

American Psychological Association. "The Truth About Lie Detectors (aka Polygraph Tests)." August 5, 2004. https://www.apa.org/research/action/polygraph.

Anderson, Jack. *Beatrice Daily Sun*, March 9, 1970. https://newspaperarchive.com/beatrice-daily-sun-mar-09-1970-p-4/.

Anderson, Jack. "Mystery Kissinger-Dobrynin Meeting." *Washington Post*, December 16, 1980, B15.

"A Popular Russian." *New York Times*, May 11, 1959. https://timesmachine.nytimes.com/timesmachine/1959/05/11/80575833.html?pageNumber=7.

App, Austin. "The Sudeten-German Tragedy." *Reason*, February 1976. https://reason.com/1976/02/01/the-sudeten-german-tragedy/.

Barnes, Clive. "Drama: Public Theater Presents 'Memorandum.'" *New York Times*, May 6, 1968. https://timesmachine.nytimes.com/timesmachine/1968/05/06/91229093.html?pageNumber=55.

Belousek, Daniel. "Rak, který zmizel beze stopy" [Rak, who disappeared without a trace]. Paměť a dějiny 3 (2008): 25–35.

Berman, Daphna. "Natan Sharansky: Act II, Scene I." *Moment*, July–August 2012, https://momentmag.com/natan-sharansky-act-iii-scene-i-2/.

BIBLIOGRAPHY

Boyajian, William E. "An Economic Review of the Past Decade in Diamonds." *Gems & Gemology* (Fall 1988): 134–153.

"Charles Frankel Resigned a Post Under Johnson." *New York Times*, May 11, 1979. https://www.nytimes.com/1979/05/11/archives/charles-frankel-resigned-a-post-under-johnson-he-left-state.html.

Cunningham, Benjamin. "Cult Classic." *Los Angeles Review of Books*, March 26, 2016. https://lareviewofbooks.org/article/cult-classic/.

Dalin, David. "President Ronald Reagan and the Jews." *Jewish Ledger*, February 26, 2011. http://www.jewishledger.com/2011/02/president-ronald-reagan-and-the-jews/.

Dickins, Tom. "The Political Slogan in Communist Czechoslovakia (1948–89)." *Central Europe* 15, no. 1–2 (2017): 58–87. https://doi.org/910.1080/14790963.2017.1412719/.

Eder, Richard. "Some Interesting Happenings in Prague." *New York Times Magazine*, November 12, 1967. https://timesmachine.nytimes.com/timesmachine/1967/11/12/83642882.html?pageNumber=265.

Eisenhower, Dwight D. 1961. "Military-Industrial Complex Speech." Transcript of a speech given in Washington, DC, January 17, 1961. https://avalon.law.yale.edu/20th_century/eisenhower001.asp.

Feron, James. "Police Link 4 Slayings in Bedford Hills to Same Burglars." *New York Times*, May 12, 1979. https://timesmachine.nytimes.com/timesmachine/1979/05/12/111024284.html.

"From the Archive, 14 September 1978: Bulgarian Dissident Killed by Poisoned Umbrella at London Bus Stop." *Guardian*, September 14, 1978. https://www.theguardian.com/theguardian/2012/sep/14/bulgaria-umbrella-murder-archive-1978.

Gallup. "Satisfaction with the United States." https://news.gallup.com/poll/1669/general-mood-country.aspx.

Harrison, Mark. "Soviet Economic Growth Since 1928: The Alternative Statistics of G.I. Khanin." *Europe-Asia Studies* 45, no. 1 (1993): 141–167.

Havel, Václav. "The Power of the Powerless." Hannah Arendt Center for Politics and Humanities. December 23, 2011. https://hac.bard.edu/amor-mundi/the-power-of-the-powerless-vaclav-havel-2011-12-23.

Klaidman, Stephen. "Czech Writer, Here, Sees Opportunity for Liberals." *New York Times*, May 5, 1968. https://timesmachine.nytimes.com/timesmachine/1968/05/05/89323539.html?pageNumber=14.

Krpec, O. "Czechoslovakian Trade Policy After World War I (1918–1927): Nationalism and Capitalism." Working paper presented at the GERG conference,

Geopolitical Economy of the 21st Century World, Winnipeg, Canada, 2015. https://gergconference.ca/wp-content/uploads/2015/09/Krpec-paper -Czechoslovak-Trade-Policy-in-1920s-2.pdf.

Kundera, Milan. "Český úděl" [Czech destiny]. Translated by T. West. *Listy* 7–8 (1968): 1–5. https://www.academia.edu/2503513/Czech_Destiny_Milan_Kundera_.

le Carré, John. "My New Friends in the New Russia: In Search of a Few Good Crooks, Cops and Former Agents." *New York Times Book Review*, February 19, 1995. https://timesmachine.nytimes.com/timesmachine/1995/02/19 /464195.html?pageNumber=114.

Letter to the editor. *New York Times Book Review*, April 2, 1995. https://timesmachine .nytimes.com/timesmachine/1995/04/02/576895.html?pageNumber=100.

Markham, James M. "Shcharansky Wins Freedom in Berlin in Prisoner Trade." *New York Times*, February 12, 1986. https://www.nytimes.com/1986/02/12 /world/shcharansky-wins-freedom-in-berlin-in-prisoner-trade.html.

Maxa, Rudy, and Phil Stanford. "The Swinging Spies." *Washingtonian*, February 1987.

"Москвашпионская" [Moscow spy]. *Trud*, August 24, 2012, 4.

Nixon, Richard M. "Second Inaugural Address." Transcript of a speech given in Washington, DC, January 20, 1973. https://avalon.law.yale.edu/20th_century /nixon2.asp.

Pryor, Zora P., and Fredric L. Pryor, "Foreign Trade and Interwar Czechoslovak Economic Development, 1918–1938." *VSWG: Vierteljahrschrift für Sozial- und Wirtschaftsgeschichte* 62, no. 4 (1975): 500–533.

Reagan, Ronald. "First Inaugural Address." Transcript of a speech given in Washington, DC, January 20, 1981. https://avalon.law.yale.edu/20th_century /reagan1.asp.

Sciolino, Elaine. *New York Times*, January 20, 1992. https://www.nytimes.com /1992/01/20/world/kgb-telltale-is-tattling-but-is-he-telling-us-all.html.

Sheraton, Mimi. "A Third Ave. Pub and a Village Storefront." Restaurants, *New York Times*, April 14, 1978. https://www.nytimes.com/1978/04/14/archives /restaurants-a-third-ave-pub-and-a-village-storefront.html.

Taranto, James. "Leonid Brezhnev Lives." *Wall Street Journal*, March 30, 2012. https:// www.wsj.com/articles/SB10001424052702303404704577313750705052134.

"The Trigon Caper." *New Republic*, October 4, 1980, 17.

West, Tim. "Destiny as Alibi: Milan Kundera, Václav Havel and the 'Czech Question' After 1968." *The Slavonic and East European Review* 87, no. 3 (July 2009): 401–428.

Whitney, Craig R. "Wolfgang Vogel, East German Spy Swapper, Dies at 82." *New York Times*, August 24, 2008. https://www.nytimes.com/2008/08/24/world /europe/24iht-obits.4.15590555.html.

Wolf, Daniel. "The Bizarre Secrets of a Lost Empire." *Sunday Times* (London), February 12, 1995. https://www.julianlewis.net/selected-news-coverage/3283:the -bizarre-secrets-of-a-lost-empire-23.

Wolfe, Tom. "The 'Me' Decade and the Third Great Awakening." *New York* magazine, April 8, 2008. https://nymag.com/news/features/45938/.

Žáček, Pavel. "Případ 'Rino': Náš člověk v CIA. Řízení čs. špičkové agentury sovětskou rozvědkou, 1973–1976" [The 'Rino' case: Our man in the CIA. The management of the top Czechoslovak agency by Soviet intelligence, 1973– 1976]. *Securitas Imperii* 29 (2016): 190–242.

ARCHIVAL MATERIALS

Doolittle, James H., William B. Franke, Morris Hadley, and William D. Pawley. Presidential Panel of Consultants, *Report on the Covert Activities of the Central Intelligence Agency*. September 30, 1954.

Palmieri, Edmund L. "In Re Grand Jury Subpoena Koecher." 601 F. Supp. 385 (S.D.N.Y. 1984), December 11, 1984.

Record of Telephone Conversation Between Henry Kissinger and President Richard Nixon, September 16, 1973. NSA Archives. https://nsarchive2.gwu.edu /NSAEBB/NSAEBB255/19730916KP5.pdf.

State Security Archives of the Czech Republic

Karel Koecher, files 44503, 816105

Hana Koecher, file 48181

AUDIOVISUAL MATERIALS

Carlin, George. "Monologue: George Carlin on Football and Baseball—SNL." October 11, 1975, Saturday Night Live, video, 4:06, October 24, 2013. https:// www.youtube.com/watch?v=5ebyLkCaAL0.

Clark, Dick. "1973 New Year's Ball Drop." December 31, 1972, AwardsShowNetwork, video, 0:59, May 6, 2010. https://www.youtube.com/watch?v=6iw0C5F5cwI.

Kaufman, Matthew, and J. Hart, dirs. *American Swing*. HDNet Films, 2009. 1 hour, 21 min.

New, David, dir. *Stranger in a Strange Land.* Associated Producers Ltd., 2004. 47 min.

Runnette, Brooke, M. Smith, and O. Zill de Granados, writers. *Frontline*, 2000, Season 18, Episode 14, "Drug Wars Part 1," aired October 9, 2000, on PBS. https://vimeo.com/14154434.

INTERVIEWS

Joseph Calluori, February 1, 2021.

Joseph Downs, July 7, 2021.

Joseph Fierer, February 18, 2021.

Loren Graham, July 1, 2021.

Pavel Illner, September 8, 2021.

Karel Kaplan, August 31, 2015.

Ronald Kessler, August 31, 2015.

Hana Koecher, September 7, 2015.

Karel Koecher, August 3, 2015.

Karel Koecher, August 17, 2015.

Karel Koecher, September 7, 2015.

Karel Koecher, November 3, 2016.

Karel Koecher, November 30, 2016.

Ian Leigh, September 11, 2015.

Gerard Lynch, September 16, 2015.

David Major, September 15, 2015.

Marti Peterson, April 14, 2021.

Alejandra Suárez Barcala, October 18, 2021.

NOTES

CHAPTER 1: REBEL WITHOUT A CAUSE

1. Krpec.
2. Heimann 48.
3. Zweig 383.
4. Kennan, *Memoirs*, 60.
5. Kennan, *Memoirs*, 67.
6. Heimann 109.
7. Kennan, *Memoirs*, 63.
8. Kennan, *Memoirs*, 65.
9. Kennan, *Memoirs*, 70.
10. Heimann 125.
11. Heimann 139.
12. Heimann 341.
13. Heimann 159.
14. Heimann 156.
15. Heimann 174.
16. August and Rees XV.
17. Gaddis 163.
18. Maddison 185.
19. Gaddis 58.
20. Judt 437.
21. August and Rees 50.
22. August and Rees XVIII.
23. August and Rees 42.
24. August and Rees 43.
25. Judt 186.

26. Gaddis 100.
27. Gaddis 104.

CHAPTER 2: EXISTENTIAL STRUGGLE

1. Judt 310.
2. Roberts 422.
3. Judt 311.
4. August and Rees 58.
5. The literal translation of Stalin.
6. Hrabal 121.
7. Ševela 25.
8. Short for Filmová a televizní fakulta Akademie múzických umění.
9. As part of the FAMU admission process, Karel wrote the aforementioned 1956 autobiographical motivational essay.
10. Camus 1.
11. Frankel 198.
12. Gleason 143.
13. Judt 170.
14. Judt 437.
15. Kennan, "The Sources of Soviet Conduct," 125.
16. Kennan, "The Sources of Soviet Conduct," 132.
17. Doolittle, Franke, Hadley, and Pawley.
18. Goldman 23.
19. Galeano 113.
20. Galaeno 113.
21. Westad 5.

CHAPTER 3: JOINING UP

1. Ševela 67.
2. Kafka 152.
3. Tuckerova.
4. Heimann 207.
5. Eder.
6. Gaddis 66.
7. Eisenhower.
8. Gaddis 78.

9. Allison and Zelikow 92.
10. Gaddis 75.

CHAPTER 4: PASSING THE TEST

1. Josef Pardametz is often referred to as Hana's uncle, because of their generational divide, but he is a second cousin.
2. Ševela 77.
3. Kline is now deceased, but before his death, Czech journalist Vladimir Ševela communicated with Kline via email, and Kline denied any connections to American intelligence agencies.
4. Ševela 97.

CHAPTER 5: INNOCENTS ABROAD

1. le Carré, *Pigeon Tunnel*, 8–9.
2. Ševela 96.
3. Ševela 102–103.
4. Partner channel Radio Liberty targeted the Soviet Union specifically, and today, ironically, RFE/RL's joint headquarters are in Prague. They no longer operate under the direct remit of the CIA.
5. Andrew and Mitrokhin 324.
6. Heimann 221.
7. Gaddis 192.
8. Frankel 196.
9. The original text on this StB document uses the name Maricyn, but this seems nonsensical, and future documents reference Marilyn.
10. Eder.
11. Harrison 146.
12. August and Rees 103.
13. Eder.

CHAPTER 6: THE END OF THE BEGINNING

1. Andrew and Mitrokhin 325.
2. Golan 163–164.
3. Heimann 203–232.

4. Andrew and Mitrokhin 327.
5. Andrew and Mitrokhin 331.
6. Klaidman.
7. Barnes.
8. Westad 375.
9. Westad 375–376.
10. Heimann 247.
11. Dobrynin 180.
12. Dobrynin 179–181.
13. Dobrynin 179.
14. Heimann 250.
15. Andrew and Mitrokhin 339.
16. Taranto.
17. Dobrynin 183–184.
18. Judt 447.
19. Andrew 341.
20. Kundera 4.

CHAPTER 7: DOUBLE AGENT

1. Schulman 7.
2. Gaddis 171.
3. Schulman 9.
4. Schulman 10.
5. Schulman 12.
6. Cohen and Taylor 468.
7. Schulman 3.
8. Schulman 37.
9. Schulman 7.
10. Schulman 26.
11. Westad 381.
12. Harrison 146.
13. Schulman 5.
14. Gaddis 147.
15. Westad 382.
16. Gaddis 171.
17. Roth 60–61.
18. Ševela 137.

19. To anyone who reads it in its entirety, it's almost demonstrably correct.
20. Westad 365.
21. Philips-Fein 37.
22. Schulman 16.
23. Gaddis 145.
24. The prior description of lie detector tests comes from the American Psychological Association.

CHAPTER 8: COMPANY MAN

1. Andrew 262.
2. Schulman 33.
3. Philips-Fein 53.
4. Philips-Fein 44.
5. Philips-Fein 21.
6. Philips-Fein 55.
7. Nixon.
8. Žáček 194.
9. Žáček 195.
10. Žáček 200.
11. Westad 340.
12. Westad 356.
13. Westad 358.
14. In 1928, the Colombian military shot two thousand workers who were on strike from local banana plantations. The same company, the United Fruit Company, that had successfully lobbied for the 1954 coup in Guatemala urged intervention in Colombia. After the US government threatened to deploy marines, the Colombian military took action.
15. Runnette, Smith, and Zill de Granados.
16. Westad 359.
17. Žáček 201.
18. Žáček 203.
19. Ševela 247.
20. Gaddis 177.
21. Žáček 205.
22. Ward, Kiernan, and Mabrey 280.
23. Harward 181.
24. Rozell 118.

25. Rozell 118.
26. Though it was just called *Saturday Night* for its first two years.
27. Carlin.
28. Gaddis 179.

CHAPTER 9: HIGHS AND LOWS

1. Záček 211–213.
2. Sheraton.
3. Mahler 155.
4. Kessler 260.
5. Roth 73.
6. Philips-Fein 57.
7. Mahler 289.
8. Philips Fein 2.
9. Philips-Fein 99.
10. Mahler 274.
11. Mahler 30.
12. Mahler 224.
13. Mahler 124.
14. Kaufman and Hart.
15. Mahler 126.
16. Kaufman and Hart.
17. Bevins 266–267.
18. Ševela 236.
19. Sciolino.

CHAPTER 10: BEHIND THE CURTAIN

1. le Carré, *Pigeon Tunnel*, 114.
2. Kalugin 1.
3. Kalugin 6.
4. Kalugin 22.
5. *New York Times*, "A Popular Russian."
6. Kalugin 45.
7. Kalugin 73.
8. Kalugin 139.
9. Kalugin 116.

10. Anderson, *Beatrice Daily*.

11. Anderson, *Beatrice Daily*.

12. Anderson, *Beatrice Daily*.

13. Kalugin 113–114.

14. I called Oleg Kalugin in September 2015 and briefly spoke to him on the phone. I told him I was writing about Karel Koecher and wondered if he would be willing to answer a few questions. Kalugin asked me to call him back in thirty minutes at his office. He gave me an alternate phone number. When I later called that number, it turned out to be the office of a Russian scholar at the Washington, DC–based think tank called the Cato Institute. He had no idea why Kalugin had given me his number. In fact, Kalugin had given me a fake phone number—and the slip. All subsequent attempts to contact him were unsuccessful.

15. Sciolino.

16. Kalugin 74.

17. Kalugin 143.

18. Kalugin 202.

19. le Carré, *New York Times Book Review*.

20. "From the Archive," *Guardian*.

21. le Carré, *New York Times Book Review*.

22. le Carré, *New York Times Book Review*.

23. Letter to the editor, *New York Times*.

24. Letter to the editor, *New York Times*.

25. Letter to the editor, *New York Times*.

26. Letter to the editor, *New York Times*.

27. Kalugin 77.

28. Kalugin 214.

29. New.

30. New.

CHAPTER 11: TRIGON

1. Record of Telephone Conversation between Henry Kissinger and President Richard Nixon, NSA Archives.

2. This quotation comes from an interview with Alejandra Suárez Barcala, who quoted from another forthcoming book detailing her father's diaries.

3. Peterson 123.

4. This statistic comes from Kalugin's memoirs. As far as I can tell, it is actually close to correct.

5. Peterson 130.

6. Goldman 291.

7. The account of these events comes from Peterson 208–214.

8. Peretruchin 173.

9. Peretruchin 173–180.

10. A decade and change later, he would tell the Soviets about several CIA assets inside the KGB in exchange for cash.

11. In a minor deviation from an otherwise common narrative, the KGB suggested that Ogorodnik used the first to murder yet another pregnant girlfriend of his.

12. Kalugin later settled comfortably in the Washington suburbs with a summer home on Maryland's Eastern Shore.

13. Anderson 2.

14. Clarridge 167–168.

15. Bearden and Risen 26.

16. "Москвашпионская," *Trud*.

CHAPTER 12: THE BEGINNING OF THE END

1. Judt 582.

2. Judt 577, Harrison 146.

3. Bren 112.

4. Roth 8.

5. Judt 502.

6. Judt 569.

7. Judt 569.

8. Roth 18.

9. Judt 570.

10. Havel.

11. Havel.

12. Havel.

13. Dobrynin 365.

14. Dobrynin 370–371.

15. Gaddis 217.

16. Wolf.

17. Boyajian 134.

18. Lasch 209.

19. Lasch 68.

20. Gaddis 213.
21. Gaddis 211.
22. "Charles Frankel," *New York Times*.
23. Feron.
24. Gallup.
25. Schulman 145.
26. Reagan.

CHAPTER 13: OUT OF THE WILDERNESS

1. Dobrynin 523.
2. Kennan, *Memoirs* 82.
3. An acronym for the Russian words for nuclear missile attack, Raketno-Yadernoye Napadenie.
4. Boyajian 134.
5. Dobrynin 477.
6. Ševela 276.
7. Kessler 129.
8. The portion of the dialogue with Kenneth Geide comes from Kessler's account of the FBI investigation of the Koechers, 132.
9. Ševela 293.
10. Kessler 135–139.

CHAPTER 14: EXCHANGE

1. Palmieri.
2. Ševela 314–315.
3. For the sake of consistency, I will refer to him as Natan Sharansky, the Hebraized version of the name that he later adopted, except in cases where the Russian transliteration is relevant.
4. Dalin.
5. Berman.
6. New.
7. Solzhenitsyn 238.
8. Sharansky 420.
9. Gaddis 228.
10. New.
11. New.

12. Whitney.
13. New.
14. Sharansky 395.
15. Sharansky 396.
16. Sharansky 399.
17. Sharansky 399.
18. Sharansky 406.
18. Sharansky 402.
20. Sharansky 403.
21. New.
22. Markham.
23. Sharansky 408.
24. Sharansky 408.
25. Sharansky 408.
26. Markham.

EPILOGUE

1. Addison 185.
2. Gaddis 265.
3. He later did send them to me. One book was *Everything Under the Heavens: How the Past Helps Shape China's Push for Global Power*, by Howard W. French. The other was *Destined for War: Can America and China Escape the Thucydides Trap?*, by Graham Allison.

INDEX

Abel, Rudolf, 51
Afghanistan, 189
Alexander, Sandy, 209–210, 213–214
Allende, Salvador, 123, 160
American Civil Liberties Union
  (ACLU), 212
American Fund for Czechoslovak
  Refugees, 70
Ames, Aldrich, 170, 175
Anderson, Jack, 149–150, 172
Andrew, Christopher, 90, 134
Andropov, Yuri, 8, 11, 78, 85, 124,
  132, 194, 199–200, 204
Angola, 129
Arbenz Guzmán, Jacobo, 39
Argentina, 123, 141
Austria, 102

Barnes, Clive, 87
Batista, Fulgencio, 46
Bay of Pigs invasion, 51
Beneš, Edvard, 17, 24
Bolivia, 123, 141
Brazil, 141
Brezhnev, Leonid, 8, 63, 84, 86–88,
  90–91, 182–183, 188, 199
Brod, Max, 43

Brodsky, Josef, 42
Brown, Jerry, 205, 207
Brzezinski, Zbigniew: Carter
  administration and, 183–184;
  Kalugin and, 148; Kissinger's
  alleged undermining of, 173;
  Koecher's access to, 9–10, 74, 105,
  107, 183–184; Koecher's CIA
  application and, 110; Russian
  Institute and, 76, 103
Burth, Richard, 225
Bush, George H. W., 128, 131, 141, 191

Camponeschi, Philip, 189
Camus, Albert, 36
Carlin, George, 128–129
Carter, Jimmy, 9, 172–173, 183,
  188–189
Case for Modern Man, The (Frankel),
  37, 76
Castro, Fidel, 46, 123
Central Intelligence Agency (CIA):
  AE Screen department/Soviet East
  European Division, 115; Church
  Committee investigation and, 127;
  Cold War hiring increases of, 27;
  creation of, 25; ex-Vlasovci and,

116–117; Foreign Intelligence Surveillance Act (FISA) and, 127; Koecher's application to, 110–112; Latin America and, 123–124, 141–142, 160; offer to turn Koecher, 206–207, 210; Office of Political Research, 7, 126; Operation Condor, 141–142; Radio Free Europe (RFE) and, 72

Černá, Jana, 43–44

Chamberlain, Neville, 17

Charter 77, 180

Cheney, Dick, 128, 183

Chernenko, Konstantin, 200, 217

Chile, 123, 141

Church, Frank, 127

CIA. See Central Intelligence Agency (CIA)

Closely Watched Trains, 73

Colby, William, 128, 143

Colombia, 123–124, 130–131, 255n14

Columbia University, 3, 75–76, 79, 94–95

Confessions of a Spy (Earley), 173

Cuba, 46, 51–52

Czechoslovak Communist Party, 22–24, 28–29, 46–48, 50, 84–86, 232

Czechoslovakia: aftermath of World War II in, 21–22; assassination of Heydrich and, 20; birth of, 15; Charter 77 and, 180; Communist Party and, 24; as Czechoslovak Socialist Republic (CSSR), 46; effect of Communist rule on, 28; ethnic tensions in, 16; genocide of Jews and Roma under Nazi occupation in, 19–20; Helsinki

Accords and, 179; Jews in, 16–19, 28–29, 33; Munich Agreement (1938) and, 17; Nazi occupation of, 17–18; in 1950s, 38; in 1960s, 78, 84; Operation Anthropoid and, 20–21; period of normalizace in, 98–99, 178; political dissent within, 72–73, 180–182; Prague Spring, 43, 85–88; purges and, 28–29; removal of Stalin statue, 52; Soviet 1968 invasion of, 88–90; under Novotný, 31–32, 46; Velvet Revolution and, 231; Vlasovci fighters and, 21–22; between the wars, 15–16

Czechoslovak Socialist Republic (CSSR). See Czechoslovakia

Czechoslovak Union of Writers, 84

de Gaulle, Charles, 94

Democratic National Convention (1968), 96

diplomatic cover, 69

Dobrynin, Anatoly, 89, 91, 149, 172–173, 194, 200

Doolittle Report, 39, 127

Downs, Joseph, 201, 204–205

Dubček, Alexander, 85–89

East Germany, 49, 179, 220

Eder, Richard, 78–79

Eichmann, Adolf, 19

Eisenhower, Dwight D., 39, 40, 46, 50, 128

existentialism, 35–36

Facelle, Thomas A., 190

FAMU, 35–37

Fear No Evil (Sharansky), 222

Federal Bureau of Investigation: counterintelligence and, 200; interest in Koecher and, 201–203; interrogation of, 204–207; Koecher's 1970 approach of, 106; surveillance of Koechers, 207

Fedjanin, Viktor V., 125, 130–131

Fierer, Robert, 211–215, 218–219, 224

Fila, Jan (Šturma): background of, 122–123; defection of, 234–235; handling of Koechers in 1980s, 201, 203–204; meeting with Fierer and, 218–219; as potential informant for United States intelligence, 234; reactivation of Koecher and, 185, 192–194, 195–196, 197; StB concerns about, 185–186, 234–235

Filatov, Anatoli, 172

Ford, Gerald, 9, 128–129, 183

Foreign Intelligence Surveillance Act (FISA), 127

Forman, Miloš, 35

France, 75, 94

Frankel, Charles, 10, 37, 76, 190

Frohn, Wolf-Georg, 224

Gaddis, John Lewis, 94, 98, 217, 230

Geide, Kenneth, 204–206, 208

Germany, 16–17, 19. See also East Germany; West Germany

Giuliani, Rudolph, 207, 210–211

Glienicke Bridge, 51, 224

Gorbachev, Mikhail, 217–219, 224

Gordievsky, Oleg, 91

Gottwald, Klement, 19, 23, 29

Graham, Loren, 76, 79, 99

Grechko, Andrei, 88

Green, Ashbel, 151

Green, Bruce, 219–220

Gromyko, Andrei, 189

Guatemala, 39

Guevara, Che, 123

Gvozdek, Miloslav (Grulich), 55

Haig, Alexander, 191

Hájek, Jiří, 90, 95–96

Harutinyan, Alexandra, 159

Hašek, Jaroslav, 73

Havel, Václav, 73, 78–79, 84, 86–87, 99, 177–178, 180–182, 232

Helms, Richard, 123

Helsinki Accords, 179

Helsinki Group, 215

Heydrich, Reinhard, 19–20

Hitler, Adolf, 16–18

Ho Chi Minh, 40

Holland, Agnieszka, 35

Honecker, Erich, 220

Hrabal, Bohumil, 32, 73

Hungarian uprising, 8, 85–86

Husák, Gustáv, 99, 180–181

"Ideology, Philosophy and Science" (Koecher dissertation), 101

Illner, Pavel, 18, 33, 86, 92

Indiana University, 3, 74–75

Iran, 28, 189

Jandová, Jana, 100

Javorsky, Jaroslav, 225

Jesenská, Milena, 44

John Paul II, Pope. See Wotyla, Karol

Johnson, Lyndon, 89, 94, 98

Kaczmarek, Jerzy, 224

Kafka, Franz, 42–44

Kalugin, Oleg (Felix): background of,
144–146; concern about CIA agent
in Bogotá and, 158; intelligence
career of, 144, 146–150, 152, 156,
191; interference with Koecher of,
13, 150, 155–156, 171; interview
with le Carré, 153–155; meeting
with Koecher in Čtyřkoly, 2–13,
144, 150, 155; memoirs of, 151–152;
Ogorodnik and, 164–165, 170;
outing of as KGB agent, 149–150;
as possible CIA asset, 144, 150,
154, 156–157, 170–172
Kazakov, Sergei, 130
Kennan, George, 17–19, 38–39, 195
Kennedy, John F., 51, 59, 123–124
Kennedy, Robert, 94
Kessler, Ronald, 135–136
KGB: concern about Bogotá embassy
and, 123–124, 130–131, 158;
decision to deal with Koecher
directly, 132–133, 142; Koecher's
letter for Andropov and, 11, 132;
Koechers' 1976 trip to
Czechoslovakia and, 142–143;
Latin America and, 123–124;
notice of Koecher and, 117, 132; as
rebranded NKVD, 30
Khrushchev, Nikita, 8, 30–31, 46–47,
51, 63, 85
King, Martin Luther, Jr., 94, 127
Kirk, Grayson, 94
Kirkpatrick, Jeanne, 191
Kissinger, Henry, 126, 160, 172–173
Klíma, Ivan, 99
Klimová, Rita, 23
Kline, George: first meeting with
Koecher, 42–44, 55; Koecher's CIA
application and, 110; Koecher's

defection to US and, 62, 66, 70–71;
Koecher's entrance into Columbia
and, 75–76; Sarah Lawrence
position and, 120; ties to American
intelligence and, 62–63, 253n3
Kodeš, Jiří, 26
Koecher, Irena, 15–19, 33
Koecher, Jaroslav, 16, 18–19, 33–37,
236–237
Koecher, Karel: animosity toward StB
after 1968 invasion and, 103–107;
arrest for espionage, 208; birth of,
15; Catholicism and, 23–24; CIA
information passed to the StB and,
119–122, 124–126, 130–131;
codenames of, 55, 71, 117; on Cold
War, 229; defection and, 64–66;
deployment to US for StB and,
61–63; difficulties with Czech
authorities, 26–27, 47–50, 52–55,
60; entrance into Charles
University, 31–33; espionage case
and, 211–213; exchange of for
Sharansky and, 214–215, 220–221,
224–226; explosive meeting with
Kralík and, 103–105; family and,
33–37, 60, 236–237; FAMU and,
35–37, 40–41; FBI interest in,
201–203; FBI interrogation and
cooperation, 204–207; on Fila, 234;
financial struggles in United States
and, 81, 103–104, 107, 132, 187–188;
hiring of at CIA, 110–112;
intelligence from 1980s, 198–199,
202; initial intelligence goals in
United States, 68–69; jail attack on,
213–214; Jandová and, 100;
Kalugin's interference with, 13,
150, 155–156, 171; KGB's decision

to deal with, 132–133; life in post–
Cold War Czech Republic,
227–228; meeting with Kalugin in
Čtyřkoly, 2–13, 144, 150, 155; on
morality and spywork, 235–236;
Novissa and, 184–185, 188,
196–197; PhD thesis of, 101; on
post-Communist Czech and
Slovak republics, 232–233; Radio
Free Europe (RFE) and, 3, 72–77,
90, 92, 97, 99, 104; reactivation of
in 1980s, 196–197, 201, 203–204;
recruitment into StB, 54–57;
refusal to denounce dissidents as
American spies and, 177–178;
relationship with Hana and,
58–60, 79–80, 82–84, 100,
136–138; Soviet 1968 invasion of
Czechoslovakia and, 90; swinger
lifestyle and, 134–138, 140; theory
on Ogorodnik of, 175; training
and, 64; United States citizenship
and, 3, 108, 220; work at CIA,
115–117, 126, 131–132
Korean War, 27
Kovalev, Nikolai, 174
Kozák, Jan, 24
Kralík, Václav, 100, 103–108,
119–120, 130–131
Kryuchkov, Vladimir, 157, 215, 219
Kukla, George, 207
Kundera, Milan, 35, 85, 91
Kusturica, Emir, 35

Lasch, Christopher, 186–187
le Carré, John, 145, 153–155
Lehrman, Lewis, 199
Levenson, Larry, 136, 139
lie detector tests, 64, 111–112

Liška, Jan, 53–54, 61
Lynch, Gerard, 212

Mailer, Norman, 190
Major, David, 211
Markov, Georgi, 153–154
Martin, John, 219, 221, 225
Masaryk, Jan, 24
Memorandum, The (Havel), 87
Menzel, Jiří, 35, 73
Metropolitan Correctional Center
(MCC), 209
Millingen (security official), 74–75
Mills, C. Wright, 44, 69
Mlynář, Zdeněk, 91
Molotov-Ribbentrop Pact, 19
Mosaddegh, Mohammed, 28
Munich Agreement (1938), 17

National Liberation Army (ELN), 124
NATO, 75
New York City, 138–139
New York Post, 210
New York Times, 73, 87, 147, 171, 189,
233
New York Times Book Review, 153
New York Times Magazine, 78
Ngo Dinh Diem, 59
Nistroy, Dietrich, 225
Nixon, Richard, 96–97, 101–102,
118–119, 123, 126
Novissa business, 184–185, 188,
196–197
Novotný, Antonín, 31, 46, 78, 84–85
NSC-68, 27, 94, 127

Ogorodnik, Alexandr (Trigon): affair
with Pilar Suárez Barcala and,
161–162; arrest of, 168–169;

INDEX

background of, 158–159; as CIA source in Moscow, 163–165; in Colombia, 160–163, 165; disenchantment with Soviet Union and, 160–161; Kalugin and, 164–165, 170; Koecher's suspicions about, 125, 131, 164–165; in Moscow, 164–165, 168–169, 171–172; official CIA blame for capture of and, 173, 175; poisoning of, 169–170; post-Soviet questions about, 174–175; recruitment by CIA and, 162–163
Old Westbury College, 189

Panama, 123
Paraguay, 141
Pardamcová, Hana (Adrid): background of, 58–59; defection and, 64–66; deployment of Koecher to US and, 61–62; desire to have a child, 82, 141; detention is United States as material witness, 208, 211–212; exchange of for Sharansky and, 220–221, 225–226; Fila and, 123, 141, 194, 196; job at Harry Winston's and, 71; life in post–Cold War Czech Republic, 228; Novissa and, 184, 188, 196–197; relationship with Koecher and, 58–59, 79–80, 82–84, 136–138; spy training and, 64; StB assessments of, 82–83, 120, 199; swinger lifestyle and, 134–138, 140; United States citizenship and, 108, 220–221; work for Savion and, 117; Zítek and, 141
Pardamec, Josef (Valentín), 58, 65
Pardametz, Josef, 59, 63–66, 75, 78

Peretruchin, Igor, 168–169, 171
Perle, Richard, 191
Peterson, John, 165
Peterson, Marti, 165–168, 175
Pinochet, Augusto, 123, 160
Plášek, Miroslav, 199, 201
Poland, 73; Nazi invasion of, 19
Polreich, Miroslav "Mirek" (Patera), 73–74, 76–78, 90, 95
"Power of the Powerless, The" (Havel), 181
Powers, Gary, 51
"Pragmatic and Ideological Factors in Soviet Decision Making" (Koecher), 132
Prague Orgy, The (Roth), 138, 179
Prague Spring, 43, 85–88
Pravda, 7
Putin, Vladimir, 156

Radio Free Europe (RFE), 3, 72–77, 90, 92, 97, 99, 104
Radio Moscow, 147
RAND Corporation, 103
Reagan, Ronald, 128, 183, 190–191, 195, 200, 218–219, 224
Revolutionary Armed Forces of Colombia (FARC), 124
Rockefeller, Jay, 147–148
Roth, Philip, 99, 180
Rudé pravo, 24
Rumsfeld, Donald, 128, 138–139, 183

Sakharov, Andrei, 215
Sakharovksy, Alexander, 148
Sartre, Jean Paul, 38
Saturday Night Live, 128–129
Savion, Joseph, 114, 116, 184
Scharfenorth, Detlef, 224

INDEX

Schlesinger, James, 128

Schmidt, Helmut, 220

Seeger, Pete, 73

Seifert, Jaroslav, 31

Sevareid, Eric, 96

Ševela, Vladimír, 100

Sharansky, Avital, 216, 226

Sharansky, Natan, 180, 214–217, 222–223

Shcharansky, Anatoly. *See* Sharansky, Natan

Shultz, George, 191

Slánský, Rudolf, 28, 31

Solzhenitsyn, Aleksandr, 216–217

"Some Interesting Happenings in Prague" (Eder), 78

Soviet Ministry of Foreign Affairs, 164

Soviet Union: blockade of West Berlin and, 24–25; Brezhnev Doctrine and, 90–91; Cold War narrative and, 230–231; Cuban Missile Crisis and, 51–52; Czech communists in, 19; Helsinki Accords and, 179; Hungarian uprising and, 85–86; invasion of Afghanistan and, 189; invasion of Czechoslovakia in 1968 of, 88–90; Latin America and, 141; Molotov-Ribbentrop Pact and, 19; Nazi attack on, 19; in 1950s, 38; nuclear arms and, 27–28, 97–98, 118, 172–173, 188–189; Prague Spring and, 43, 85–88; project RYAN and, 195; purges and, 28–29; Reagan and, 191; U-2 spy plane incident and, 51

Sputnik, 46

Spy vs. Spy (Kessler), 135

Stalin, Josef, 29, 31

Státní bezpečenost (State Security, StB): anti-Semitic readings of Koecher of, 108, 114–115; arrest of Koecher's school-age anti-state group and, 26; assessment of Koechers' deployment, 108–110; assessments of Hana and, 82–83, 120, 199; communications with Koecher and, 65–66, 73–74, 76–77, 100–105; concerns about Fila and, 185–186, 234–235; creation of, 24; decision to denounce Koecher and, 177, 183–184, 188; funding of Koechers, 121, 126, 198–199, 200–201, 203; Jandová and, 100; Jaroslav Koecher's letter to FAMU and, 37; Kalugin's interference in Koecher's case, 13, 150, 155–156, 171; Koecher's CIA work and, 115–117, 119–122; Koecher's refusal to denounce dissidents as spies and, 177–178; Kralík's requests of Koecher, 105; overtures to Koecher in 1980s, 191–192; preparations to recall, 111, 113; state of intelligence abroad, 67–68; Tomek and, 48; uncertainly about Koecher, 105–108, 110, 113, 142; view of America in 1968 of, 96–97

Strategic Arms Limitations Talks (SALT) I treaty, 118

Strategic Arms Limitations Talks (SALT) II treaty, 172–173, 188–189

Suárez Barcala, Alejandra, 160–163

Suárez Barcala, Pilar, 161–163

Surmach, Myron Jr., 70

Surmach, Yaroslava, 44, 55, 63, 69

Suslov, Mikhail, 7–8

Tanabauer, Michal, 26–27
Tehran hostages, 189
Tiso, Josef, 18
Tito, Josip Broz, 25
Tomek, Vladivoj, 48
Trau, Solomon, 82
Treaty on the Non-Proliferation of
    Nuclear Weapons, 97–98
Trial, The (Kafka), 43
Trud, 174
Turner, Stansfield, 174

Ulík, Stanislav, 203
Unbearable Lightness of Being, The
    (Kundera), 91
United Fruit Company, 39, 255n14
United States: Berlin airlift and,
    24–25; Cold War narrative and,
    230–231; Cuban Missile crisis and,
    51; Doolittle Report and, 39, 127;
    economic malaise and, 101–102;
    Helsinki Accords and, 179;
    internal surveillance and, 98;
    Johnson's Great Society platform
    and, 98; Latin America and,
    123–124; National Security
    Council, 25, 27; neoconservative
    movement and, 127–128; New York
    City insolvency and, 138–139;
    NSC-68, 27, 94, 127; nuclear arms
    and, 27–28, 97–98, 118, 172–173,
    188–189, 195; recession of 1970s
    and, 117–118; Single Integrated
    Operational Plan (SIOP), 195;
    Soviet 1968 invasion of
    Czechoslovakia and, 89; U-2 spy

plane incident and, 51. *See also*
    Central Intelligence Agency (CIA)
Urban, Josef, 26
Uruguay, 123, 141

Vaculík, Ludvík, 84
Velvet Revolution, 231–232
Vergangenheitspolitik, 56
Vietnam War, 40, 70, 75, 77–78,
    93–94, 101, 125–126
Vlasov, Andrei, 21–22
Vogel, Wolfgang, 220, 224, 226
Voskovec, George, 86–87
Vukasin, Maria, 197–198
Vukasin, Milos, 116, 126, 197–198

Wagner College, 99
Walker, John Anthony, 149
Wallace, George, 96
Wall Street Journal, 128
Washingtonian magazine, 135
Watergate break-ins, 98, 118, 126
Westad, Odd Arne, 40, 97–98, 123
West Germany, 49, 56, 220
Wotyla, Karol, 73, 78, 188

Young Men's Hebrew Association
    (YMHA), 140
Yugoslavia, 25, 73

Zápotocký, Antonín, 31, 46
Zemlyakov, Yevgeni, 224
Zhikov, Todor, 153
Zítek, Richard, 5–6, 11, 102, 120–121,
    141, 144
Zweig, Stefan, 16

Benjamin Cunningham is a Barcelona-based writer. He is a former correspondent for *The Economist*, editor in chief for the *Prague Post*, and copy boy at the *Saginaw News*.